Canada's North   *R. A. J. PHILLIPS*

1967/Macmillan of Canada/Toronto

Library of Congress Catalogue Card No. 67-21265

Printed in Canada for The Macmillan Company of Canada Limited
70 Bond Street, Toronto
by McCorquodale & Blades Printers Limited

To the people who made the North,
and to Margaret, Brigid, and Jennifer who will inherit it.

Contents

List of photographs viii

Introduction x

1. The Setting 2

2. The Coming of Man 26

3. Enter the European 40

4. Fish and Fur 56

5. Gold 84

6. Whose North? 98

7. The Settlers 114

8. The Quiet Years 142

9. Change 160

10. The Modern North: Transportation and Communications 178

11. The Modern North: An Inventory of Resources 198

12. The Modern North: The Social Legacy 218

13. The Modern North: Political Development 242

14. Science, Literature, and the Arts 262

15. The Still Point 282

Index 300

MAPS   (*between pages 18 and 19*)
prepared by C. C. J. Bond

The Canadian North

The Yukon

Circumpolar map

The North-west

The Canadian Shield

Photographs

(between pages 146 and 147)

1. The Yukon River (*R. A. J. Phillips*)
2. Dawson, Yukon Territory (*National Film Board, Ottawa*)
3. Mid-winter's day near the Arctic Circle (*NFB*)
4. Arrival of the steamer *Seattle No. 1* at Dawson (*NFB*)
5. Partial view of the town of Inuvik (*NFB*)
6. Eskimo family after fishing for arctic char at Pelly Bay (*NFB*)
7. Typical tundra country in the Cape Dorset area (*NFB*)
8. Eskimo fisherman at Fort Chimo, Quebec (*NFB*)
9. Eskimos outside their summer tent at Pelly Bay (*NFB*)
10. Eskimos fishing in the sapotit at Pelly Bay (*NFB*)
11. A fine example of a glacier (*NFB*)
12. Indian village of Old Crow in the Yukon (*R. A. J. Phillips*)
13. Grandmother Eskimo Manny with grandson at Chesterfield Inlet (*NFB*)
14. Young Eskimo girl in a class at Resolute Bay (*NFB*)
15. Eskimo oil-driller at Winter Harbour, Melville Island (*NFB*)
16. 'Enchanted Owl' by Kenojuak (*NFB*)
17. 'Complex of Birds' by Kenojuak (*NFB*)
18. Eskimo artist preparing a stone block at Cape Dorset (*NFB*)
19. Large herd of reindeer owned by the Eskimos at Mackenzie Delta (*NFB*)
20. Musk-oxen on Devon Island (*NFB*)
21. Eskimo hunters at Resolute Bay (*NFB*)
22. Polar bears on Baffin Island (*NFB*)
23. Mould Bay weather station, Prince Patrick Island (*T. C. Fairley*)
24. Selwyn Mountains in the Yukon (*NFB*)
25. Terrain around an Eskimo camp-site, northern Baffin Island (*NFB*)
26. Cambridge Bay Station on the Distant Early Warning Line (*R. A. J. Phillips*)
27. Government survey helicopter on the airstrip at Isachsen (*Herb Taylor*)
28. Barge assembly on the Mackenzie River (*NFB*)
29. C.G.S. *C. D. Howe* at Pangnirtung (*NFB*)
30. St. David's Anglican Church at Fort Simpson (*R. A. J. Phillips*)

Introduction

Today only a few people are caught by the magnetism of the North.

The penetration of this farthest kingdom is no longer a compelling vocation that drags men from reasonable pursuits into the terrors of the unknown, harsh, arctic wasteland. Now, in less time than it takes to read a James Bond thriller, one can fly from Montreal past the horizons that Frobisher or Mackenzie knew, look down upon the scene of Jens Munk's agony, or cruise over the final mystery of Franklin.

Yet somehow the force that drew these men, and others after them, has not dissipated. The towns and telephones, the sound of generators, the grinding of sewage trucks, the ugliness of oil tanks and wires: all this human defilement has not robbed the North of its strange power. When men live in the North, their values change. They build new civilizations on a mud flat in the Klondike. They live a lifetime alone, and die when they emerge. They become citizens of a different kind of country, a country where nature is overwhelmingly stronger than man.

When we speak of the North that draws and holds men, and makes a silent fellowship of those who share it, we are not talking of high drama. Almost any newcomer may be astonished by the crescendo of northern lights above the silent winter earth. The tourist's first sight of a Yukon mountain or the marvellous sculpture of ancient ice in a summer sea provokes a natural wonder. For those who learn to know and love this land, there are quieter pleasures. Footprints on top of the hard arctic surface, the snow around etched away by the wind. The first cold red light of the sun as the High Arctic winter passes its zenith. The chant of dogs or the quiet abrasion of sled runners. The softness of the bending black spruce boughs in the sub-Arctic snow. The long straight lines of smoke, balanced from the chimneys of the village like rope in the Hindu rope trick.

For some men, the North holds nothing beyond what was there ten centuries ago. For others, the North is the smell of coffee on the stove like burning incense. It is the secure intimacy of the village which has its own peculiar society and which has made an uncomplicated peace within its boundaries. It is the notes of the accordion, the smells and laughter of the Saturday dance, the sound of song – old songs sung with glasses of strong rum and the camaraderie that comes of nostalgia. It's the comfortable monotony of the store, and the fact that people smile when they pass. It's the welcome roar of the plane arriving, and the more welcome roar as it departs.

Northern travellers seem to have found an extraordinary fulfilment in this unlikeliest of lands and seas. They were moved to literary heights they had not reached before, and would never reach again. In success or in failure, almost all became missionaries for their cause. When they could return, they did. When they could not return, they relived their northern voyagings throughout their days, the way other men have spent their lives experiencing over and over the trauma of war-time.

We are the pilgrims, master, we shall go
Always a little further: it may be
Beyond that last blue mountain barred with snow
Across that angry or that glimmering sea.

Of all who travelled north, few have been heroes. Most have been ordinary people, at least until they went. Some have been bureaucrats, and I was one of these. The literature on the Canadian North is extensive, though it has gaps. There is little current writing that sets out to discuss with the friendly stranger what the North is all about, what it looks like, how it all began, and what is there for today and for tomorrow. That, approximately, is the gap this book is intended to fill. It is meant to be a point of departure for those who believe that part of the price of Canadian citizenship is acquaintance with the northern third of their country. To paraphrase the parliamentary statement often referred to in this book, it is for those who wish no longer to treat these vast territories in a continuing state of absence of mind.

To encompass so broad a theme as Canada's North, past and present, within a single volume, one must risk accusations of superficiality. One must risk the charge that here is little that has not been said before. What is new, and possibly useful, is the attempt to look at the Canadian North as a whole within itself, and as part of a developing nation whose character affected the North, and was affected by it.

The definition of 'the North' is difficult. This book deals only with Canada north of 60 degrees, where almost all of Canada's Arctic, and most of its sub-Arctic, lies. It is, therefore, concerned with the Yukon and the Northwest Territories. The Arctic or sub-Arctic areas of the provinces are discussed only briefly, mainly in their part of the Eskimo story.

Not the least of the problems in such a book is regional balance. It must be acknowledged that this book has been less than just to some areas, to some people, and to some events. For example, the proportions are in favour of the Northwest Territories and the Arctic. Such a decision is no reflection of intrinsic importance, or of contribution to the Canadian whole. It is rather a reflection of the nature of the present problem, and the present questions about the future of the North.

As in any commentary about the North, the writer has a bias. Mine is in the sense of a profound admiration for many of the men and women who have given so much to build something they intensely believe in: the North and Canada. They are not alone in their determination on behalf of the North, but they are most often on the firing-line without ammunition. They are shot at, sometimes justly, for every disappointment and frustration. In accordance with the proper rules of public service, they do not shoot back. It is to their credit that their will to serve enables them to live with these misunderstandings, while building better than they know.

A dynamic administration is one that puts the greatest emphasis on intellectual integrity and freedom of thought. It is such an administration that I had the privilege to serve. While I am indebted to those in charge of the Department of Northern Affairs and National Resources for the freedom to write this book, and much else, without censorship, curtailment, or direction, I must point out that the opinions and errors in these pages are mine, not theirs. To further emphasize this statement, I should add that my direct association with the administration of the North came to an end long before this book was finished. Nevertheless, my respect for those who continue to serve will last as long as my interest in the North itself. I hope that a few more Canadians may share it.

R. A. J. Phillips

Cantley, Quebec

Canada's North

1 | The Setting

At the still point of the turning world
Neither arrest nor movement. And do not call it fixity
Where past and future are gathered.

T. S. Eliot

At the ends of the earth, it is cold.

At that point where the earth stands still, and time stands still, it is dark for half the year. When the sun rises above the horizon at the North Pole on the twenty-first of every March, it is a glowing orb seemingly without heat and almost without light.

When it is summer by the calendars of men in friendlier climates, the polar landscape is glaring bright, though the sun is only a quarter of the way from the horizon to the top of the sky. There is no colour on the surface of the earth, except what it borrows from the refracted sunlight.

This is the permanently frozen sea. It has no form, except as the oceans or sands have form. It stretches forever to the south: there is no north, or east, or west. Here or there runs a smooth walk of glaring white, a pathway suddenly interrupted by vicious, jagged hillocks thrust upwards. Once these were water in the open seas; then they were caught in some winter that has not ended. The still mass of ice is moving imperceptibly around the polar regions. Some day, in years or decades, these shapes may move to latitudes where the seas are open. In a warmer sun, the brittle mountains will dissolve, their only trace a cooler air above some sea or coastline.

No human beings live within hundreds of miles of the North Pole except scientists, who stay briefly and then depart. It seems devoid of life. Only the wind moves. The temperature may be $-50°$ Fahrenheit in winter, though on summer days some ice melts. Many places in the world are colder. Few are more desolate, unless one finds in this antiseptic wilderness an ultimate form of beauty.

The North was long a symbolic goal for man voyaging to discover the most distant parts of his earth. Though the polar seas were probed for centuries, seemingly impenetrable barriers stretched between the Pole and the farthest points the sailing-ships could reach. For one man, more than most, the Pole was an obsession. Peary claimed to have reached it on foot. Only he ever knew the justice of his claim, and he is long since dead. Others have started the long walk. None made it.

Now, technology quickly moves man to the Pole, not on the surface of the ice, but in the air above and in the water below. By plane it is an easy flight from the nearest arctic airfield, perhaps three hours away. It is easier to look down on this ultimate destination than to land on it. A submarine can break through six feet of ice to the surface. Then one can stand, if he is so inclined, where the earth is still. He will stand for only a moment; there is nothing here but the symbolic victory over distance, and ice and cold.

The Pole itself can be a casual goal for men today. For a thousand years before, the polar regions were an often-fatal lure: some sailors came to seek new routes for trade; some came to escape an old world; some came because it was there. The history of their northward wanderings is very much a part of the history of Canada.

For many horizons from the Pole, the frozen seas stretch unchangingly. Below the crust of ice there is life within the moving seas; mountains and valleys score the ocean's bed. The floor of the ocean dips two miles below the surface. Across the Pole, the Lomonosov Ridge rises to within a thousand yards of the ice-crust, dividing the ocean in two. This marker is along a line from the New Siberian Islands to Ellesmere Island, and in these little-known depths there may be another ridge on the Canadian side. These are undiscovered lands, as new to man as the surface of the polar regions was five hundred years ago. The five million square miles of polar ice, or its four million cubic miles of water, lie between Siberia, Greenland, Canada, and Alaska.

The Frozen Seas. Some of the ice within the polar seas sticks fast to the land, growing thicker each year until May, when it is attacked by the summer sun. Then it breaks off to become part of the slowly drifting polar pack. Sometimes it doubles its depth as it pursues its languid clockwise course. On the Canadian side of the Pole it lingers close to land, a continuing hazard to the passage of ships. On the European side the pack is loose enough to be brushed aside by ships.

The ice is complex. The Eskimos use twenty-five different words to identify it, and as many more for snow. Thick, jagged pans of pack-ice are constantly drifting until they meet the shore, or ice fastened immovably to the shore. Then they slide, piece over piece, or are pushed end over end in a slowly moving jumble. The so-called polar ice has its own character. It is formed, not by the breaking of gigantic pieces from the land, but by the freezing of open water. It is older, tougher, and less salty than the frozen pack. When it stays about the Pole, little melts in the near-freezing temperatures of July and August. It may grow slowly for years before it is carried to a place where warmer water and air can erode it. Even when it remains in the northernmost parts of the Arctic Ocean, though, it rarely grows much more than ten feet thick.

The drifting ice of the polar seas moves at the instance of the wind. Fridtjof Nansen set the bow of the *Fram* within it in 1893, and waited three years to find the answers to questions about the drifting mass. The direction of the drift was 25° to 45° to the right of the wind. He measured the speed of drift as one-fiftieth of the wind. It may be so, but sometimes when the seas are solid the motion is less than half that. At other times and places, the ice may drift at one-fortieth of the speed of the wind that drives it.

As well as winds above, there are currents beneath the sea. On the Canadian side of the Pole an eddy moves slowly clockwise. Ice-islands, sometimes miles in length and breadth, and rising as much as twenty feet above the surface, float like unwieldy ships in courses that are monotonously predictable. Scientists have lived upon the larger of them, drifting as in motionless vessels, heedless of national boundaries. Peary camped on one in 1909. Forty-five years later the site remained preserved, still drifting in its predetermined eddy, pushed by winds and currents.

To a casual beholder the polar sea appears to stand still. Though it stretches outward from the end of the earth, a monotonous and apparently unchanging wilderness, it *has* changed through advancing and receding ice ages. It is only in the last fifteen thousand years that it has been revealed in something like its present shape. Before that, a large part of the world's oceans was, in the most literal sense, in cold storage across Canada and half of the United States. These areas were no colder than the polar regions, and perhaps more of these oceans were free of ice. The Lomonosov Ridge, for example, probably reached above the surface. Even more dramatically different were the outlines of distant continents affected by all this ice. Since so much of the earth's water was frozen, sea-level was probably about three hundred feet lower than it is now. One could easily walk from Siberia to Alaska, and from England to France. Conversely, if all the ice of the polar regions were suddenly melted, scientists estimate that the seas would rise 120 feet, and every seaport in the world would be engulfed.

The Islands. From the Pole, the nearest land is nearly five hundred miles away, at Cape Morris Jesup on Greenland's tip, or Cape Columbia at the uttermost reaches of Ellesmere Island. Both are uninhabited by man. At Alert, on the north-east corner of Ellesmere, man has staked his northernmost observation post. Beyond that, no-man's-land, or rather no-man's-sea, stretches to the other side of the world.

To the south lie the arctic islands. East of the Canadian Arctic Archipelago is Greenland, whose peaks rise two miles above the sea. The massive cap of ice covering four-fifths of its area reaches in many places below sea-level. The school-books that called Greenland the world's largest island were wrong. Large it is, but it is an archipelago rather than a single island. Suppose, however, that by some reversal of climate the temperatures were to rise and that the mother lode of glaciers were to melt, Greenland might then become an island after all: relieved of the unimaginable weight of ice, the land could move upwards to form a plateau, perhaps three thousand feet above the sea.

Thus, too, would the maps of arctic Canada change if the land beneath the ice were relieved of its frozen burden. The land has risen from the times when it was entirely encumbered by ice, and it still rises – about three feet a century. The ice-caps on Ellesmere, Devon, Baffin, and Axel Heiberg islands are small in comparison with the immense mantle lying upon Greenland. In the highlands of the Eastern Arctic, new glaciers still grow, and move slowly towards the sea. This is where the icebergs start. These glaciers are the ice-machines of the giants; the greatest machine of all is in Greenland – a fiord near Jacobshavn that each day discharges a million tons of ice to move slowly and menacingly into the water-currents of the Atlantic. These icy mountains, as they dwindle and die, cool the seas and continents.

North of Europe and Asia are few islands, and beyond Alaska there are none. Between the Canadian mainland and the Pole, the archipelago is divided in two by the Parry Channel, running westwards from Lancaster Sound to Viscount Melville Sound. To the north are the Queen Elizabeth Islands, collectively named in tribute to a newly crowned monarch. The islands of the archipelago south of the channel are fewer and larger. Baffin Island, with fewer than three thousand inhabitants, has three times the area of the United Kingdom, and a more trying climate. Victoria Island is bigger than the whole of Canada's Atlantic provinces.

It took nearly ten centuries of effort for man to thread his way through these islands; today an airplane crosses them in less than ten hours. Such a flight across the northernmost lands of the world brings home a vivid truth about the nature of the North.

One can generalize about the polar seas, but on the land there are many norths. Each one looks startlingly different, as different as a darkened Baffin coastline, when winter has put all nature in hibernation, and a Whitehorse living-room, blue-lit by a television screen. The North may mean igloos or water-skiing. The North is the table-top monotony of the barrens, the dramatic pinnacles of Ellesmere, and the mountain ranges of the Yukon.

The islands themselves show something of this spectrum of arctic landscape. They are cold – no sun-bathing here in a July whose temperature rarely touches 50°. The winters are, so to speak, more dark than cold. It is the dark that quenches the human *élan*. One cannot clothe oneself against the dark, or dispel it by turning on the lights. The extreme temperatures, rarely below –50°, look worse on paper than they feel in fact, unless the wind is keen. The warm days are balmy compared to Siberia's record –100°. One Siberian town has a mean January temperature of –58.2° – twenty-seven degrees lower than that of Resolute Bay in the Queen Elizabeth Islands.

In the summer, the cluttered seas are open to the ice-breaker, which can choose its route. Cornwallis Island, and Eureka and Grise Fiord on Ellesmere, are the most northerly ports of call. For many years, an ice-breaker fought its way to the weather-station at Alert, on the tip of Ellesmere, but the sea has won the battle. The narrow passage is now uncut by hulls of ships; aircraft bring in the tons of supplies needed each year. Though the southern arctic waters are generally warmer than the northern, this is not a generalization to be carried too far. For centuries, the cruel legend of an ice-free sea at the top of the world drew many an early mariner towards the Pole. In fact, there is an area called the North Water, between Lancaster and Smith Sounds – about 75° north – that is free of ice at all seasons. The whalers of a century ago knew it, and sought it out through ice-filled barriers to the south. They did not know why it was there; nor do we. Off Cape Dorset, on Baffin Island's south-western reach, is more open water, and half the western coast of Greenland is remarkably free of ice in winter.

On the land there is evidence everywhere of glaciers long gone. It is not unexpected that beaches are covered with the gravel created and transported by these gigantic rock-crushers. It *is* surprising that the beaches reach far inland and climb as high as five hundred feet. These upper levels were once the shore. Radio Carbon 14 dating has now traced the history of these beaches to over a hundred centuries ago. As the pressure of the ice lifted, the land escalated to a height nearly as high as the tallest man-made structure in Canada.

Even an untrained eye can see the marks of past glaciation in a progressive movement across the arctic islands. Sand-gravel ridges, called eskers, are left by glacial streams. Long, deep scratches across the surface of the rock were clawed by the moving ice. These are found in other regions as well as in the High Arctic; but here they are revealed as in a classroom model — trees, plants, and earth removed, so that man can see the power of a glacier.

The islands in the far west are low and flat beside the dramatic shapes of Ellesmere or Baffin to the east. The hills of Ellesmere rise eight thousand feet, and the edges of the land are notched in deep fiords. This is the country that brings out the worst prose of the tourist-writer, and leaves the sensitive new-comer without words.

Some will say that winter is the North's true season — that summer is an aberration, a contradiction in the Arctic, as well as a time of insects. Winter brings the cleanliness of shapes, the subtlety of faintly spreading red or purple in the sunlight, and the purity of ice and snow in the crisp brilliance of the moon. Winter brings the howl of wolves or dogs, and the comforting sound of a hostile wind kept at bay by a wall of snow or plastic insulation.

Summer is for the amateur, the easy traveller, the man with colour film in all his cameras. Anyone can see the strange enchantment of the High Arctic in summer. The shapes are there among the inland hills, or in cliffs reaching down to the sea. The ice has gone from the land, and even from the sea, depending on the latitude; the rocks have emerged: white rocks streaked with green or red, rich brown hills without a trace of earth, bands of gravel laid with the order of a Japanese garden. There may be no tree for a thousand miles, or even a bush, but there is a carpeting of floral life, from the lichens clinging to the boulders to the boldly blooming flowers finding an uncertain life in pockets of soil. The sea and sky are rich blue in the long sunny days. Towards midnight, in midsummer, the brilliance of the colour slips to softer tones. When the day ends, the cameras of the new-comers are still clicking.

The Mainland. To the south is the arctic mainland, from Ungava in the east, across the coastal regions of the Northwest Territories, to the delta of the Mackenzie River. It is at this point that each man needs his definition of the Arctic. For some, 'Arctic' means all the globe north of the Arctic Circle, 66° 33′ north latitude. The definition is admirably simple, but hardly useful. It merely divides the world by sunlight. At the Arctic Circle, during the course of a year, the sun does not set on one day, and on one day it does not rise. Northward, the number of sunless and nightless days increases until, at the Pole, there are roughly 183 of each – one long day and one long night.

Sometimes the Arctic is defined by the permafrost line – the line north of which the ground is permanently frozen. Permafrost has a tendency towards great irregularity in its southern reaches: it may appear well south of beaches where the townspeople swim on the long summer days. Even if scientists were to produce a strong case for using the permafrost as a standard of the Arctic, it is a definition that would annoy Boards of Trade in towns that claim agreeable climates.

For a few, the auroral zone is a reasonable delineation of the Arctic. Oceanographers have their own definition, in terms of water temperature and salinity. If the water is at freezing-point, with a salt content of thirty parts per thousand, it is considered Arctic.

The most useful and most widely accepted definition of the Arctic is that area whose average July temperature is below 50° Fahrenheit. This, by and large, is the temperature required for the growth of trees. They can withstand the severest winter cold if they have that brief summer respite.

The boundary of the Arctic, then, is the temperature-line – the tree-line. It is the edge between the barrens and the bush. It divides not only land-forms but cultures. The tree-line was the farthest limit past which the Indian did not venture. Beyond was the terror of the cold, shelterless barrens, and of the Eskimo, who shunned the bush.

This division of the North has always been enormously important to every northern operation. The tree-line gives vivid evidence of the apparent unpredictability of climate. It does not follow a regular line from east to west. From the Mackenzie Delta the tree-line runs in a wavering diagonal to Churchill, Manitoba. On the eastern shore of Hudson Bay, the barrens of Quebec lie north-west of a line from Great Whale River to eastern Ungava Bay.

All points on the line have similar July weather. The summer is just about as warm in the Mackenzie, well above the Arctic Circle, as in northern Manitoba. The depth of temperature in winter has little effect on trees, as Russia's northern forests show.

The northern limit of the sub-Arctic is the tree-line but its southern edge is harder to define. Certainly it stretches south of the permafrost line. Sometimes the definition is economic, in terms of transportation. The sub-Arctic is said to lie beyond the railways: hardly a reliable criterion, when a railway can advance a mile a day into the North. Sometimes the line of the sub-Arctic is considered in terms of settlement, and placed at 55° across the Canadian West. Perhaps the most convenient line is 60°, the northern boundary of the western provinces. Land north of the sixtieth parallel is commonly considered the North, whether it lies in Canada or in the Soviet. Using this definition, we assume that Canada's North includes north-western Quebec and the rest of the million and a half square miles between the western provinces and the Pole. This is forty per cent of Canada.

From the Pole through the arctic islands to the Canadian mainland is roughly fifteen hundred miles – about as far as from the Pacific Ocean to the Great Lakes. The mainland, unlike its Soviet counterpart, is a barrier for those who must travel by surface. With one great exception – the Mackenzie – it has no major rivers flowing northwards to the sea. Most of the arctic mainland is part of the great Canadian Shield, which reaches from southern Canada to where land ends. Here are the barrens, thoroughly rocky, their granite and gneiss naked of earth, unlike comparable latitudes in the Soviet North. The Canadian North is rolling or hilly, without soaring heights or deep valleys. It has uncounted lakes, more than all the rest of the world together.

To the amateur map-reader the barrens are a nightmare. The heights and dips are indistinguishable, and each lake seems to merge into the next. Sometimes there will be a striking esker: a ridge of gravel, perhaps 150 miles long, left by glaciers, a landmark for pilots and construction crews.

For hundreds of square miles the surface of the land may be shaped by drumlins: debris in long whaleback shapes marking forever the direction in which the glaciers moved. Then for hundreds of miles the ground may have no regular pattern at all. Here are immense and lonely boulders, marooned in the undistinguished sea of gravel and untidy rock. There are few rivers to shape the face of the land, only streams that have their moment of power when the spring sun melts the snows. When the glaciers went, or the sea retreated, it was the silent frost that made most marks, shattering rock and reducing giant monoliths to rubble as the centuries wore on. Frost, too, is the force to move rocky soil down even the gentlest slopes, like a slow landslide that tends to fill the hollows and leave the hilltops bare.

In the Mackenzie Delta, cones of gravel and debris called pingos sprout from the flat ground like ant-hills. Most are less than a hundred feet high, though some rise over twice as far above an otherwise flat and featureless lake bottom. The centres of some of them may be collapsed like volcanoes, though in fact they are caused by an eruption of the permanently frozen ground through a lake that may have since disappeared.

In winter, of course, all the land is frozen. Since snowfall is light, the traveller is usually very much aware of the detailed contours of the ground – the large boulders, the sharp rocks, the rough grain of the drumlins (which he hopes he will not have to cross), the ridges of the eskers. Any rise of more than a few inches is probably swept bare, and the hardy wisps of grass may still stick up like short wires sprouting from the flat ground. Sometimes the light snow has treacherously filled the crevasses, the straight-lined cracks of polygons on land, or the dangerous caverns in the ice of the sea.

In summer the perils of the ground are clear, but with the melting snow goes the sled, the one reasonable means of non-mechanical land transportation. Tramping across the barrens may be an exhilarating experience, or an exasperating feat of endurance. If the rock is flat, or the gravel even like the surface of an esker, there is no problem. If the route is across low, water-soaked soil or muskeg, it gives the feeling of slow progress through a bowl of porridge sown with knife-blades.

Arctic Climate. The summer weather of the Arctic varies relatively little across the Northwest Territories, from the end of the trees to the farthest land at 82°. While it is generally colder in the arctic islands than on the mainland to the south, Resolution Island, at the mouth of Hudson Strait, normally has lower summer temperatures than Ellesmere Island. The mean temperature in July, even in these farthest reaches of the inhabited Arctic, ranges between 40° and 50° — a great deal warmer than central Greenland. At Alert, the mean temperature is as high as 40° in July. Along the coast of the arctic mainland to the west, the summer days are relatively warm, with average July temperatures near the 50° point that marks the end of the Arctic and the beginning of more temperate zones. When the mean July temperature is below 50°, the afternoons may still produce a sunny 60°. The thermometer, even in such arctic zones, sometimes has its brief moment of drama with a reading of 80°. Then the southern Canadians are sometimes seen with cameras and bathing-suits, while those more accustomed to these vagaries through the centuries look on knowingly.

The record winter temperature belongs far from the Arctic. Snag, in the Yukon, boasts with nervous pride a reading of –81° in February 1947. Though winters are undeniably chilly in Snag, its average temperature at this time of year is a modest –19°.

At that most northerly recording point, Alert, the winter temperatures are only ten degrees lower than in the north-west Yukon, but the winter with its darkness and cold persists far longer than in the lower latitudes. The coldest ever recorded in the whole of the Northwest Territories was –63°. High in the arctic islands there is little to choose between January, February, and March, in temperature. For most humans, the sunless January is more of an ordeal than March, whose twenty-first day brings an equal division between sunlight and darkness, just as it does at Montreal, Rio de Janeiro, or on the Equator.

In arctic communities, winter tends to be regarded as an absolute state rather than one of degree. People who live in the arctic winter are like ocean travellers who think in terms of land or sea but not of the depths of the water. For human – or animal – comfort, temperature is of far less consequence than the wind. An intensely cold, calm day is infinitely more tolerable than a more moderate one with winds of gale force. The effect of wind-chill, the rapid loss of the body's warmth through radiation, is keenly felt. Winds lower visibility as they pick up the sparse granules of snow and create a white, directionless wilderness. A wind unbroken by trees, hills, or human shelter creates sheer hard work if the clumsily clad human or his dogs are pushing into its face. The shorter prairie winter has the same cold and biting wind.

Though strong wind may be the traveller's worst enemy, throwing for days a barrage that keeps all life clinging to shelter, there are many days of light breeze or wondrous calm. The Arctic is, in this respect, generally kinder to man than the south-polar regions.

The vast whiteness of the arctic winter, when the wind stirs air and snow into a featureless nothing, or when the landscape lies glaring below a blue sunlit sky, may give the impression of a heavy snowfall. But there is little snow or rain. The Arctic is, in fact, a frozen desert. About the same amount of annual precipitation is found by weather-stations reporting from Canada's Far North and from Cairo. Baker Lake, in the Keewatin District, has about one-eighth the snowfall of Seven Islands, Quebec, less than a quarter as much as Montreal, and not a great deal more than Vancouver or Victoria. Vancouver has ten times as much rain as Baker Lake and seventy times as much as Alert.

Annual rainfall in the Arctic varies from half an inch (Alert) to about eight inches (Lake Harbour). Snowfall may be as little as fifteen inches (Eureka), or as much as eighty-six inches (Resolution Island). Total annual precipitation, calculated on the basis of ten inches of snow equalling one inch of rain, is less than ten inches for almost all of the Arctic, and about five inches for the arctic islands. This is fortunate, for the little snow that falls is constantly lifted from the shelterless plains and deposited in enormous drifts wherever obstructions arise.

The Aurora. On a winter's night the northern heavens may take on the fluorescent colours of the aurora borealis. Though the northern lights are sometimes seen south of the Arctic, they are most brilliant in the polar latitudes, especially in March and April, September and October. The colours range the spectrum; the most common is the bluish green that darts in rays and crowns, spreads like enormous erupting flowers, or shifts like the coloured arc-lights of a pageant. Northerners say that when the aurora is most intense it crackles. The cause of the display is the bombardment of the earth's outer atmosphere by protons and electrons travelling at hundreds of thousands of miles a second; they release energy in the form of light. The aurora is most active during magnetic storms, and, simultaneously, radio communications are either blacked out or seriously disturbed. The electrically charged particles sent out from the sun are guided to the earth's magnetic field. The auroral zone, from seventy to a hundred miles high, lies 20° to 25° from the earth's magnetic pole. During an average display, a hundred million protons and electrons strike one square inch of the earth's atmosphere each second, so that the air seems to be on fire.

The Living Arctic – the Plants. At a distance, the winter Arctic may seem to be a land in which all life has been extinguished, or in which none has been born. Yet in the Canadian Arctic 834 different flowering plants and ferns have been identified.

The growing season is short, but during those few weeks when the ground is exposed to the life-giving sun of summer the sun shines almost constantly. The amount of summer sunlight depends, of course, both on the latitude and on the weather of the day, but the polar regions as a whole naturally have far more summer light than any other part of the planet.

Though rainfall is light, precious traces of moisture are trapped by the permanently frozen ground. Without this permafrost, the Arctic would be a lifeless desert. Were it to be melted through the warming of the polar regions, and were there no accompanying revolution in rainfall patterns, the moisture that falls would quickly drain through the coarse porous soil. The surface would be dry, bleak, and utterly arid.

Life for arctic plants is not such a hopeless proposition as it might seem. When the temperature of the air begins each day to climb close to 32°, plants that find some shelter from the wind are helped by the heat absorbed in the dark soil. That soil, and the air around it, may be as much as twenty-five degrees warmer than the meteorological temperature. Somehow the plants manage to survive the constant freezing and thawing.

Almost all the plants of the Arctic are perennial because the summer is too short for the completion of a life-cycle. Most species need many years from germination to first flowering. The Arctic has no climbing plants; none that sting or poison; none with spines or thorns. Most arctic plants have light, tiny seeds that are carried far by the wind. Many almost identical plants grow across the polar regions of the world.

At the southern edges of the Arctic, willows and junipers hold precariously to life. Some, no thicker in the trunk than a man's thumb, are four hundred years old. The rings marking each summer's growth can be counted only with a microscope. The arctic willow on Cornwallis Island adds only a third of its own weight each year. In southern Canada such a plant can grow as much in a single week. The weight of plant material on Cornwallis Island is only about one per cent of the weight in a similar area in a temperate climate.

The height and weight of arctic plants is small, but their extent is a cause for wonder. Tropical deserts usually nurture plants where the land is low and traces of moisture collect. In the tundra, it is the higher ground that is first carpeted with flowers. As soon as the snow melts in late May or June, the blossom of the saxifrage appears. The sparse soil generally lacks nitrogen, but where the ground is fertilized – for example, near a bird colony – the growth is lush.

Across the rocky desert of the Arctic, lichens and mosses cling to the stone and give it warm colours. Where the gravel looks least promising, the bright arctic poppy has a foothold. Creeping willows, dwarf birch, berry-bearing plants, and heathers develop large root systems to support their stunted growth. The leaves of arctic plants are usually thick and juicy, or stiff and leathery. There are no trees big enough for use in construction, though some can be burned as fuel. Their real importance in the arctic scheme of things lies in the fact that they support birds and the rodents on which fur-bearing animals feed.

The Arctic Animals. Though the Arctic is scarcely teeming with wildlife, on land and sea a remarkable number of animals have made their peace with the cold. Some are small, like the lemming, and some large, like the polar bear and the musk-ox. They range from the tiniest of marine creatures to the walrus and the whale and the narwhal.

Not surprisingly, arctic animals are examples of masterful insulation. Intensive modern research has designed no fabric to equal the properties of the caribou skin, which is almost as useful to man as to the caribou. The musk-ox has a coat of wool so fine that it has been made into garments softer and warmer than the highest grade of cashmere; this wool is covered by guard-hairs almost two feet long, creating the effect of a shapeless gown concealing the wearer's feet. The fur of the white fox is so effective as insulation that the animal does not need to move for warmth until the temperature drops to $-40°$. The ptarmigan has feathers on the soles of its feet.

Only a few animals, such as the arctic ground squirrel, sleep through the winter. The lemming disappears from view, sometimes searching for food, sometimes remaining inactive. The polar bear roams the ice-pack, the musk-ox wanders across the tundra. The caribou migrates from the northern prairies almost to the Arctic Ocean. The raven, unchangingly black through every season, raucously remains when others go. The owl (Ookpik) and the ptarmigan also spend their winters in the Arctic.

Even sea mammals often migrate, not to escape the excesses of the cold, but to avoid the perils of a canopy of ice which cuts them off from breathing. The jar seal and the bearded, or square-flipper, seal stay behind, clawing out breathing-holes over which, if they are unlucky, the patient hunter waits. A persistent arctic legend is that seals use stones as hammers to keep open these vital breathing-spaces. The truth is that they simply scratch newly formed ice, though it is scarcely less remarkable that they prefer such an arduous existence to an annual migration.

Many animals of the Arctic live in cycles of scarcity and abundance. The white fox reaches a population peak every four years, then declines, predictably, to a tenth of its former population. This was disastrous for the trapper in the days when fur was the only source of income. In a cycle interlocking with that of the fox is the lemming, on which the fox feeds. When foxes are scarce, these tiny animals increase prodigiously. They can sweep a landscape as clean as a plague of locusts does. Then they suddenly disappear, from starvation or virus infection. Millions of them are said to end their lives in spectacular mass suicides in the sea, a story more honoured in the long arctic nights than in university lectures. Arctic hares, like their southern cousins, die off in cycles of nine or ten years.

The caribou has dwindled drastically. The explorer David Thompson said he saw three and a half million. The Canadian Wildlife Service estimated 1,750,000 in all Canada at the turn of this century, a sixty-per-cent decline in the next fifty years, and another sixty-per-cent decline in the following six years. Today, their numbers have been cut to a little over two hundred thousand by wolves, disease, destruction of the lichen as prospectors burned their way down to rock, and most of all by the rifle. (This new weapon was given without any lessons in conservation.) The decline appears now to be arrested.

Wherever modern man has gone, the risk of destruction to entire species has loomed. The musk-ox was almost lost. Polar bears were too often hunted for their skins. Control has saved them from extinction, but they will never again spread across the Arctic in great numbers.

The wildlife of the sea has fared generally better, largely because dispersal has made destruction more difficult. The char population has suffered because it is accessible to anglers in fresh water. Only in the fifth year of life does it swim to salt water for a few weeks of summer.

The jar, or ring, seal, the bearded seal, and the harp seal are almost everywhere in arctic sea waters. The walrus feeds on clams and other animal life at the bottom of the sea that fall prey to its enormous tusks. It was making a reasonable peace with the world until the arrival of man; a walrus basking on rocky benches is much too easy a target for the hunter with harpoon or rifle. Though its numbers decline, it is not in danger of extinction. It is more fortunate than the Greenland whale, which was almost swept from the polar seas half a century ago. The white whale, or beluga, can still be found in many parts of the Arctic. So can the narwhal, with its

Maps *(on the next seven pages)*

prepared by C. C. J. Bond

The Canadian North
The Yukon
Circumpolar map
The North-West
The Canadian Shield

On this page:
a portion of Luke Foxe's
circumpolar map, 1635

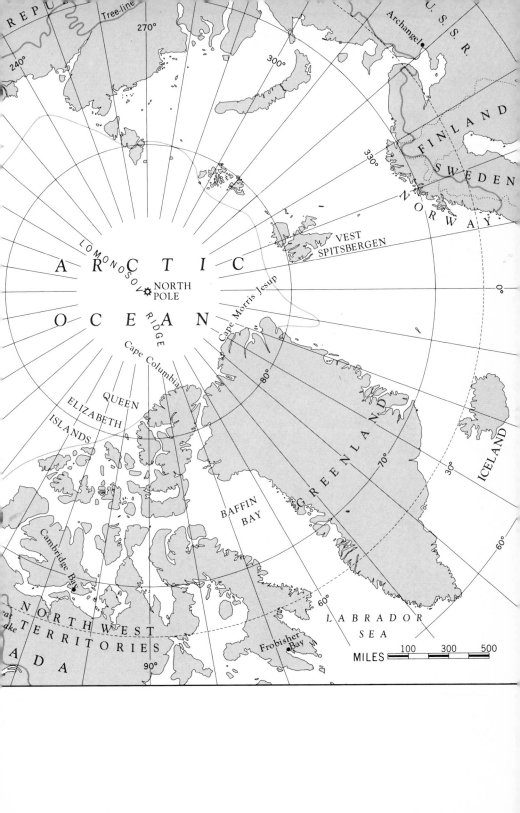

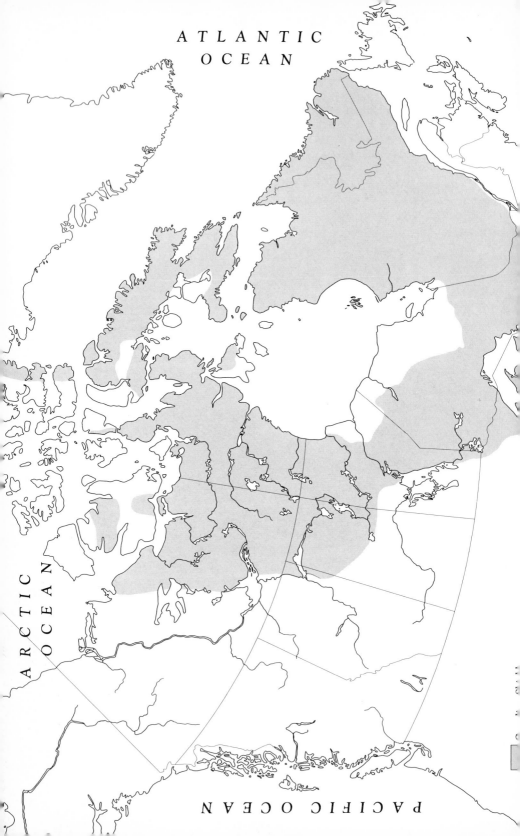

ATLANTIC
OCEAN

ARCTIC
OCEAN

PACIFIC OCEAN

strange, ungainly single tusk up to nine feet long. The narwhal's survival through the ages is the more surprising; its tusk was highly prized for the powers it was believed to possess, both as an aphrodisiac and as an antidote to all manner of poison. In the stories of the narwhal was born the legend of the unicorn.

Of all life in the arctic air, man is most conscious of the mosquito, prodigious in numbers and in fierceness. It can make life a living hell for the unprotected man or beast. Though mosquitoes are sensitive to cold and wind, nearly every part of the inhabited North can expect summer clouds of droning, ravenous insects, and a winter in which the larvae wait dormant like a time-bomb. Repellents are effective, but spraying does little good because these flying predators can drift so far in the wind. If in a philosophical mood, the victim of the mosquito can reflect on the healthy diet these insects provide for birds.

The raven and the ptarmigan – permanent Arctic-dwellers – are joined by about seventy-five other species that come to the Arctic to breed. They arrive noisily in the earliest days of spring to settle in enormous colonies that generally change little from year to year. They lay their eggs in the scantiest of nests, or on the bare ground.

Though some gulls stay the year round, the commonest goes to the Atlantic for the winter. One of the smallest of the gulls, the tern, winters in the Antarctic. This means an annual flight of twenty thousand miles, a remarkable commuting distance which must indicate the tern's high regard for the Arctic. The commonest sea-bird is the murre. It is sometimes likened to the penguin because of its colouring and its habit of walking erect. There are no penguins in the Arctic, and none would survive among the many predators of the North.

Permafrost. Permafrost, or permanently frozen ground, underlies about a quarter of the land surface of the earth, including most of Canada above the sixtieth parallel. The southern limit tends to coincide with the 23° annual mean-temperature line, though there are irregularities, depending on drainage and temperature. The permafrost goes back to the Pleistocene epoch. In some places the permafrost is advancing, but more commonly it is receding at an estimated rate of about twenty-five miles a century.

In the permafrost zone, the ground at the surface freezes and thaws with the seasons. This active layer may be as little as a few inches and as much as a yard deep. Below is the rock-hard frozen ground into which neither roots nor water will penetrate. It may be largely ice, or in well-drained gravels it can be dry permafrost. Little is known about the general thickness of the permafrost. In a mine-shaft at Yellowknife, the sporadic lenses of ice are visible for a few yards below the surface. At Point Barrow, the layer is about a thousand feet thick. A two-thousand-foot test hole in Greenland showed permafrost all the way. On Melville Island in the Canadian Arctic Archipelago, permafrost has been found for fifteen hundred feet in a two-mile hole dug by oil-drillers.

Permafrost creates turbulent effects on land, on roads, and on buildings. Enormous pressures push fine materials into the active layer or up to the surface. The result may be forms of nature such as mud-spots, silt-boils, frost-blisters, ice-mounds, or pingos. Permafrost can cause landslides when the surface soil, thawing soggily in the spring, moves like a glacier downhill over an immovable ice foundation. It makes construction more expensive and hazardous.

Man has only recently learned how to build on permafrost. His failures have sometimes been spectacular. Any heated building disturbs the permafrost. The uneven melting and refreezing change the contour of the ground; the structures are pushed aside as if weightless. The small Presbyterian church in Dawson City is distinguished by a floor about four feet higher at the centre than at the walls. Before engineers learned how to handle permafrost, living-rooms with wildly tilting floors and walls or roads that almost disappeared in spring were common.

Now man tries to leave permafrost as it is. Almost any building affects the radiation of the ground. A road removes the bush cover and allows heat to penetrate. A house generates its own heat. The accepted technique is to insulate this disturbing situation from the underlying permafrost. Thick, well-drained gravel pads provide the cheapest insulating layer. A surer but much more expensive way is to drive wooden piles thirty or forty feet into the permafrost, and to build upon them. Several feet of air space should be left between the building and the ground, to allow heat to be carried away.

The piles are wood because it is a good insulator; in arctic conditions they will last for a hundred years without rotting. They must be hammered in with the aid of steam to melt their path, and then left to freeze. Even after that, it has not been unknown for the piles to edge irrepressibly upwards against tons of dead-weight building, or to twist uselessly from their upright position.

The permafrost layer may be anything from solid rock to muddy water. The layer under Aklavik is more than half water, the rest silt. If it all should suddenly melt, the village would sink or float away. That is not likely to happen for a few thousand years, but the summer bogs of Aklavik give a good indication of how permafrost usually seems to win any feud with man. Communities built later have more successfully avoided the clash.

The permafrost is well below the sub-Arctic ground. It is usually undetectable from above, unless there is a clue in the trees which become unstable when their roots cannot grow downwards into the icy barrier. They heave, fall with the wind, or are pushed sideways by the restless earth.

The Sub-Arctic. The bush sets off the sub-Arctic. This is the Land of Little Sticks. No timber grows on the high mountains of the Yukon. In the southern reaches of both Territories, the trees grow to a fair size. There is wood for local use, for piles, for mine pit-props, and for the telephone poles whose wires join the provinces to the Arctic. There is wood for lumber to build the log cabins of old, or the ranch-style and split-level houses of today's northern towns. There may be wood for plywood. Still, the black spruce, birch, and willow are small by the standards of Canada's forest industries. A northern tree with a diameter of more than twelve inches is uncommon.

From the air much of the sub-Arctic looks like a carpet of bush, with lakes like holes in its even fabric. The form of the land varies widely across the sub-Arctic. On its western edge, the Yukon, part of the Cordilleran region, is high, like the mountainous interior of British Columbia. Most of the Yukon is a large basin between two and three thousand feet above sea-level; its eastern, western, and northern sides are rimmed by peaks of more than ten thousand feet. Mount Logan, nearly twenty thousand feet, is the highest peak in Canada.

The plateau is cut by rivers. Dominating all is the Yukon River, one of the longest navigable waterways in North America. Rising near the boundary of the Yukon and British Columbia, it flows 1,980 miles through Alaska into the Bering Sea. It is fed by the Pelly, the Stewart, and a host of smaller rivers, including the golden Klondike.

A second plateau in the northern Yukon, the Peel Plateau, is drained by the Peel River, which flows north-west into the North-west Territories to join the Mackenzie, just before it loses itself in its delta and the arctic seas. A third and smaller plateau in the south-west is cut by the Liard River which also empties into the Mackenzie.

The special majesty of the Yukon may lie in its dramatic arctic seashore, its rolling, well-used farmlands of the settled south, or the turmoil of its peaks and valleys. It may be powerful river torrents close to the mountain-tops that have left the trees behind. It may be the richness of the sky, the still lakes in summer, or the golden hills in autumn. Or it may be merely that there are not many people about.

In one flat valley a mountain suddenly erupts, perfect in propor-tion, isolated from all other mountains, a simple decoration on the face of the land. 'God put a mountain there,' the Yukoners say, 'so that man may know what a mountain should really look like.'

Across the mountain barrier to the east is the valley of the Mac-kenzie River, a prodigious waterway. It is Canada's longest, and ranks tenth among the rivers of the world. It drains two of Can-ada's largest lakes, Great Slave and Great Bear. Great Bear Lake, a quarter the size of England, is so cold that no plankton lives in its deep waters, and all the fish stay close to shore.

The Mackenzie valley is an extension of the Great Central Plain. Unlike the arctic barrens to the east, it has thick soil. It is a sedi-mentary formation, rich in possibilities for oil and gas. Though the mountains rise to the west, the valley is broad and relatively flat. Despite the immense size of this country, it has only a few spectacular scenes: the Headless Valley of the Nahanni River; the imposing Alexandra and Louise Falls on the Hay River, not far north of the sixtieth parallel; the Ramparts, 250-foot-high cliffs that line the Mackenzie for seven miles; and Prelude Lake, near the north shore of Great Slave Lake.

To the east of the Mackenzie valley is the arctic tundra. To the north again is the sprawling delta of the Mackenzie. This delta is surely the most confusing country in the world. The thin, flat bush is cut up by a million ponds, lakes, and channels whose shapes change as the earth is refashioned. It is brutal country for the amateur navigator, but a paradise for muskrats, which produce excellent pelts on which the delta fur industry is based.

Sub-Arctic Climate. Although the sub-Arctic is not as dry as the desert of the Arctic, Watson Lake in the southern Yukon, with more than six feet of snow and nine inches of rain a year, is the wettest recording station in the Yukon. For Yukon farmers, lack of rain creates a greater problem than low temperature. A few miles nearer the Pacific Ocean, the situation is sharply different. In the Alaskan panhandle, summers are humid and the winter piles snow on snow. This is beyond the boundaries of the Yukon, but not beyond the Yukon's concern: the routes inland from the ocean lie through the panhandle.

The Mackenzie valley has less rain and snow than the Pacific coast. Fort Smith, Yellowknife, and Aklavik, with less than four feet of snow and less than eight inches of rain a year, are drier than prairie cities in both winter and summer. In the east, Toronto has more snow than these Mackenzie towns and more than three times the rainfall.

Whitehorse has a mean annual temperature of 31°, averaging 5° in January and 56° in July, about nine degrees lower than the comparable figures for Quebec City. Yellowknife is colder. Its mean temperature over the year is 22°, with an average of −18° in the coldest month and 60° in the warmest. The towns of the southern Mackenzie are much like the prairies in summer, but in winter the northern temperature is much lower. Fort Smith once reached a summer temperature of 103°; Canada's southernmost city, Windsor, has never been so hot. Right through the Mackenzie valley, July days of 80° are common.

The summer days are long. In Yellowknife, a golf tournament is held at midnight on June 21, and visitors to Dawson are urged to climb the Dome to see the afterglow of yesterday merging with the promise of tomorrow. The summer explodes with a brief and vivid glory. Plants and flowers grow to enormous proportions with the urging of almost endless daylight. Then the frosts come, and with them the anticipation of winter.

In the Yukon plateau, there are generally about forty-five frost-free days when agriculture is possible. In the southern Mackenzie, nearly three and a half months are frost-free; around Fort Simpson, there are nearly three frost-free months. Even on the edge of the Mackenzie Delta, at the Arctic Circle, still within the tree-line, there are more than fifty frost-free days.

Sub-Arctic Plants and Animals. Wildflowers appear with the disappearing snow. The magenta-coloured fireweed, floral emblem of the Yukon, is the most common. The vast variety runs from the delicate mountain avens of the alpine regions to half a dozen varieties of orchid. Along the valley of the Mackenzie River, the wildflowers range from the large bluish-purple flowers of the wild crocus found at the mouth of the Mackenzie Delta to the pink or white blooms of the wild roses that line the Mackenzie Highway.

The boundary between Arctic and sub-Arctic is observed by most animals, but not by the caribou, known as the walking department store because it traditionally provided food, clothing, and summer shelter for the people of the north. Its antlers and bones were the material for tools, and its fat was used for fuel. In spring, caribou herds move from the bush-lands, where they spend the winter, deep into the barrens. For years they may follow the same route, and then mysteriously change course. It is commonly supposed that the caribou is driven north each spring by insects, but better fodder and cooler summer days are likelier incentives. Its route may depend on changing patterns of forage.

In the days before the European came, hunters tried to channel the moving herds into defiles. There, or in shallow water, the caribou was vulnerable to their relatively crude weapons. When the rifle shifted the balance sharply in favour of the hunter, the caribou began its fast decline, to the intense hardship of Indians and Eskimos alike.

Biggest of all the animals of the sub-Arctic is the wood buffalo, found only in a small region near the Northwest Territories–Alberta boundary. A wood buffalo sometimes weighs a ton and measures twelve feet in length. Herds have been reduced not by ignorant destruction but by an ill-advised bureaucratic decision. In the mid 1920s six thousand plains buffalo were shipped north, and breeding with these much smaller animals almost destroyed the once-remarkable strain. Now only five hundred wood buffalo remain.

Moose range far across the Yukon and the Northwest Territories. Other major land animals found across the sub-Arctic are Dall sheep, mountain goat, black bear, grizzly bear, and wolf. There are also fur-bearers – beaver, muskrat, mink, marten, fisher, and lynx. Even hare and squirrel pelts yield minor cash.

The Yukon and the Mackenzie valley are renowned for their fish: salmon, rainbow, steelhead, Great Lake trout, arctic grayling, inconnu, northern chub, northern pike, sculpin, trout, perch, Mackenzie whitefish, the rare Coulter's whitefish, flounder, Great Bear Lake herring, pike, and smelt. In northerly waters the rate of growth and reproduction is slow, but the fact that most of the lakes are seldom fished ensures huge trophies, and a sustained yield in relatively small commercial fisheries.

To summarize or generalize about fauna, flora, climate, or any other aspect of the North is to invite misconceptions. The North is a hundred regions. Its common denominators are few, and its differences are enormous. The Queen Elizabeth Islands are as distant a world to the southern Mackenzie as they are to Ontario. The rock-wall between the Yukon and the east is rarely penetrated. The land and water, the resources beneath the earth, the behaviour of the elements in the atmosphere above – all shape the country and the men who live there. The people of the North have been strangers to one another and strangers to the country of which they have now become consciously a part.

2 | The Coming of Man

Until twelve thousand years ago, Canada was covered by ice.

The glacial, or Pleistocene, period, or the Ice Age, started about six hundred thousand years ago. In the next half-million years the ice retreated and advanced four times. Nearly all the northern latitudes were buried in ice, and nearer the Equator the climate was unusually humid. During the times of greatest ice-cover, North America from the air would have looked much as Greenland does today. None but the highest mountains showed above a sheet of ice a mile thick. The glaciers of Alaska and British Columbia formed a continuous ice-field. The ice spread eastward across the prairies and south below the fortieth parallel, filling the Great Lakes with tongues reaching farther down into the mountains of east and west.

The ice not only hid the face of the northern world: it twisted it. In many places the unbelievable weight pushed down the land

below the level of the sea. At the same time, the gathering of so much water into a frozen blanket on the land lowered the oceans and left exposed what today is covered by sea.

Between the cold periods the climate was temperate; probably it was not very different from today, though some of the exposed land was warmer than now, and other parts colder. We may now be living in a typical pause between glacial periods. When the ice advanced at the end of a warm spell, Canada grew very cold – too severe for human settlement. Long after the ice had retreated far enough from its Pacific edge to permit passage down North America from north to south, the central plains of Canada were covered. As the last phase of the Ice Age began to retreat, perhaps fifteen thousand years ago, a human flow passed across what is today the Bering Strait but was then a land-bridge between the continents. The new-comers made their way southwards towards Mexico and the central plains of the United States, for the way to the north and west was blocked by ice. The path they took was close to the route of today's Alaska Highway. From earliest times, Canada was used as a pathway for people going somewhere else.

As the ice retreated from Canada's western provinces, and as the population pressures built up within the United States, many of the later immigrants chose to move in a direction more east than south. They gradually moved across the plains into Ontario, Quebec, and the Atlantic provinces. These movements took place at least fifteen thousand years ago. They were, of course, not so well ordered as sweeping arrows on a map might suggest. Some of those who were later known as Canadian Indians moved northwards from the United States, while others never ventured much below what is today the international boundary. In one respect we can be clear about their movements: they almost never settled north of the tree-line, though they might make summer forays across the barrens in search of caribou. The tree-line remained as real and as solid a boundary as an ocean's shore. And so it is today.

To explain the origins of the Eskimos, one theory suggests that some had been pushed north from southern Canada. It has, for example, been held that those who came to depend upon the caribou gradually followed the northern migration route from Manitoba and Saskatchewan into Keewatin. This theory is no longer in

favour. It is generally accepted that the Eskimos were a later migration of people from the north-west corner of the continent, people who never moved south of the tree-line.

Beringia (as those parts of Asia and America near the Bering Strait are often called) is generally believed to have been the homeland of Eskimo culture. It was on the shores of Alaska and Siberia, as well as on land now submerged by the Bering Sea, that the Eskimos learned the arts of arctic living. This proposition is supported by archaeologists who have found rich evidence of succeeding layers both of static settlement and of apparent migration. The identification of this ancient homeland has another form of support which, while of doubtful scientific weight, is intriguing to the imagination. The Eskimos, like so many primitive peoples, preserve in their legends the tradition of a great flood that inundated the hunting-grounds of their forebears. Could the explanation be the sinking of the Bering Strait, perhaps ten thousand years ago? If so, the unwritten folk tales of the Eskimos have shown a wondrous tenacity.

Those who seek the history of the Canadian Eskimos before their life in Beringia have, so far, little evidence to build on. The Eskimo language provides virtually no clues, for it seems to be akin to no other language on earth. The appearance of the Eskimos themselves is Mongoloid, but this does no more than suggest an eastern Asiatic background. Some say that Peking Man is the forerunner of the Mongoloid people who developed physical characteristics best adapted to the cold. This early pre-history is highly conjectural. The only safe starting-point is Beringia, and even from that point history is far from clear.

It was probably around 4000 B.C. that the Eskimos arrived in North America. Some stayed in the Aleutian Islands and on the coasts of Alaska. Others spread eastwards into the Canadian barrens because of population pressures and altering patterns in hunting, or as a result of a changing climate. Diggings in Alaska have turned up Eskimo tools made around 3000 B.C. Remains at Independence indicate a movement into north Greenland at least four thousand years ago. Archaeologists have not yet found evidence to identify the time and place of movements east from Alaska into Canada.

At some stage, two quite different patterns of Eskimo culture began to emerge. They have been given the names of the communities where they were first identified: Thule and Dorset. Apparently the Dorset Eskimos occupied the Canadian Arctic from about 700 B.C. to A.D. 1200. Unlike the Eskimos we know today, they had no long sleds or dogs, but in winter travelled on foot. Their houses, partly underground, were made of stone slabs and boulders with turf. Although a few Dorset Eskimos may have survived on Southampton Island until the beginning of the twentieth century, the Dorset culture was gradually overtaken by the more advanced Thule culture in Canada, from about a thousand years ago. The Thule Eskimos had been thriving in the extreme north-west of the continent long before they moved to the east, following a life similar to the customs recorded by European explorers of recent times. These Thule Eskimos seem to have moved right across the top of the continent into Labrador and Greenland, reaching there about the tenth century A.D., just as the Norsemen were arriving from the east. Remains of early Thule communities have been found all over the Canadian Arctic, except in the Queen Elizabeth Islands.

There may well have been Eskimo groups other than the Dorset and the Thule. Eskimo legends speak of a race of people called the Tunit, or Tornit, who were supposedly very powerful. Though many theories have been advanced to explain who they were, it now seems that they could have been a group of the Dorset people. Excavations on the shores of Foxe Basin suggest the existence of a quite different civilization, earlier than any of the Dorset or Thule cultures. These people probably lived four or five thousand years ago, and came not long after the ice retreated.

Although present-day Eskimos evince many differences in dialect, clothing, and tools, all of the Canadian Eskimos are more or less similar because they share a common heritage from the Thule Eskimos.

One group of Canadian Eskimos remained distinctly different from the rest. Only they declined to make their homes beside the sea. They lived in the interior of Keewatin, depending for food, clothing, and summer shelter upon the caribou. They took no sea animals. Hence they lacked the traditional Eskimo oil-lamp, burning a kind of local heather for heat. When European ways invaded the Arctic, the Caribou Eskimos proved peculiarly vulnerable to the upset in the balance of nature. The caribou could be destroyed by the rifle more readily than could any other arctic animal. When the caribou had gone, life ebbed away for the people of the deer.

The Traditional Eskimo Way of Life. With Sir Edward Parry as he journeyed into western Hudson Bay between 1821 and 1824 was Captain George Francis Lyon. Like many of his profession in an earlier age, he possessed an unusual gift for writing and sketching. His journal recorded in detail the life of the Eskimos he encountered during the unusually prolonged contact between the members of the expedition and the permanent residents of north-western Hudson Bay. More than any other source, this finely illustrated record has formed the basis of popular writing about the Eskimos, even in modern times when Eskimo life has changed. After Lyon, many distinguished anthropologists and explorers described in great detail the life of the Eskimo community before and after the invasion of European culture. The Eskimos have been among the most copiously recorded peoples on earth. It seems certain that they have had more words lavished on them per capita than have any others. The contrast with their nearest neighbours, the northern Indians, is sadly striking.

Before European contact there may have been as many as two hundred thousand Eskimos, but more likely there were about one hundred thousand throughout the world, or twice as many as there are now. In Canada, where there are now about twelve thousand, there were probably never more than twenty to twenty-five thousand. None lived in large communities. Except for the relatively few Caribou Eskimos, they were spread along the sea-coasts from Alaska to Labrador: even within historic times they made their homes as far south as the lower St. Lawrence, when the climate and water of the gulf were cooler than now.

All Eskimos, before the substantial inter-breeding with Europeans, had Mongoloid characteristics: black hair, dark brown eyes, high cheek-bones, and wide faces. They appear short and stout, but this is partly an illusion created by bulky, loose-fitting clothing. The Eskimo's legs and arms are short, but his torso is long and powerful. Although the nose appears broad, the bony nasal passage is one of the shortest known. Though his skin appears to be dark, actually it is fair except where face and hands have been exposed to sun and wind. Eskimos seem to be somewhat more resistant to cold than are Europeans, and to be able more easily to digest and assimilate fat.

Only with extraordinary ingenuity could any human beings live in the harsh climate of the Canadian Arctic. The best-known invention to meet such a climate was the igloo, which was a creation of the Canadian Eskimos. 'Igloo' means merely house, but to non-Eskimos it has come to mean the unique dome-shaped structure of snow. It has the combined advantages of strength, insulation, and speed of construction. A simple shelter for the night can be well built within an hour. Even more elaborate, semi-permanent dwellings can be quickly erected and readily abandoned when they become dirty. The igloo is made of snow blocks, not layer on layer, but as a continuous spiral that depends for its success on the slight angling given to each apparently rectangular block. The building material is the hard, wind-packed snow; the hole made by cutting out the blocks becomes the centre of the igloo; to the back, the snow is left to serve as a sleeping-platform. As the spiral goes up, the builder stands inside, cutting and fitting each block with his snow-knife. When the key block is finally slipped into place, the structure is strong enough to take the weight of a man.

Inside the snow house, the temperature can be raised by oil lamp, as well as body heat, to forty or fifty degrees higher than the wind-swept outdoors. There is, of course, a limitation on its temperature, for if the air rises much above freezing-point the melting snow can be exceedingly uncomfortable and unhealthful. All joints are chinked with loose snow. As further protection from the outdoors, the entrance to the snow house is reached by a low passage which is used as a storehouse for meat. The door is a snow block, the window a piece of clear ice or seal intestine. Such elaborations are not necessary in an igloo for the night.

The snow house was an excellent dwelling in the circumstances of the old Arctic, when skins for clothing and for sleeping-platforms were plentiful. The igloo was more hygienic than the traditional stone and turf house of the Dorset or Thule cultures, or the sod house common in Greenland and Alaska. The snow house met its most serious limitation at the beginning and end of the season, when the intense cold preceded the snow and when the spring sun melted the walls. When finally the snow house had to be abandoned, the skin tent took its place for the summer months. Skins were sewn together so skilfully as to be completely waterproof, and the centre was suspended by a pole of driftwood or bone. Outside, around the edge, boulders were placed in a ring to keep the skins from blowing. When the family went away, naturally they did not bother to shift the boulders. The tent-ring remained — often for centuries — as the record of the temporary sojourn of some long-forgotten family. Since tents were pitched close to shore, the present distance of ancient tent-rings from the sea indicates the upward movement of the land.

Another renowned Eskimo invention was the skin kayak which enabled the Thule Eskimos to pursue mammals in the sea. It is exceedingly light, its hull designed to present a minimum of resistance. The sole occupant of the kayak could attain great speeds with his double paddle. The boat's deck was a good weapon base for the hunter. It held the harpoon and line, as well as an inflatable sealskin known as an avatak. This device, blown up like a balloon and attached to the line, slowed the progress of the wounded beast and exhausted it.

The kayak was useful for hunting, but not for travelling. Water transportation in summer was by umiak, a larger open boat, also with skin hull. Its skeleton was made with driftwood, lashed together with skin thongs. An umiak was sometimes big enough to carry thirty people, with their dogs and other possessions. Lacking such a boat, the family would have to travel by land, each dog carrying a pack of thirty or forty pounds. Since the rest of their belongings were on human backs, this form of transportation discouraged the accumulation of worldly goods.

In winter, travel was easier, though any kind of transportation was fraught with problems. The sled and dog-team moved everything. The number of dogs varied with the affluence of the owner. Generally, a team of more than ten created an undue food problem. Two, or even one, might be used in adversity, but fewer than four would generally give too little motive power. As a rough rule, dog teams under reasonable conditions carried about one hundred pounds per dog. The sleds, as long as thirty feet, would stick in granular snow as though it were sand, unless the runners were specially treated. Since ice will not adhere well to wood or bone, a coating of mud and reindeer moss was plastered on, a few inches thick, then smoothed before freezing. This coating, with minor repairs, would last all winter, but a glazing of ice had to be applied each day.

The Eskimos' winter clothing was light and efficient. They wore two layers of caribou skin. Next to the body was a hooded parka and trousers, the fur turned inside. This was the standard dress for inside the snow house. For outdoor wear, a second parka and trousers were added, the fur turned outside. Double stockings were worn in moccasins. The women's parka had a large hood in which to carry a baby. This caribou skin was not only extremely warm, but unequalled in its ability to shed snow. In summer, sealskin was substituted. Boots, also of sealskin, were kept soft by the women's chewing them.

For hunting on land, the Eskimo used a bow made of wood, antler, or musk-ox horn, its short pieces carefully spliced together. Arrows might be tipped with flint, bone, or ivory. On the water, the harpoon with detachable ivory head tipped with flint or stone was the standard weapon. Spears were used at close quarters. Fish were caught with a three-pronged spear, or with a hook and ivory lure.

Eskimos used a number of cleverly made implements for sewing and scraping, most of them of stone. Around Coppermine, native copper was common, and occasionally farther east bits of meteoric iron were hammered into parts for implements. Entirely made of stone was the long, shallow lamp called the kudlik, in which animal oil was burned. Bits of the arctic cotton plant or moss along the edge served as a wick, though it took some skill to ensure an even flame.

In the days before the European came, the Eskimo was nomadic, moving at the dictates of the hunt and of the seasons. The family was the social unit, and a few families often lived and hunted together in a loose community relationship. There was, of course, no village to act as a pole-star in their wanderings. While their predictable travels were between summer and winter hunting areas, they were equipped and ready to move much greater distances, according to the exigencies of game or of neighbours. Life could be brutal and short, especially when the hunt was poor. Infanticide was an economic necessity, for the family was in greater need of males for hunting than of females for domestic tasks. Those too old to contribute to the search for food knew that they must no longer be a burden: custom told them what to do. They were commonly left in a snow house to die when the camp moved on.

Sudden death by misadventure, or the agonizing failure of the food supply, were accidents to be accepted with a certain fatalism. When things went well, the dark moments were quickly forgotten. The Eskimo has always had a reputation among Europeans for good cheer, a quality that the visitors have almost universally found endearing. It would be misleading, though, to regard this generous nature and good-hearted attitude as indicative of a simple, happy life. Asen Balikci's study of the suicide rate among certain Caribou Eskimos suggests tensions as great as in a modern city.

The average Eskimo community was very loosely organized. Since there were no hereditary chiefs, one man would lead because of his skill in the hunt or his real or imagined occult powers. Discipline was easy. Although individual and family independence were marked, the power of public opinion made formal regulation unnecessary. Eskimos worked together, sharing in the bounty of the hunt, or taking responsibility for the sick. Theft and lying were apparently unknown.

Eskimo religion centred on supernatural characters that controlled the weather or the hunt. There was a rigid system of taboos, some with a rational basis. The shaman was respected for his supposed power to intercede with supernatural forces.

The Eskimos had no written language. There was, however, a strong oral tradition, which ensured the transmission of legends through generation after generation. The Eskimos' only musical instrument was the drum, and their major form of recreation was the drum dance. This was the occasion for the telling of old tales by a singer beating time on the drum and dancing, or for recounting recent exploits of the hunt. One unusual feature of these gatherings was the settlement of disputes by a song duel: one man sang a song ridiculing his opponent, the other replied in kind. The verdict of the audience was bloodlessly accepted. There were, however, other occasions when passions transcended this civilized kind of safety-valve.

Besides the drum dance, there were other forms of amusement. Eskimos were skilled jugglers. They worked string figures of great complexity. They carved stone and ivory for pleasure, or to evoke the spirits of the animals they hunted. They also played a form of football.

To the Arctic new-comer, all this seemed an exotic and fascinating life. With the exception of those whose minds had already been warped by racial prejudices in other climates, almost everyone has accepted the Eskimos. They have been studied, written about, and, above all, romanticized. Many new-comers have paid the final compliment of trying to follow their way of life and be 'adopted' by them for greater or lesser periods. These amicable gestures were, alas, usually quite unfamiliar to the northern Indian

The Indians. The Athapaskan Indians who settled in the Mackenzie valley may well have been among the last of the Indian immigrants to Canada. Even so, they were probably long established when the first Eskimos moved into the barrens to the north of them. No one can say with conviction when and how the Indians came. It seems a reasonable guess that about ten thousand years ago they migrated from Beringia, down the Alaska Highway route, then east through British Columbia towards Alberta, for by then the plains were free of ice. It also seems reasonable to conjecture that this was not a single movement, for they probably settled in Alberta before some combination of pressures from the south and the attractions of a virgin wilderness led them into the Mackenzie valley. Gradually they spread northwards to the Mackenzie Delta, as far as the tree-line. Their eastern boundary was also the edge of the bush.

All the tribes occupying the Mackenzie and Yukon valleys belonged to the Athapaskans, a language group that reached from near the Arctic Ocean to New Mexico and Arizona. There were nine tribes in the Yukon and the Northwest Territories — the Kutchin, Hare, Nahanni, Yellowknife, Dog-Rib, Slave, Chipewyan, Sekani, and Beaver. While tribal decisions had a little more meaning among Indians than among Eskimos, the northern Indian had a much vaguer tribal structure than most Indians to the south. The real social unit was the family. Like Eskimos, Indians would band together in groups of several families to hunt or to withstand some human danger. Although they sometimes intermarried, the lack of agriculture and the relative sparseness of game encouraged the Indians to disperse. They could rarely hold large meetings.

Each family group and band had a leader chosen, as in the Arctic, for qualities of leadership or skill in the hunt. There was no hereditary title to power. The families moved about freely within a well-defined territorial preserve claimed by the band. The customs, and even the dialects, of the bands differed. It might be generally concluded that in their organization the northern Indians were closer to Eskimos than to other Indians, for the sparseness of the occupation of the land and the frailty of communications were barriers to the sort of cohesion − not to mention the military friction − common to many southern tribes. To the Eskimos, who possessed no word for war in their whole rich language, the Indians were a blood-thirsty lot. Among the Indians as a whole, the residents of the North seemed relatively amiable, spending more time struggling with nature than with their neighbours.

The northern Indians were people of moderate stature and slender build, without the prominent beaked nose of the Plains Indians. Their faces were usually dark, their hair black and straight, their cheek-bones slightly prominent.

Life was harsh and uncertain for these nomadic hunters. A surplus of game or fish was rare, and famine was common. Living in the bush, the Indian could use wood for fuel and shelter. He travelled in the soft snow with snowshoes or toboggans. Like the Eskimo, he used dog-drawn sleds; but the Indian, tracking along a narrow path through the woods, had to harness the dogs in tandem, rather than with the fan-hitch that was practical in the treeless Arctic. In summer, the Indian used a canoe made of birch bark, spruce bark, or moose hide.

Bows and arrows, spears, and snares were the weapons of the hunt. Caribou were killed after they were led into a pound, or herded into water where they could be speared from canoes. Fish were caught with bone fish-hooks trolled from canoes, or jigged through the winter ice. Unhindered by game wardens, they fished at night with torches and three-pronged spears. Ambitious fish-seines were often made from willow bark or caribou thongs, but no fishing device was as spectacular as the Yukon Indians' fish-wheel, left in the water during the salmon run. The fish swim in and cannot get out; and the power of the flowing stream turns the large wooden drum, lifts the fish, and drops them into a trough at the end of the drum.

The Indians of the more southern regions lived in caribou-skin tepees throughout the year. Farther north, they covered their tents with spruce bark. In winter, they made lodges with poles chinked with moss and topped with boughs or spruce bark.

Clothing was made mainly from caribou or moose hide. The men wore shirts of caribou or rabbit, with a hood or separate hat in winter. The women's skirts were long. Women also wore moccasins and leggings. While the men's leggings came up to the thigh, the women's reached only to the knee. Clothing was often richly embroidered with dyed porcupine quills or moose hair. Both men and women favoured tattooing. In contrast to modern practice, only the men painted their faces.

Implements and weapons were made of wood, bone, horn, and antler, and sometimes had blades or tips of native copper or stone. Bark or woven spruce root was used for cooking-vessels. Since these could not be exposed to flame, stones were heated and then dropped into the container of water.

Social life was not particularly rich or varied. There were few large gatherings, and lavish entertainment was never popular among these northern groups. There was no great oral tradition in song, as in the Arctic, though dancing and gambling were popular diversions.

Some Indian bands had shamans who claimed supernatural powers. Lacking a variety of medicaments, the shaman's approach was generally psychiatric. When he lost his patient, the fates were blamed. Religious dogma was simple. The Indian looked to the spirits of animals or birds to help him in the hunt. Despite, or because of, the travails of the present world, he gave little thought to the Valhallas that were so vivid in the imagination of more southern tribes.

From the earliest European accounts, the Indian seems to have had a gloomier outlook than the Eskimo, though they were presumably moulded by somewhat the same forces. When faced with heavy odds, the Indian lacked nothing in bravery, but he apparently leaned more to pessimism than to fatalism. He developed a reputation for unreliability among the Europeans. It might well be unfair, though, to lay upon the shoulders of the Indian the full blame for the lack of rapport that has often characterized inter-ethnic relations in the sub-Arctic.

Whatever their attitude to society, Canada's oldest citizens in the Arctic and sub-Arctic had made their own peace with the elements. For both peoples, it was a tough, uneasy life. Perhaps it was also an uncomplicated life, free of the material rewards and dangers of a more sophisticated society, free of the complex competition of the world outside. Whether the old life was a better life than the one that was to come with the European, no man will ever know.

3 | Enter the European

When Columbus made his well-remembered voyage to the Caribbean, Canada had been known to Europeans for more than five hundred years.

The early years of Canada and of the United States were therefore sharply different. The fifteenth-century European discovery of the United States was the result of a bold, almost desperate attempt to break the barrier of the unknown in search of a short trade route to Asia. Though Canada was also a barrier for adventurers on the path to Asia, Canadian history in its European beginnings had quite another focus. Northern Canada was the frontier of northern Europe.

The ferment that led explorers to the Canadian frontier did not begin in the fifteenth-century courts of Lisbon and Madrid, or in the counting-houses of London and Bristol. It started much earlier, in Scandinavia. During the ninth century Vikings had advanced, by sword and sail, over much of Europe. They had penetrated as far as Italy and North Africa, and had settled a good part of the British Isles. By 870 they were moving farther outwards and northwards into Iceland. By 930 Iceland was settled to the point of overcrowding. The path of empire, or merely the flow of population expansion, was towards Greenland. In 982, the first Vikings set foot there, led by Eric the Red. Eric was probably born in Iceland. Outlawed from 982 to 985 for killing one of his countrymen, he spent his time exploring Greenland. 'Eric the Red', says the Saga of Frode, 'was the name of the man who sailed thither from thence and there took land at the place which is since called Eriksfiord. He gave the land a name and called it Greenland, and said that having a good name would entice men to go thither.'

The Vikings wintered on the west coast of Greenland. Like the American frontiersmen who pushed westwards into the middle of the North American continent in the nineteenth century, they were attracted by uninhabited open spaces, with plenty of game and the promise of good farmland. In Greenland, the new-comers apparently found no human opposition. Later the Vikings were to meet Eskimos whom they called Skraelings. No one knows what happened when they met. Some historians argue that there was more marriage than murder, and that the early colonists, who were lost to sight for centuries, were absorbed into the Eskimo population. Others say that the fierce Eskimos killed them off. Again, they may have died of disease or starvation.

In 986 Eric the Red, his exile over, returned to Iceland and organized a flotilla of twenty-five ships, fourteen of which reached the west coast of Greenland. The son of one of Eric's immigrants set out to join his father for the Yuletide of the same year. Through the perils of weather or through poor navigation, this Bjarni Herjolfsson apparently reached Canada instead. Though he did not land, he was probably the first European to see Canada. This was 506 years before the voyage of Columbus.

These early Vikings were skilled and active colonizers who brought farm animals and implements. They built substantial barns and houses; the remains of one of their fourteen churches are still standing today. The sheep of south-west Greenland still graze around the walls where the Vikings first began farming a thousand years ago.

A few years later, probably about 1000, the son of Eric the Red, known appropriately as Leif the Lucky, did land in Canada. In the next two decades, the Vikings made many landings in those parts of North America they called Markland and Vinland. Differing opinions about the identification of Vinland have placed it at spots all the way from James Bay to New England. The likeliest location long seemed to be in the neighbourhood of Cape Cod. Markland was thought to be the Labrador coast until 1961, when Helge and Anne Ingstad, by identifying Viking ruins at L'Anse-aux-Meadows, showed that Markland was really in the northern tip of Newfoundland. For two centuries Newfoundland, or Markland, was a source of timber and perhaps other supplies for the Greenlanders who lived beyond the tree-line. These voyages between Canada and Greenland seem to have been common. They were economically more useful to Labrador and the Greenlandic colonies than were the probings into the mysterious Vinland.

The well-established colonies of Greenland were probably a base for many voyages to the west, but the sailors who undertook them were better navigators than chroniclers. Perhaps it was orally that word spread of this new Ultima Thule, the present Canadian Eastern Arctic. Throughout the Middle Ages it was known not as a curiosity, or as a route to somewhere else, but for two prized resources: falcons and polar bears.

In the early thirteenth century, Frederick II referred to Greenland in his definitive work *The Art of Falconry*. He knew of Greenland because the Viking falconers brought their birds there from the Canadian Arctic. The Canadian islands were known as the Falcon Islands. The Arab Abu'l-Hasan 'Ali Ibn Sa'id wrote of Baffin Island where 'men get good falcons'. Marco Polo in the thirteenth century wrote of the abundant 'gerfalcons' and peregrine falcons apparently from the Canadian archipelago. By the fourteenth century the Canadian arctic islands often appeared on maps as a source of falcons and polar bears, regarded by royalty as precious gifts. The trading monopoly that the Vikings maintained over the Canadian islands, Greenland, and Iceland was of commercial significance because of the enormous prices paid for falcons and polar bears.

By the fifteenth century, the Danish kings ruled Scandinavia. In a treaty of 1432 the English respected their monopoly. About 1470, King Christian I of Denmark undertook to show two Portuguese emissaries his western possessions, and the expedition may have visited Baffin Island and Labrador. Thus, from the earliest days of European discovery in the Canadian Eastern Arctic there was frequent, if not constant, contact between Canada and Greenland, and between Greenland and Scandinavia. The well-established Danish claims to all these northern possessions were tacitly recognized in the Papal Bull of 1493, which divided the world between Spain and Portugal. No mention was made of the known lands of the North Atlantic, presumably because these were recognized to be already ruled by a Christian king.

By the end of the fifteenth century, the spirit that had driven the Viking frontiersmen west had dwindled and died. They probably maintained contact with the arctic islands because of the immediately lucrative resources there, but they did not push farther west or south. The pressures of population that once led the adventurous from Iceland to Greenland were no longer strong. The population dwindled as many colonists slipped from agriculture into the hunting life of the Eskimo who, by the eleventh century, had crossed from Canada into Greenland and settled along the west coast. The resources for imperial adventurings had disappeared. Thus, although no European power had questioned Scandinavian suzerainty over the north-eastern reaches of Canada for five hundred years, these reaches were now about to be dominated by the English for the next five hundred years. The twentieth century would bring another age, in which Canadians would develop their own resources.

English sailors may have sighted Canada a few years before John Cabot's journey. Certainly the merchants of Bristol were enterprising promoters of fisheries, rivals of the Icelanders. Their sailors may have penetrated the Grand Banks and seen land. Of immensely more significance were the voyages of John Cabot in 1497 and 1498. Although he was an Italian, it was Bristol money that took him west, and it was for the King of England that he claimed Newfoundland.

Cabot, looking for Asia, was the first of a line of searchers that was to stretch down through the nineteenth century. Almost all saw Canada as a route to somewhere else. Cabot's discovery of a formidable barrier on the way to his goal was more disappointing to him than to his backers in Bristol. Cabot described the Atlantic fisheries with the hyperbole of a promoter. In the years after his voyages, the Grand Banks swarmed with the fishing-boats of England and other European nations.

Meanwhile, men of even broader vision were looking northwards to a route that would circumvent the land barrier. Martin Frobisher was born in Yorkshire in 1540, and within fourteen years he was sailing foreign seas. He became obsessed with the dream of finding a passage to the north-west, but none would share his vision. At last, through the Earl of Warwick, he was able to launch an expedition. His ships were the *Gabriel* and the *Michael*, neither over thirty tons, and a small pinnace just one-third their size. They were pitiably small to venture into the North Atlantic, let alone into the unknown ice of the Eastern Arctic. His crew in all numbered only thirty-five. The equipment and supplies were no more adequate than the vessels and the knowledge of the men who manned them.

He set sail down the Thames on June 19, 1576. Queen Elizabeth took note of this imperial adventure and waved her handkerchief to the departing sailors. On July 11 they saw Greenland. On July 29 they first sighted Canada. The land they scanned was Resolution Island, at the entrance to Hudson Strait. Frobisher called it Elizabeth Foreland. Thence they moved to the north along the eastern shore of Baffin Island. They sailed up Frobisher Bay to an island where, on August 19, an historic meeting took place. Frobisher's encounter with Eskimos was an unhappy affair on both sides. There was some communication between them, and Frobisher was shown their houses and 'their manner of food and life, which is very strange and beastly'. The episode ended in a skirmish, and the loss of five of the Englishmen, who either were captured or decided to settle. The captain took an Eskimo hostage back to England, arriving in London on October 9. It is said that in England the Eskimo died of cold.

Frobisher was bitterly disappointed that the wretched condition of his crews forced him to go back after his men had spied 'two headlands at the further ends of the straits and a great opening between them which, by reason of the great flooding tides, which they found coming out of the same, they judged to be the West Sea, whereby to pass to Cathay and to East India' (from the account of Michael Lok, who with George Beste chronicled the expedition).

Among his souvenirs, Frobisher brought back a piece of black rock. When a friend inexplicably threw it into a fire, shining flecks were disovered. This touched off Canada's first gold rush. After all his years of struggle for financial support for the finding of a passage that would change the world, Frobisher now found no problem in raising money for an expedition in the following year, but he was commissioned 'to deferre further searching for the passage, and to look only unto the golde'. He returned to Frobisher Bay with the *Michael* and the *Gabriel*, and a new ship as well. Things did not go well. Frobisher's party again encountered Eskimos, who 'hurt the General in the buttocks with an arrow' (George Beste). They did no exploration of consequence beyond Frobisher Bay, but they 'brought aboard almost two hundred tons of gold ore in the space of twenty days'. This evoked enormous excitement, and generous financial support. In 1578, Frobisher set out a third time, now with a veritable armada of fifteen vessels. They intended to winter on Baffin Island, and to that end built a house of lime and stone on Countess of Warwick's Island in Frobisher Bay. Unfortunately, they encountered unusually bad weather. They lost part of their supplies, cached the remainder, and set sail for England well burdened with their ore.

Up to this point it appeared that Frobisher, who visited the Arctic only as an explorer, had stumbled on its mineral resources and the true significance of the Canadian North. But it was not to be. The ore was not gold but almost worthless iron pyrites. His important pioneering voyages forgotten, Frobisher was to be known, instead, for a distinguished naval career, including service against the Spanish Armada. He died in action in 1594.

As Frobisher Bay slipped back into the anonymity of the ages, even the map-makers ignored the discoverer of Baffin Island. It was not until 1861 that Frobisher emerged in his proper perspective in history. During the preceding winter, Captain Charles Hall dis-

covered the remains of Frobisher's expedition, including the house
of lime and stone. Much more remarkably, he heard from the
Eskimos the story of the encounter between their ancestors and
Frobisher's party, nearly three hundred years before. The Arctic is
an extraordinary preserver of more than wood, lime, and stone.

The last footnote to Frobisher's arctic career was written another
hundred years later. In the reign of Queen Elizabeth the Second
men sought Baffin Island, not for gold, but for the richest iron ore
in the world.

Today we can scarcely imagine the difficulties faced by mariners
like Frobisher, and the explorers who followed him in the search for
the Northwest Passage. In comparison with Frobisher, even astro-
nauts have every advantage. Frobisher's ships were no larger than
the pleasure vessels one sees today on the Great Lakes. They were
utterly unfitted for the ice, all trust being placed in the stoutness of
the English oak. Though they were propelled only by sail, even at
rest the force of the relentless ice-pack could crush such vessels
utterly. The early explorer had no maps, and only vague notions of
what lay beyond even Iceland. Every fog-enshrouded bay or indenta-
tion in the coast might be the Passage. For days, these early mariners
might probe gingerly through the ice, praying each moment for the
fabled sea that would open upon the imagined palaces, the silk, the
spices, and immortality. They edged, and waited, and drifted back;
or, when they had found a lead into the endless maze of ice, the wind
might fail them. Eventually they moved forward, straining for a
change in the bordering coastlines. Then at last, at the end – land
again. It was not the Passage. Once more all the agony of extrication,
while one more mark was placed on the map of northern Canada.

Always there was the race against time. Even when an expedition
took what seemed ample stores, storms and other accidents often
brought disastrous losses. No one could live off the land; indeed,
they could not live from the provisions they had brought. Scurvy
was as menacing as the ice itself, and even more mysterious.

And yet they persevered. Like the participants in the Klondike
gold rush, these sailors suffered unbelievable agonies of body and
spirit in the pursuit of their goal. Like them, they sought the riches
that lay 'beyond that last blue mountain flecked with snow, beyond
that angry or that glimmering sea'. As the years wore on, it must

have been painfully clear to all who would see that there was no real
hope of instant wealth. Yet the North drew men. The failure of one
generation served only as a spur to the next, until all the pathways
had been traced, until the whole North itself would be possessed by
man.

John Davis was the first to follow Frobisher. Only seven years
later he skirted the western shore of Greenland, sailed west to Cape
Dyer on Baffin Island, went south to Cumberland Sound, and then
made for home. The belief was then strong that, if one could but
reach the polar seas, one would find open water leading to the
Passage. He made two more voyages in this direction, each time
turned back by a shortage of supplies.

George Weymouth took the famous little barque *Discovery* into
Hudson Strait in 1602, but did not persist into the great inland sea
beyond. This was left to Henry Hudson, one of the most remarkable men ever to seek the Passage. After one attempt straight for the
Pole east of Greenland, and equally unsuccessful probes into the
Northeast Passage, he was able, after the discovery of Manhattan
Island and the Hudson River, to get support for an expedition to follow up Weymouth's voyage. In 1610 he took the *Discovery* through
Hudson Strait into Hudson Bay, sailing south right to James Bay,
where he wintered. The following June he was defeated, not by the
long odds of the Arctic, but by his ill-assorted, mutinous crew. With
his son and seven companions Hudson was cut adrift in a boat.

Now the map of the New World was changed. Englishmen had
penetrated nearly half a continent in a season. This was the sea on
whose shores China must surely be. There was mercy for the mutineers who had murdered Hudson, for upon their knowledge depended the success of the oriental trading voyages to come. The *Discovery*, now under the command of Sir Thomas Button, entered
this new frontier again in 1612. Button sailed straight across Hudson Bay to winter in Manitoba. He added to the maps of Canada the
estuaries of the Nelson and Churchill rivers, and six hundred miles
of coastline to the north. All was land. This was indeed a bay, and
not the sea.

Robert Bylot and William Baffin followed soon afterwards. Bylot
sailed in with the *Discovery*, on which he had served as a mate

under Hudson, and as captain when the mutineers took over. In 1615 he and Baffin went north-west in Hudson Bay. The following year they returned to explore Baffin Island. Reaching farther than anyone else in this region for 237 years, they sailed past Lancaster Sound, unaware that it was the beginning of the passage to the Pacific Ocean. Today, when every square mile of Canada has been photographed and entered on maps, when every strait and headland is within the knowledge of any school-boy, when those who sail the Arctic are armed, not only with every aid to navigation, but often with the helicopter that raises man's vision thirty miles or more, these probings seem like a diabolical game of snakes and ladders. The prolonged search for the Passage through the labyrinth of scattered land and ice persisted simply because of the failures of the past, because of the conviction that the Passage was there. By the time man sailed through it, in the twentieth century, it no longer mattered, commercially.

Through the cycles of despair and hope, the explorers of arctic Canada were building more than they knew. They made maps. Frobisher's Meta Incognita gradually became a little better known. Knowledge of the routes was no more important than being able to cope with the problems of travelling: how to handle ice, how to provision ships, and, above all, how men should live to make an accommodation with the Arctic. Each voyage not only sketched a little more of the navigation map, but also made the Arctic more familiar. After five centuries of exploration, in the mid twentieth century, ordinary people began to accept the fact that the North was not an island in space. Like any other part of Canada, it was a region for which equations could be written: equations that balanced problems of travel, ice, and cold, against resources.

Canada had nation-builders like Champlain, La Vérendrye, and John A. Macdonald. Men like Frobisher are also part of the story. So were Leif the Lucky, and those who learned the breeding-grounds of the gyrfalcon, and the bush pilots, and the men who switched on the motor at the first arctic oil well. Each in his age was driving back a frontier.

By the late seventeenth century, the search for fur was adding an extra impetus to activities in the Canadian North. The effect on the dogged search for the Passage was at first only indirect and slow. The mariners of the High Arctic were aloof from the fur-rack and the cross.

Early in the seventeenth century, Danish interest in Greenland and in the Canadian Arctic was reawakened. Danes apparently wanted not only to re-forge the link with Denmark's former outposts of empire, but to take a full part in the search for the Passage. For this search they chose the remarkable Jens Munk, notable less for the knowledge he added to the northern geography than for his vivid example of heroism.

In 1619, Jens Munk sailed from Denmark with all the hopes of spring. By September, he and his sixty-odd companions in the *Unicorn* and *Lamprey* reached Churchill, where they decided to winter. Things went well enough until early in the new year, when scurvy struck. By mid February, a third of his men were dead, and all but seven of the rest were too ill to walk. The doctor and the padre died. By April 10, only four could walk, and forty-one were dead. By June 4, three, including Munk, were left, scarcely alive amid the stench of bodies they were too sick to move. Yet, by July 16, these three were able to regain enough strength to make ready the smaller of their ships, and they got it back to Bergen on the day of the equinox. After surviving this terrible ordeal, Munk was killed in the Thirty Years' War. With his passing, Danish interest in the Canadian North faded and all but died.

In the summer of 1631 Luke Foxe and Thomas James sailed separately into Hudson Bay. Foxe had the greater triumph. He journeyed down the bay to the Churchill and Nelson rivers, across the south coast to Cape Henrietta Maria, then north above the Arctic Circle into Foxe Basin. The more inept James not only lost his ship on the shoals of James Bay, but was the only recorded arctic explorer to have endangered his life in a forest fire, when he set fire to some trees in the hope of attracting the attention of any natives. If the natives saw it, they apparently ran in the opposite direction. James, however, was an able publicist who attracted acclaim through his account of *The Strange and Dangerous Voyage of Captain Thomas James*. Foxe, like many another able arctic hand, suffered from a certain dullness of style.

With Foxe and James, interest in exploration waned, even in

England. John Knight made a disastrous trip to Hudson Bay at the age of eighty. Between 1719 and 1721, he and all his company perished on Marble Island, a bleak patch of ground sixteen miles off the coast of Keewatin at Rankin Inlet. The voyages that followed were devoted to the pursuit of fur, rather than to routes to China. Hudson Bay was increasingly frequented by traders, but they did not form part of the story of the Passage. It was only after the Napoleonic Wars that interest in the Canadian Arctic quickened again.

With the beginning of the long peace, after the long turmoil, English ships had too little to do. Their use in the Canadian Arctic had a good deal to commend it, for this half-continent was now British. London had done little about its northern reaches. The exploration of the mouths of the Coppermine and Mackenzie rivers had thrown a new light on the edge of the Arctic far to the west, but the passage by sea was still elusive.

In 1818, the British navy sent John Ross to the Canadian Arctic. He penetrated Lancaster Sound for fifty miles, more firmly on the track to the Pacific than any man had been. Then he saw what he took to be a range of mountains barring his progress. Probably it was ice fog. No one can know how little ice, or how much, barred his way to the west.

Sir Edward Parry, who had sailed with him, was much luckier. He was able, the next year, to organize an expedition of his own which went right through Lancaster Sound as far as Melville Island. In 1821 he went again, to see if the Passage could be reached from Hudson Bay itself, instead of along such a northern route. It took him two years to learn that he could not penetrate Fury and Hecla Strait, which does indeed lead north and west from Hudson Bay towards Lancaster Sound. The strait is like a funnel through which the ice of the High Arctic disgorges into Hudson Bay. (Arctic hands, in the long nights, argue about what would happen if it were dammed, and the bay were insulated from this chilly cargo each spring.) When Parry returned to Lancaster Sound by the old route, around Baffin Island, he ran into bad luck, being stopped by ice far short of his previous farthest point. So ended most of the enthusiasm of the Royal Navy.

When John Ross returned with his nephew James to the Arctic in 1829, he did so without naval support. Felix Booth, rich from

gin, contributed £20,000 to his expeditions. Ross's ship, the *Victory*,
had been on the run between Liverpool and the Isle of Man where
it attracted attention as one of the first side-wheel steamers ever
built. Now it was to cross the Atlantic and enter the Arctic. It was
no pleasure cruise. After the *Victory* was marooned for two winters
in the ice of the Gulf of Boothia, James Ross crossed the Boothia
Isthmus to reach the North Magnetic Pole on May 31, 1831. By the
summer of 1832, young Ross and his men pulled their boats to Fury
Beach and reached Lancaster Sound. Then they had to return to the
ice-bound ship at Fury Beach for a fourth terrible winter. In 1833
the Rosses again reached Lancaster Sound where, miraculously,
they were rescued by a passing whaling-ship going back to England. Strangest of all, it was the ship John Ross himself had
commanded on his first arctic voyage. Of the twenty-two men who
had started with him, nineteen were still with him. It was an incredible end to an incredible adventure.

A major tragedy was now to help fill in the maps of the High
Arctic more quickly in a decade than possibly all the voyages were
able to do during the previous hundred years. In 1845 the navy sent
Sir John Franklin to the Arctic. The expedition was a sort of
Titanic of Canadian arctic exploration. This was the most lavishly
equipped expedition ever sent to the polar seas. The *Erebus* and
Terror were reinforced with iron to meet the ice, and had engines
and screw propellers. There was hot-water heating in the cabins, cut
glass, delicate china, heavy silver, a library of twelve hundred books,
a barrel organ that could play fifty tunes, food for three years – and
not a single sledge, tent, or pair of snowshoes. It was under the
command of the ageing Sir John Franklin, whose name was thought
to be synonymous with 'arctic expert'. The expedition could not
fail to find the Passage at last. It did more than fail: it vanished from
the face of the earth. Within the next ten years, forty expeditions
sailed and sledged back and forth across the Arctic seeking, first,
the missing men, and, later, clues to the disaster that struck them.
While Lady Franklin waited patiently at home, the best men and
materials of the age were thrown into the search for a man who
stood as a symbol of England's naval greatness. The newspapers
took it up, and for the first time the Canadian Arctic became some-

thing of a household word. The Americans joined the search and took a new interest in the Arctic.

A British expedition starting from the Western Arctic included Robert M'Clure, commanding the *Investigator*. For three years he was hopelessly ice-bound. Then he crossed the sea-ice on foot, first to Melville Island, which Parry had reached, then to Beechey Island, which they came to in 1854. From there he and his men were carried by ship back to England. This was not the Northwest Passage as men had dreamed of it, but it was the Northwest Passage, and M'Clure had crossed it to win the Admiralty's prize of £10,000.

A less heroic chapter was written by Sir Edward Belcher, who had been leading his four well-equipped search ships in Wellington Channel, north-west of Lancaster Sound. This was a long way from the place where Franklin probably died. In the spring of 1854 he inexplicably abandoned his ships and left for England on a transport. The epilogue to this sordid tale is that one of his ships, the *Resolute*, piloted herself out of the ice and sailed with no human being aboard for a thousand miles towards England. She was boarded by American whalers, and given back to the British government by the United States. It was not the way the Royal Navy liked to see things done.

News of Franklin was at last brought back to England by the able explorer John Rae of the Hudson's Bay Company. He learned from Eskimos that the whole Franklin party had died from starvation at, or near, King William Island in 1847 and 1848. Though the Franklin search was now officially over, Lady Franklin herself was able to finance one final expedition. It was under the command of another great explorer, Leopold M'Clintock. In the summer of 1857 he reached Melville Bay, where he was frozen in. For eight months his ship, the *Fox*, drifted with the ice, edging 1,385 miles away from his goal, down into Davis Strait. Then he was almost destroyed as the ice broke up and the ship was freed. Immediately he turned north again. Running into more bad ice, he was stuck in Bellot Strait. M'Clintock, like Rae – and unlike Franklin and most of his predecessors – had learned to adapt himself to the Arctic, to travel light, and to use the resources of the land. He made a series of remarkable sled journeys in the course of which he collected the only written remains of the Franklin expedition ever to be found. In 1859 his ship was at last freed from the ice and he returned to England.

For one man, the Franklin search still had an enormous appeal. This was the American Charles Hall. In 1860 he shipped aboard a New England whaler to Baffin Island with the wild hope of making his own way in a little open boat to the scene of the Franklin tragedy in the central Arctic. Although he was soon shipwrecked, Hall was wise enough to learn about the Arctic from those who knew it best, the Eskimos. Stranded for two years on Baffin Island, he made an intensive study of Eskimo ways and was probably the first non-Eskimo to make a conscious effort to live in the manner of those who had mastered the Arctic. In the course of this first trip, Hall added something to the knowledge of the Frobisher Bay area, and redeemed Frobisher's arctic reputation. Again carried by whaler, from 1864 to 1869 he lived among the Eskimos in the area of Committee Bay and Repulse Bay. In 1871, he began his last journey in a tugboat, under instructions from the United States Navy to start for the North Pole. That was too tall an order, but he did sail farther north than man had ever sailed before – to 82° 11′ north. That fall he died, apparently poisoned by a member of his crew.

The dash for the North Pole opened an often unimportant and sometimes unsavoury era of exploration. Markham, with Nares's expedition, made an heroic trip north to 83° 20′ north in 1876. The British navy had learned so little in two hundred years that Nares was beaten by scurvy. The field was then left to Dr. Frederick Cook and Captain Robert Peary, both of whom claimed to have reached the Pole. There is no clear evidence that either did, and considerable indication that both failed. Peary's claim in 1909 rests on doubtful records of an alleged dash of 133 miles over the ice in five forced marches after he had left behind all literate members of his party and anyone capable of corroborating his statements. It is a pity that this questionable showmanship should have marred a distinguished career. Peary's place in arctic history should have rested on his stature as a member of the new school that believed in conquering the Arctic by understanding it.

Almost as a neglected side-show, the Northwest Passage was at last discovered. Roald Amundsen bought a small herring-boat called the *Gjoa* when he was twenty-eight. He had more enthusiasm for arctic exploration than he had money. In 1903, when Amundsen was thirty-one, he and six companions had to sail secretly from Norway to avoid their creditors. They spent two winters at Gjoahavn on King William Island making magnetic observations. In 1905 they sailed west as far as King Point in the Yukon, where they spent a third winter. In August 1906 they reached the Pacific Ocean. They had finally sailed the Northwest Passage. Nineteen years later, Amundsen and Lincoln Ellsworth almost reached the Pole in an airplane. In 1926 they were with Umberto Nobile in the Italian dirigible *Norge* when it was navigated across the Pole. Two years later Amundsen was lost in a seaplane as he set forth to rescue Nobile on a fatal arctic voyage.

In 1940-2 the *St. Roch*, the vessel of the Royal Canadian Mounted Police, became the first vessel to sail the passage from west to east. In 1944 it gained the further distinction of being the first to sail the Passage in a single season.

In the twentieth century, voyages of exploration have been superseded by arctic expeditions with more varied purposes. Greely went north in 1881 to establish meteorological stations on Ellesmere Island. The German Polar Year Expedition of 1882 had the same purpose on Baffin Island. In 1883 Franz Boas went north to study anthropology. Commercial, religious, and political impulses were soon to lead new generations to the northern frontier. With the new century, a different arctic age was starting. Whether the shape of the new Arctic was worthy of those who had come from afar to build its foundations will be left to the judgement of history.

4 | Fish and Fur

The North Atlantic, according to John Cabot in 1497, was 'swarming with fish, which can be taken not only with the net, but in a basket let down with a stone'. 'At times,' his brother wrote, 'they stayed the passage of our ships.'

The fishermen of England and western Europe needed little encouragement to be lured from the shadow of the Icelanders into waters both virgin and rich. Some may already have known the Grand Banks when Cabot started his voyages, but it was Cabot's reports that started the trickle, then the flood. The waters off the Canadian seaboard became enormously populated each season; all this activity was in strange contrast to the unknown and empty land a few miles away. Fishermen, like falconers, are not notable colonizers.

Yet fish lured the Europeans farther inland. Cartier was drawn

into the St. Lawrence River to form the foundation of a new commercial empire, although he himself disdained trading. His chief
interest was information, which could serve the scientific objectives
of the explorer and the ends of imperial endeavour. The farther the
fishermen penetrated, the greater the contact with the Indians. At
first there were casual meetings of sailors with natives, and passing
of trinkets. It was the beginning of a story that was to be repeated
on the human frontier of Canada until the twentieth century: the
little luxuries of trade, such as metal weapons and utensils, turned
into necessities. The dependence of native peoples on the new-
comer soon became so fixed and complete that ways of life had to
be changed to fit the European's whims and his economy. Gradually, the contact with the fishermen became more regular and prolonged, as they took to drying their fish on land before transporting
them back to European markets. The French, who possessed greater
natural sources of salt, ordinarily salted their fish on shipboard.
The English were forced to land and to air-dry their fish on Newfoundland shores, which they gradually occupied.

The Indians, who had only a few kinds of goods to trade, soon
found that the most acceptable was fur. In the winter months, while
the fishermen were away, the Indians set about accumulating stocks
of fur enormously greater than they had ever needed for themselves.
Gradually, as the fur trade was established as a major industry during the sixteenth century, lines began to reach out from Canada's
eastern gateways to meet, join, and link the north and south of
Canada.

The habits of the beaver had much to do with the way Canada
was shaped. The beaver quickly became the focus of the fur trade.
It advertised itself, not only by its houses, but by alteration of the
whole landscape when its house-building caused rivers to flood and
meadows to become swamps. It could be caught by trapping or by
breaking into the beaver houses to kill the occupants. The beaver
survived partly because it was prolific enough to withstand the relatively light pressure of the pre-European Indian trapper; the hunter
did not need much fur, and it was hard work to get it without
steel axes to demolish the dams. When the Europeans brought
metal implements, beaver could be cleared away from settled areas
with devastating efficiency. The beaver then led the trapper and

the trader farther and farther into the interior. The St. Lawrence Basin provided admirable routes south, west, and north. The best pelts were in the country to the north.

It was not until the mid seventeenth century that the paths of the fur-traders began to have a direct importance to the opening of the North. The unconscious agents of this grand national design were two improbable adventurers, Pierre Esprit Radisson and Médard Chouart des Groseilliers. Between 1654 and 1657 they made extensive travels at least as far as Lake Superior, though exactly where they went is by no means certain from their narratives. Most important, they realized that the fur trade needed new methods. Probing deeper into the interior, traders could no longer be certain of a food supply from either agricultural Indians or the light freight they carried in their own boats. The future success of the fur trade depended upon a new solution to the problems of transportation. Depots would have to be established along the extending routes. In the course of his travels in 1659-60, which took him at least as far as Lake Winnipeg, Radisson hit upon a far bolder answer to the mounting obstacles, not only of transportation, but of increasingly troublesome Indian middlemen along the route. He advocated penetration from the north, through Hudson Bay.

Neither the successful trading expedition nor the commercial visions of Radisson and Des Groseilliers won them favour back in Montreal. They were equally unsuccessful in France. In 1663 they went to New England, where they got a ship. They took it as far as Hudson Strait, but they could not persuade their captain to go on. And so in 1664 they went to England, where they told Charles II a good story. It was on those conversations that much of the future of the Canadian North depended: for if England should prove cool, the Dutch were decidedly interested in enlisting the services of Radisson and Des Groseilliers to develop a new commercial route to the Canadian North. England was not cool. Charles II indicated his enthusiasm by maintaining the Frenchmen in England, and by giving them two ships with which to penetrate Hudson Bay. In 1668 Des Groseilliers succeeded, and reached Rupert Bay, where no European had sailed since Henry Hudson fifty-eight years before. He built a fort and persuaded the Indians to bring skins in quantity.

Thus began a rivalry of enormous consequence. It was a rivalry between two fur routes, the northern and the southern. It was a rivalry between two imperial powers, and the beginning of a pincer movement on French Canada. It was the beginning of English commercial interest in Canada; that interest made it necessary to consolidate English rule in the following century. Slowly, London abandoned its assumption that the northern reaches of North America were of little importance in the horse-trading of peace conferences. That first voyage of Des Groseilliers may have had an effect on the Canadian mosaic.

Had the fur trade's one and undisputed capital remained in Montreal, how different would have been the ethnic map of Canada today? How different in character would have been the aspirations of French-speaking Canada in the late twentieth century?

'We were Caesars, being nobody to contradict us,' Radisson wrote with a truth that was to survive two centuries. The instrument of the British Caesars was 'The Governor and Company of Adventurers of England Trading into Hudson's Bay'. On May 2, 1670, it received its royal charter, which, in seven thousand words of tortured prose, staked out a gigantic empire whose dimensions no one of that generation could vaguely suspect. The Hudson's Bay Company was granted 'the whole trade of all those seas, streights and bays, rivers, lakes, creeks and sounds ... within the streights commonly called Hudson's Streights together with all lands, countries, and territories upon the coasts and confines of the seas, streights, bays, lakes, rivers, creeks and sounds aforesaid. . . .' Eventually this sweeping grant was interpreted to include 1,486,000 square miles of north-western Quebec, northern Ontario, all of Manitoba, most of Saskatchewan, southern Alberta, and a large part of the Northwest Territories. More than a trading monopoly, it conferred power to build fortifications, to wage war, and to seize trespassers.

The Hudson's Bay Company nourished grandiose schemes at a time when England could ill afford imperial adventures. It was nevertheless important that the claim be made. The Danes, who saw the possibility of a fur-trading post on Hudson Bay long before, lost their enthusiasm in the agony of Jens Munk and never again tried to colonize Canada. The spoils of Canada's east coast, dimly perceived, were left to be divided by English and French; farther west, inquisitive eyes were cast by Spain and later the United States.

The French soon grasped the importance of the new trading route. They saw that it would not only short-circuit the flow of furs from the north, but that it would stop the flow of natives into the influence of the Jesuit missions. Church and State were united against the English threat. To combat it, the French sent an expedition through Quebec from the Saguenay to James Bay, in 1672. Led by Father Albanel of the Jesuits, its purpose was to claim the region for France. At first, the English found that they could set up their trading-posts practically from their ships, but then the harassment of the French became more effective and cut them off from their sources of fur. The English, like the French, had to embark upon permanent inland posts, though they did so with the advantage of a much shorter land route.

To secure its sources of fur, the Hudson's Bay Company first had to explore. Henry Kelsey, between 1690 and 1692, penetrated from York Factory into the prairies of Saskatchewan. Though just entering his twenties, Kelsey was a remarkable frontiersman. He learned to travel light and to live off the land. He apparently enjoyed tremendous success as a peacemaker among quarrelsome Indian tribes. He was the earliest of the company's representatives to carry out a policy of Indian relations in contrast to the practices of most previous traders. Though the company was not always renowned for its philanthropy towards the native peoples of the North, it did cultivate, rather than mine, the fur trade. It always assumed that it was in the country to stay: it could out-wait its impatient and bumptious rivals. One good effect of this policy was a relatively responsible attitude by the Hudson's Bay Company towards the use of alcohol as an item of trade.

After Kelsey's journeys, northern explorations by land came to a virtual end for half a century. The servants of the Hudson's Bay Company at that time proved competent as traders but unenterprising as explorers. Where the Indians had a choice between English and French goods they usually chose English. The Hudson's Bay Company was securing the fur trade without the bother of going much farther out to meet it. In 1717 the first company fort north of York Factory was established at Churchill, where Jens Munk had undergone his ghastly ordeal. In 1731 stone-masons arrived to construct Fort Prince of Wales at the mouth of the

Churchill River. Almost on the tree-line, it protected all of Hudson Bay, the only major fortification ever built in the Canadian Arctic. It was never defended, and in 1782 it was conquered by the French, without a shot. The commander of the French forces was the Comte de la Pérouse, who recognized the merit in the work of Samuel Hearne, then in charge of the fort. The explorer's own countrymen had given him less than his due, but La Pérouse allowed Hearne and his countrymen to sail home free men, on condition that Hearne's journal be published.

Hearne was one of the seven great overland explorers of the Canadian North. To the sound of a gun-salute from the fort on November 6, 1769, he advanced for the first time into the Arctic. Thirty-six days later he returned without any salutes – destitute and deserted by most of his Indian companions. Two months later he was off again, and made an important trip to the vicinity of Chesterfield Inlet and Baker Lake. Pausing only two weeks after his return, Hearne set off on his most famous expedition on December 7, 1770, in company with the remarkable Indian guide and explorer Matonabbee. This trip, like the earlier ones, was to investigate reports of copper mines deep in the barrens. The year-and-a-half journey was a success largely because of the organizing ability of Matonabbee, as well as his knowledge of the land. The party first kept within the sub-Arctic, then emerged into the barrens on May 22, 1771, just east of Artillery Lake. On July 13 they reached the Coppermine River. Three days later, the Indians accompanying Hearne came upon a group of Eskimos fishing at Bloody Fall, near the mouth. The Indians murdered every one of them. It was an episode of wanton, senseless brutality. About thirty miles east of the mouth of the Coppermine River, Hearne found the deposit he sought. He described it as 'no more than an entire jumble of rocks and gravel'. Although it had supplied the Copper Eskimos with metal for their implements and weapons, the pieces were too slight and too distant to be of commercial interest to the company. A far more important discovery was the shore of the Arctic Ocean. The maps of Canada thus attained an enormous new depth. The work of those who had charted the Arctic from the sea could now be linked with those who were filling in the open spaces of land.

In the fifty years that followed the signing of the Treaty of Paris in 1763, Hearne's travels were the only major contribution made by the Hudson's Bay Company to the opening of the continent. The main impulse for the push into western Canada came from the North West Company of Montreal. The Montreal traders were a dynamic, sometimes wild collection of adventurers who possessed a vitality, boldness, and imagination not characteristic of the proprietors of the Hudson's Bay Company. They came from the fur routes of the Ohio or Mississippi, from the *coureurs de bois* of Canada, and from the Highlands of Scotland. Unlike their northern rivals, the senior managers of the North West Company knew the country where they traded. They had lived in the field, dealt with Indians, and endured rough weather and white water in dangerous rivers. Most of the Merchant Adventurers had never been within two thousand miles of the source of their wealth. The Montrealers, out for their own fortunes, worked with style and speed; they also destroyed as they went, for they did not share the Hudson's Bay Company's prudence in cultivating a continuing yield of fur and good relations for generations to come.

The Montreal traders were loosely grouped until 1775, when they began to pool their interests. Their organization was never without its dissensions and feuds. In 1821 it was taken over by the Honourable Company, which by then had to either absorb it or go out of business. During its short history, men in the service of the North West Company made their mark on Canadian maps: Alexander Henry in Saskatchewan, Peter Pond in the Athabasca, and Alexander Mackenzie in the Northwest Territories.

Mackenzie, a twenty-four-year-old Scot sent to relieve Peter Pond at Chipewyan, knew the ways of the land from three years in the field. During 102 days of 1789, he covered three thousand miles of the Canadian North-west, almost none of which had been mapped or even seen previously by a European. On July 14 Mackenzie reached the Arctic Ocean. He was deeply disappointed that it was not the Pacific. This northern journey gave a new perspective to the Northwest Passage – by now of doubtful commercial promise – and it provided many pieces to help complete the northern jigsaw during the next hundred years. Mackenzie's extraordinary voyage to the Arctic is too often overshadowed by his expedition to the Pacific four years later.

Activity by land and sea in the North had been slowed by the Napoleonic Wars. To the fur trade, this military struggle had threatened disaster, for London depended heavily upon the markets of the Continent. The Hudson's Bay Company, saved by its conservatism, entered the post-war period in 1815 with a reasonably sound financial position, and a distaste for a continuation of the costly struggle with the Montrealers.

The short-range policies of the North West Company were beginning to tell. Since the profits of each season were shared, there were no reserves for lean years, save in the notoriously unreliable personal fortunes of its associates. The Colonial Office encouraged a commercial union of the two companies, for the maintenance of imperial power in the Canadian West could not withstand such internecine struggles. While the Americans were the principal menace, London was aware of the growing threat of Russia in the North-west. In 1821 the deed of co-partnership was signed. It gained its sanction and its sanctity both from the original charter of 1670, and from an act of Parliament of 1821. The new monopoly was far more extensive than the grant of 1670. Most important, the union gave the Hudson's Bay Company the influence of more men who knew the Canadian frontier. The company's new vitality was as important to the making of the next stage of northern Canada as it was to the survival of the fur trade.

At the time of union, the Hudson's Bay Company had seventy-six posts, the Nor'Westers ninety-seven. The man most responsible for making commercial sense of this disparate empire and its warring factions was George Simpson, who ruled as governor-in-chief of the Hudson's Bay Company territories from 1826 until 1860. His local rule was as near to absolute dictatorship as Canada has ever seen. From the viewpoint of the company, he was an entire success. By 1828 the shareholders were earning twenty per cent per year on their investment. In 1838 the stock was earning twenty-five per cent, which was a comfortable tribute for any colony to provide. During Simpson's administration, annual dividends never dropped below ten per cent. It was an era not only of tight commercial efficiencies but of exploration and expansion in the North.

The first trading-post north of 60° was opened on Great Slave Lake in 1786 by Cuthbert Grant of the North West Company. It lasted only a year. The first permanent buildings were erected in 1796 on the north shore of the Mackenzie River near Trout River, but these were abandoned when the resident trader was murdered by Indians. In 1799 and 1800 short-lived posts appeared on the west side of Great Slave Lake and on the Liard, near the mouth of the Nahanni River. The oldest post in the Territories to survive until the present day was Fort Simpson, built in 1804 by the North West Company where the Liard empties into the Mackenzie. The Hudson's Bay Company went there in 1820 and made its key depot on the Mackenzie. There were half a dozen widely scattered trading-posts when the Admiralty turned its Canadian interest inland to seek answers to the riddle of the Northwest Passage. It attempted to relate the charted coastlines to the still unmapped lands of the northern interior.

Twenty-five years before his last journey, Sir John Franklin, with John Richardson and George Back, came to the Mackenzie District in 1820. Accompanied by Akaitcho and a number of other Indians, they went up the Yellowknife River on the north side of Great Slave Lake and built winter quarters at Fort Enterprise not far from today's hydro-electric development on the Snare River. Next spring they journeyed to the mouth of the Coppermine River where Hearne had once travelled. At Bloody Fall, the Indian guides left them, out of fear of reprisal for what their ancestors had done there fifty years before. Akaitcho remained with Franklin, who owed his life to the Indian's knowledge of the geography and conditions of the country. In mid July Franklin's party travelled through Corona-tion Gulf in birch-bark canoes, charting the coast to Kent Peninsula and Bathurst Inlet. Anxious about their lack of provisions – for they had not learned to live from the land as wiser travellers were to do – Franklin's party then made a dash to the south. They waited at Fort Enterprise, where some of the party starved to death, while Back sought relief from the Indians. By mid December, Franklin's party reached Fort Resolution, and there they spent the rest of the winter.

Franklin's next overland expedition was ambitious and more successful. Peter Warren Dease, a Chief Factor of the Hudson's Bay Company, was sent to Great Bear Lake in 1825 to open a post at Fort Franklin near the site of an old Nor'Westers' building. Meanwhile, Franklin and Kendall were making a survey of the Mackenzie Delta, and Back and Richardson were charting the shores of Great Bear Lake.

In September the whole party of fifty assembled – the largest group ever to attempt an overland reconnaissance in the Northwest. They went down to the delta where they divided into two parties. Franklin and Back explored 374 miles of the arctic coast to the west, and they were within 160 miles of a Russian expedition moving eastwards along the Alaskan coast. The gap in the charts of the arctic coastline was becoming very small.

Richardson and Kendall overcame the usual difficulties of shallow water, ice, fog, wind, and mosquitoes to chart as far as Dolphin and Union Strait. They sighted Victoria Island, landed at the mouth of the Coppermine River, and walked up its west bank, reaching Fort Franklin via Great Bear Lake in the autumn. In February 1827 Franklin made an overland winter trip to Fort Simpson.

The Mackenzie area was beginning to appear in detail. The Mackenzie and the other main rivers were known, Great Slave and Great Bear lakes were roughly mapped, the arctic coastline was almost completely charted, and the first permanent communities of Europeans were well established in the Mackenzie valley. Exploration now moved east.

In 1833 John Ross was making news in England because of his disappearance into the arctic void. George Back eagerly led a rescue party from the eastern end of Great Slave Lake to Aylmer Lake, then part way down the river later named after him. He returned to spend the winter of 1833-4 at Fort Reliance. By the following April, Back received word that Ross was safe in England, news that one suspects he heard with mixed emotions. He continued with his expedition anyway, this time following the Back River to its mouth in Chantrey Inlet.

By now the Hudson's Bay Company was feeling its imperial mantle, as well as a warm desire to harvest fur in more distant fields. George Simpson chose his able young cousin Thomas Simpson to carry on Franklin's work on the arctic coast. The year was 1837, when Upper and Lower Canada were torn by rebellion and Victoria ascended the throne of England. Sharing command with Dease, young Simpson went from the mouth of the Mackenzie right over to Point Barrow in Alaska, where he planted the Union Jack and the company ensign. The maps of the Canadian Western Arctic were now linked with the charts of the Pacific. The next year, Simpson and Dease continued where Franklin's expedition had ended its easternmost work. In 1839 they made their last and most remarkable trip. They mapped parts of Queen Maud Gulf, Victoria Island, and King William Island. The shoreline was now complete from Boothia Peninsula to the Pacific. Simpson had bold dreams of future exploration, but in 1840 he died of a gunshot wound, in circumstances that remained a mystery.

Dr. John Rae, physician, scientist, and fur-trader, took up where Thomas Simpson left off. He set out in 1846 on the first of his five expeditions. With twelve men in two open boats, he sailed from York Factory to Repulse Bay, where he and his men built a stone house, the ruins of which still remain. They brought no fuel for the house, and they gained their food from the land. Next spring they travelled by sled twelve hundred miles, mapping Boothia Peninsula to link up with Simpson's charts to the west. Parry's expedition had cost £120,000; Rae's, which accomplished far more, cost £1,400.

Rae's later expeditions mapped more of the central Arctic, including Victoria Island. On his last trip, in 1853-4, he learned from the Eskimos the story of the end of the Franklin expedition, and brought back pieces of its tableware and silver plate. It was a nice bit of symbolism – the new generation that had learned to make peace with the Arctic bearing back the relics of the old.

Sir George Simpson's interests were not confined to the opening of the Mackenzie and Keewatin districts. One of his bold imperial designs took his men right into the Russian empire. In 1838 Robert Campbell established a post at Dease Lake, in British Columbia, then went on to the Stikine River where he found himself in the country of an hospitable Indian queen. Ordinarily, the Indians of northern British Columbia and the Yukon were hostile to Campbell and his successors, and the coastal Indians were especially menacing. In 1840 Campbell found the Pelly River and Frances Lake, where he established the first Yukon trading-post two years later. In 1846, he built a post at Pelly Banks and in 1848 one at Fort Selkirk. Later he explored the Pelly, the Yukon, and the Porcupine to Fort Yukon in Alaska.

In the summer of 1847 a young clerk, Alexander Murray, who had been assigned the task of building a post at Fort Yukon, was told by Indians that they 'expected the Russians here soon'. 'This was not very agreeable news to me,' Murray wrote, 'knowing that we were on their land, but I kept my thoughts to myself, and determined to keep a sharp lookout in case of surprise.' Sir George Simpson had made an elaborate pretence of not knowing that Fort Yukon was in Russian territory, for the opportunities of this rich trade were not to be lightly abandoned. Murray was told that if a Russian representative should question his right to occupy the area, the two should refer the dispute to higher authority. Luckily for Murray, the Russians never appeared, and the fort remained in company hands until after the United States bought Alaska in 1867.

The Yukon outposts were a bold venture for the Hudson's Bay Company, but they were too far away to maintain efficiently. Between purchase of trade goods in London and the arrival there of the furs for which they were exchanged, seven years had to elapse. It was a serious strain on invested capital and on administrative resources. Alaskan-based enterprise was more competitive. Furthermore, local relations were far from satisfactory. The Indians of the Pacific coast, near Haines in Alaska, were themselves ambitious capitalists. Their deep resentment of the company's interior route which cut off their own trade prompted the burning of Fort Selkirk in 1851. No new posts were built, and the company's interests in the Yukon were extinguished for a hundred years.

The Mackenzie valley remained the focus of the northern fur trade. By the means of transportation of the early nineteenth century, the Mackenzie was remote from the supply base of the Hudson's Bay Company. Following the long sea voyage, goods were taken from York Factory to Norway House and dispatched for the Mackenzie in the middle of the following June. At the height of land called Portage La Loche between Hudson Bay and the Mackenzie, the brigade left its cargo and picked up furs from the Mackenzie and the Yukon. Each brigade had thirty men. The size of their boats changed over the years; by 1850 the standard was a light craft with a twenty-eight-foot keel, broad and shallow, drawing no more than three feet of water when loaded. It would carry about two tons of cargo, a crew of nine, and three or four passengers, with provisions. The boats cost between £20 and £25 to build and were intended to last two years.

On the Mackenzie, the pick-up of fur began in May when boats would set out from Fort Simpson to go down-river to Fort Good Hope and Fort Norman, and up the Liard River to Ford Liard. All having been collected at Fort Simpson, the boats would set out for the south in mid June, arriving at Portage La Loche at the end of July. The goods for the Yukon were at first transported via northern British Columbia; after Campbell learned that the Porcupine was a tributary of the Yukon River, the Hudson's Bay Company used the Mackenzie River route to the Peel River, then down the Porcupine to Fort Yukon.

From 1836 on, the staff of the Mackenzie and Yukon posts were recruited in England and Scotland, not because of any lack of interest among Canadians, but because it took a year longer for people from the St. Lawrence valley to get a ship to York Factory, and a canoe westwards. The railway, of course, was to change that and almost every other aspect of transportation involved in the fur trade, but by the late nineteenth century the character of the company's staff was well established. Nearly a hundred years later, the British Isles were still a major source of staff for the fur trade in the North.

The company tried hard to save money on transportation. Every device was employed to make the posts more self-sufficient or at least less dependent on goods from abroad. Small market gardens were tended by all posts, including those in the Mackenzie District. In 1852, for example, Fort Simpson harvested 700 bushels of potatoes, 120 bushels of turnips, and 180 bushels of barley. Fishing was a major occupation at Resolution, Fort Rae, and elsewhere on Great Slave Lake, as a source of food for down-river posts. Rabbit, moose, and caribou were used as much as possible for food. Where supplies could not be obtained at the post itself, it was arranged that they come from as close as possible. This led to many small local industries, which were to disappear with the coming of better transportation routes to the south. Resolution and Big Island (where the

Mackenzie River leaves Great Slave Lake) supplied boards, oars, pack cords, moose and caribou skin, and snowshoe laces cut from moose skin. Fort Liard was a source of grindstones, sledges, axe-handles, canoes, and oars. Fort Rae provided deerskin robes, and babiche or deerskin cord. From the Yukon came moose leather for the whole district. Fort Norman shipped out locally-quarried salt. In one year, the blacksmith at Fort Simpson manufactured 500 traps. Another item of (illicit) local manufacture was probably liquor. The importation of spirits was sharply reduced, or in some places prohibited, less for moral reasons than to reduce freight costs and hazards to productivity on the frontier.

The traders were constantly pressed to salvage carefully. Goods that proved unsaleable in one post might be tried in another, rather than writing off anything that had been carried so painfully so far. There were seemingly endless regulations for the re-use of packing materials. Boats were burned to salvage the nails, and old ironwork was sent to Fort Simpson for refashioning into useful objects.

The settlements at the focus of the fur trade in the mid nine-teenth century were small and without frills. The specifications for the new establishment at Fort Norman were one store, thirty feet by twenty feet, a manager's house, twenty-five by sixteen feet (divided into two rooms, one eight feet wide and the other seventeen feet wide), and a men's house, twenty feet by fifteen feet. The store was unheated, a cold-hearted regulation of the Hudson's Bay Company until very recent times, presumably designed to discourage the waste of fuel and of words. Warehouses were added to the basic complement, especially at important trans-shipment points such as Fort Simpson.

The company always began its construction program on the edge of a waterway, near the bush. Almost always, the post was put on land where no permanent settlement had been before. The presence of the company's new buildings became a magnet for Indian visitors. The Indians in the permanent employ of the company built cabins near by, but others were discouraged from the temptations of an indolent settlement life. Congregating at certain seasons was tolerated, especially when the missionaries arrived and encouraged the collective observance of religious feasts. But in the early days of the fur trade, the settlement was the company.

Although these posts were far from England, a good inter-post communication system was developed to cut down administrative costs. An express of men and sleds leaving Fort Simpson on January 22 would reach Fort Norman on February 6, Fort Good Hope on February 13, and the Peel River on February 27. On March 3 it would arrive at La Pierre's House, not far from the present-day village of Old Crow on the portage between the Rat and the Porcupine. It would end at Fort Yukon on March 19. After five days there, it would return by the same route.

The Mackenzie District, which owed much to the work of the North West Company, brought a profitable harvest of fur, especially because it remained a Hudson's Bay Company monopoly long after competitors had moved into the prairies. Between 1821 and 1844, the annual returns from the Mackenzie District rose from £12,000 to £15,000; by the mid 1850s they had doubled. In the period from amalgamation in 1821 to refinancing in 1872, there were eighty-five shares in the company, and the annual profit on each averaged over £400. At this time, clerks were being paid up to £100 a year, guides in the Mackenzie got about £25 a year, and 'strong, healthy half-breed lads' serving as apprentice tradesmen got an average of £10 a year over a seven-year period of engagement. Wages for Canadians, even in similar occupations, were substantially below those paid to young men brought from Britain.

Although their frugal lives were enriched by new material luxuries, none of the permanent residents of the North made a fortune from the fur trade. The trader, by modern standards, was no philanthropist. Here is George Simpson, in 1821, writing one of his innumerable letters of counsel to his staff:

> Their immediate wants have been fully supplied, but of course, the scenes of extravagance are at an end, and it will be a work of time to reconcile them to the new order of things. . . . I have made it my study to examine the nature and character of Indians and, however repugnant it may be to our feelings, I am convinced they must be ruled with a rod of Iron to bring and keep them in a proper state of subordination, and the most certain way to effect this is by letting them feel their dependence upon us. . . . In the woods and northern barren grounds this measure ought to be pursued rigidly next year if they do

not improve, and no credit, not so much as a load of ammunition, given them until they exhibit an inclination to renew
their habits of industry. In the plains however, this system
will not do, as they can live independent of us, and by with-
holding ammunition, tobacco and spirits, the Staple articles of
Trade, for one year, they will recover the use of their Bows
and Spears, and lose sight of their smoking and drinking
habits; it will therefore be necessary to bring those Tribes
round by mild and cautious measures which may soon be
effected.

It was this pressure towards dependence on the white man that
most profoundly altered the character of the North wherever the
trader came to settle. The orbit of operations of the Indians, and
later of the Eskimos, was changed. The rifle enabled the hunter to
get as much game as before, without having to roam so large an area
– for a while. The desire to range about the land was now reduced
by the wish to be within easy reach of the permanent trading-post.
As Simpson foresaw, the Indian trapper became dependent on the
white man's goods, and subordinate to his wishes. When the natural
economy disappeared, no one, on his own, could recapture it. The
Indian's dependence on the trader for tobacco, tea, calico, and
cooking-pots was serious enough, but his need for ammunition
became vital. In theory, a whole community might, by some tremendous exertion of will and self-discipline, return to the kind of
living it knew before the settlers came. Individuals could hardly
do so, unless to all the other hardships they were to add isolation
from their own society. To throw away these products of the new
age would have been as ineffectual as the Luddites protesting
against the Industrial Revolution by smashing machines, or workers of our own century passing resolutions against automation.

Where there was a monopoly, there was no curb on the power of
the trader to change the life of those about him. The stream of
letters and directives urging greater economies and higher returns
pressed upon every member of the trading hierarchy, including
those in the bottom layer – the trappers and the locally-hired company servants. The authority of the local trader was absolute in
more than an economic sense. In the absence of a police force or
the pressures of public opinion, he exercised life-and-death power

over the local people. It might be simply exercised by achieving a social objective through economic pressure, such as the taking of an Indian woman into the post, whatever her wishes or her family's – or indeed whatever her marital status. On a more extreme scale, if some Indian lost his life in a quarrel with the white man, there was not likely to be a judicial inquiry. The local people were, in every sense, as subordinate as Simpson had wished.

In practice, however, the company's traders operated with a sense of responsibility and of mission. The company developed the *esprit de corps* of a select priesthood, and this survived amalgamation and even the rapidly diminishing administrative power of the traders after 1870. Also hard for the company to accept was the 1857 parliamentary inquiry into its affairs, which threw unwelcome shafts of public light onto the private operations of the fur trade. Though no one would say it, there was perhaps a feeling amongst old-timers that the company was, if not above, then apart from, Parliament and other temporal realms. For all the anxiety and muttered complaints, the testimony was generally not unfavourable to the company.

'You think upon the whole, that their conduct was that of men who were doing their duty and acting in a considerate manner towards the Indians?' an artillery officer who knew their operations in the field was asked during the inquiry. 'I think so, most eminently,' he replied.

On the other hand, Dr. Rae was asked about trading. 'I will now read to you from the Indian tariff of the territory embraced within the Royal Licence, situated east of the Rocky Mountains. I find that a gun which in England costs 22 shillings, is charged to the Indian 20 beavers, equivalent in market value of £32.10; is that anything in accordance with your experience?' 'It was true many years ago, but it is not true at present.' Dr. Rae went on to explain that although an Indian in the Mackenzie still had to pay the equivalent of twenty beaver skins for the cheap rifle, he might pay the designated equivalent number of muskrat skins – that is, two hundred – on which the company could make little profit. When questioning turned from the prices, Dr. Rae told of the medical care he gave to Indians without charge.

Sir George Simpson spoke of the company management as 'my

own government'; it seemed in his mind to have a status under the Crown at least equal to the régimes of Upper Canada and Lower Canada. Concerning agricultural and settlement prospects, he was disparaging. If he was not deliberately misleading, he was wildly misinformed. The British Columbia coast, where Vancouver is today, he dismissed as 'quite unfit for colonization'. Rupert's Land was not suitable for settlement. The company would not object to settlers, as long as the fur trade was left undisturbed. 'I do not think they will do any harm, if they were restrained from interfering with the fur trade, provided the company were satisfied; they consider themselves lords of the soils, proprietors of the country in their own special territory.'

The company's dominions receded northwards as settlement came to the prairies. It did indeed interfere with the fur trade, long after Sir George Simpson was mercifully in his grave. Wheat was grown on those barren prairies concerning whose potential he had cast such serious doubts. The company lost an empire, not just because it sold its lands to Canada, but because it could thrive only where it was the only settlement 'in their own special territory'. Often the final defeat of the company's fur trade was inflicted not by governments but by the company's own merchandising departments. They ably assessed the changing times and down-graded the fur trade, to the deep disappointment of those men of the North who saw the fur trade, not as a balance-sheet, but as a way of life. The settlement of the West brought riches across the counters in a way the early traders never dreamed of. The last refuge of the fur trade was in the contracting North.

The company was slow to move beyond the bush of the Mackenzie, where it had built its fortunes for two centuries. A post was established in Aklavik at the edge of the tree-line in 1912, and a store built in Herschel Island in 1915 was the first company venture into the Western Arctic.

Here the Hudson's Bay Company was not the pioneer, for the fur trade had been brought in with the whalers. When whaling died out, the fur trade was exploited by former whaling-captains: Joe Bernard, Captain T. C. Pedersen, and, most famous of all, Captain Charles Klengenberg. By 1906, Klengenberg had travelled as far east as Victoria Island. In his autobiography he provided as revealing a picture of the fur trade as ever emerged from the parliamentary inquiries of 1857, though he was writing about Canada in the twentieth century:

> They were so innocent a people of so long ago that I had not the heart to take advantage of them in trade, so all I took was most of their clothes and stone cooking pots and copper snowknives and ice picks for steel knives and frying pans and a supply of matches. They had no raw furs with them, but their garments would be useful for my family and some of my rascally crew.

Philip Godsell, long a member of the Hudson's Bay Company in the North, described the fur trade entering the Arctic in his autobiography:

> In 1923, a .30-.30 Winchester rifle usually sold for twelve white fox skins, which was later reduced to ten. (The market value of a rifle was not much more than of a single white fox pelt.) From the very first, the rifle had proved the best seller. But at last, each Eskimo had one and the trade had reached the saturation point, a fact deplored by all. It was Captain Klengenberg who arose to the occasion in a characteristic manner by importing hard steel ramrods, giving them to the natives and telling them to scrape the insides of their rifle barrels freely to take the powder out. This, of course, soon ruined the rifling so that the guns would not shoot straight, and the erstwhile trade in rifles was resumed.

Or again:

> Now, just as Doak had told me at our campfires on the Mackenzie River, the indiscriminate sale of rifles and ammunition had led to such a slaughter of the caribou that they had become quite scarce. Not only that, but they had forsaken their customary paths of migration to and from Victoria Land to have their young. Now the natives waited in vain at the crossroads which the caribou had used as far back as the oldest man in the tribe remembered, and they could not understand. As a consequence, the erstwhile self-supporting Eskimo was becoming more dependent upon the traders and commenced to look for debt. The effect upon the Eskimos of giving up customary food and skin clothing for imported woollen and cotton goods

– quite unsuited to Arctic wear – and imported salted and canned provisions, etc., is to greatly lower their native vigor and resistance to disease. Already these natives are showing evidences of tuberculosis, diarrhea and other unaccustomed ailments resulting from the change in their mode of life.

One trader with whom I discussed the serious effects these conditions were likely to have upon the natives only laughed: 'The sooner the caribou are gone, the better,' he said, 'for the more foodstuffs can be imported and the natives will be forced to trap and become fur producers or starve.'

The coming of the trader into the Canadian Arctic had good results as well as bad. It would be grossly unfair to regard all traders as ruthless exploiters, or indeed to apply the standards of the late twentieth century's relative enlightenment to human relations of an earlier age – even the 1920s and 1930s. The government and people of Canada were content to leave undisturbed the empires of the Arctic, for to regulate trading would drain government funds which were already short, especially in the depression years.

The Hudson's Bay Company outlived all its competitors in the Arctic, and emerged as the only trading organization east of the Mackenzie Delta. The company's first post in the Eastern Arctic was opened in 1909 at Wolstenholme, near the point at which Hudson Strait opens into Hudson Bay. Lake Harbour, on the south shore of Baffin Island, followed in 1911, just two years before the whaling-station closed. Cape Dorset, to the west, and Frobisher Bay were opened in the next three years. Immediately after the First World War, the expansion continued: Coats Island (since closed) in 1918; Port Harrison, Quebec, in 1920; Povungnituk and Pond Inlet in 1921; Blacklead Island and Amadjuak (both since closed) in the same year. Clyde River came in 1923, Southampton Island in 1924, Sugluk in 1925, and Padlei in 1926. There were other posts which had a brief life and were later closed. Further establishments awaited the end of the Second World War.

The settlements of the Eastern Arctic were even smaller than the first trading-posts of the Mackenzie valley a hundred years before. Though the company by now was much less frugal in providing amenities for its staff, its establishments were small because there were no local products for building or fuel, and most food had to be brought by ship at great cost. Usually the post began in lonely splendour. Later the common pattern was a thousand miles of nothing, then a settlement consisting of an Anglican mission, a Hudson's Bay Company post, and a Roman Catholic mission, then a thousand miles of nothing. It was usually at a later stage that the police, the school, and the administrator joined the community. In the early days, when the trader's building stood alone, it attracted even fewer native dwellings than company posts in the Mackenzie, except at ship-time.

Having previously used government ships for supply, the Hudson's Bay Company built the 2,500-ton *Nascopie* in 1912. Often called an ice-breaker, though more accurately a ship strengthened to withstand the pressure of ice, it served as the supply ship of the Eastern Arctic for thirty-five years. It transported all supplies for the company, other settlers, and government parties with scientific or administrative purposes. Eventually the *Nascopie* became the pioneer in an Eastern Arctic tourist trade, taking on passengers at $650 each for a three months' arctic tour; and a good bargain it was. In 1947 the *Nascopie* was wrecked on a rock a few yards off Cape Dorset. After it broke up, the igloos of south-western Baffin Island set an impressive table of fine china and silver.

By the time the *Nascopie* was replaced by the *Rupertsland*, communications by air and radio had improved enough to take the edge off the annual institution of ship-time at an arctic post. The excitement of the annual call was at its height in the days of the *Nascopie*, when the silence of the outpost was broken only once each year. The trader received his supplies, as well as his annual inspection. There was news of the outside world from those on board, as well as from the annual mail and the periodicals which were often husbanded to while away the later evenings of isolation. It was a great event for the Eskimos, too. A tent village would sprout around the shores. The excitement reached its height when the smoke of the *Nascopie* was first sighted over the horizon. Long before the anchor was dropped, all Eskimo craft and the company boat, flying the Hudson's Bay Company ensign, would put out to meet it. It is even said that the trader would wear a tie. There was a lot of unloading to be done fast, there were gallons of tea to be drunk, there was candy for the children. There was confusion, then there was peace.

Traders used to say that the second-best day of the year was when the ship arrived: the best was when it went.

On rare occasions, the company showed the flag in a more majestic fashion that left for later generations a vivid picture of the relations of the Hudson's Bay Company with the bewildered citizens of Canada's Eastern Arctic. Such an occasion was the visit from England in 1934 of the governor of the Hudson's Bay Company himself, Sir Patrick Ashley Cooper. At each post he made a speech to the Eskimos. The company later published it in a booklet, along the style of publications that have followed major royal tours. At each outpost, Sir Patrick was borne ashore and paraded to the company compound by a personal piper whom he had brought for the occasion. There he addressed the Eskimos, in English.

> I am very pleased to see you good people here today and to have the opportunity of speaking to you. . . .
>
> Our men who live with you the year around and trade with you have often told me what good hunters you are and how you try your best to do their bidding, and I wish you to believe that we have your welfare at heart. If times are good with us, they are also good with you. If you make good hunts you benefit by them and are happy, but if the hunts are poor, we both suffer and are sorry.
>
> I know that for the past three or four years you have had hard times and so have we. In the white man's country, times are even more difficult than they are here. . . . Here God has given you plenty of fish and seals. . . . I would ask you to be more diligent in trapping so that with the foxes you catch you will be able to buy better guns, seal nets and hunting equipment. . . . The more fur you catch, the more seals you obtain, the more of the white man's goods we will bring into the country for your use.
>
> I want you to realize that we have to pay men for making these goods for you, and we have to pay men to operate our ships to bring them to you, so that if you do not pay your debts and pay us for the goods, we, in turn, will not be able to buy them. So, for your own good, I ask you to be good hunters, pay your debts, and live happily with one another.
>
> . . . Now that we have seen you, we are happy and will leave you with confidence that you will work with our post manager

as one large happy family, you following his advice as if he were your father, for he does the things which I tell him and I want you to do the things which he tells you.

The arctic traders had a sense of mission as inheritors of empire, though as time passed, the company's management was less anxious than the government to preserve the old order. Whatever else might be said about the handling of arctic affairs before the mid twentieth century, it cost the government very little.

But change was inevitable: the change from hunter to hunter/ trapper, the change from nomadic life to semi-nomadic, the rapidly growing dependence upon white man's goods. Most of all, there was the effect of the rifle in the hands of those who did not know about conservation. In the arctic, though sea mammals continued to survive at an apparently satisfactory level, the caribou dwindled disastrously. Among those who depended most heavily on them – the inland Eskimos of Keewatin – the result of the new hunting was recurring starvation and the disappearance of almost an entire people.

In the Arctic, dependence upon the white man had an especially striking effect because of the peculiarly cyclical nature of trapping. White fox so dominated the fur trade as to be almost the only pelt of importance. When world prices were strong, and the fox was at the height of its population cycle, times were good. Two years later trapping would yield only one-tenth the number of pelts. Even a price rise could not compensate for such a disaster.If a low point in the cycle coincided with a fall in markets, the consequences were all the worse – and beyond the comprehension of those who now lived and died by the fox. Naturally the company did not simply turn its back on the trappers. It issued credit, called debt, in substantial degree. This did not altogether alleviate the suffering of bad times, and it further subordinated the Eskimo to the white man. Since there were few other furs to cushion the shocks, the Eskimo felt the effects of feast and famine more than any other Canadian living in the realm of the fur trade.

Another change was the institution of the camp boss. Eskimo society had chosen its own leaders generally on the basis of skill in the hunt, though other considerations, such as age, entered into the selection. The leader's power was tempered by much collective decision-making. The white man, however, wanted to deal with a single person, not necessarily the man who would be chosen by Eskimo standards. The new camp boss had to be amenable to the white man's needs, and quick to pick up some English. The reflected white light would ensure his position among the Eskimos. He was instrumental in eroding or eliminating the process of local decision-making, except on those matters well outside the white man's interest. Later generations faced a long uphill struggle in trying to restore local decision-making.

Among the largest decisions the white man ever took in the Arctic was the movement of a whole community, lock, stock, and barrel. This has happened several times in the Arctic's brief modern history, and the results have sometimes been tragic. The earliest experiment occurred when American whalers moved their families to Southampton Island each year during the height of the whaling season and returned to Baffin Island at the end of the season. One of the last was when, in the mid 1950s, the government moved people from depleted game areas in Quebec and northern Baffin Island to Cornwallis and Ellesmere islands in the High Arctic. One of the most controversial was undertaken by the Hudson's Bay Company, with government sanction, in August 1934.

The *Nascopie*, calling at Cape Dorset, Pangnirtung, and Pond Inlet, took on board fifty-two Eskimos, one Hudson's Bay Company post manager, 109 dogs, all personal possessions, and materials for a new post. All these were deposited at Dundas Harbour which appeared to have good game. Unfortunately, rough ice made hunting there exceedingly difficult. The manager therefore sent half his party to Crocker Bay, thirty miles west. This proved equally unfortunate. The whole scheme was abandoned in 1936, and Dundas Harbour was closed. The assemblage was now re-embarked on the *Nascopie*. All the Cape Dorset and Pond Inlet Eskimos were dropped at Arctic Bay, though the two Pangnirtung families were returned to their former homes. In 1937 these displaced people were loaded once more on the *Nascopie* and deposited at another new company post, Fort Ross, near the entrance to Bellot Strait. In 1947 Fort Ross was closed, and the survivors were next moved to the west, and farther from home, to Spence Bay on the west side of Boothia Peninsula. There they remained. Any bold scheme for resettlement may fail, but resettlement without the most careful prior investigation into resources and living conditions is a responsibility few men today would dare take. While the Eskimos who were uprooted from their homes with promises of return passage were, in theory, volunteers, the story of free will and Eskimo decision-making could not withstand careful examination.

Despite the tragedy of this project, there have since been many people who have advocated the total resettlement of the Eskimos right out of the Arctic to a world more alien than Fort Ross, to hazards a thousand times more treacherous than the sea-ice of Dundas Harbour. Eskimos understandably show some caution towards the white man's schemes for ordering their lives.

The thirteen-year-long resettlement project was a heavy burden to the Hudson's Bay Company at a time when it was facing its first competition in the Eastern Arctic. In 1904 Revillon Frères began its Canadian fur-trading operations, and by 1923 it had forty-seven outposts, including a number in the Eastern Arctic. Competition was extremely keen. Often the leader of each company kept a sled loaded with all materials necessary to start an outpost, waiting for his rival to move. One might move out in dead of night, but the other would be warned of his departure and would follow, ready to begin trade wherever his rival chose to stop. Tales are still told about the strange situations when the only two white men in an empty wilderness were engaged in internecine commercial struggle. Some said that the Eskimos profited greatly, though members of the Hudson's Bay Company hold that instability never benefits the Eskimo. Whatever the effect, it ended in 1926, when the Hudson's Bay Company acquired fifty-one per cent of its rival's stock; outright ownership came ten years later. Competition erupted again before the war, when a former Hudson's Bay Company man started the South Baffin Trading Company. Though it was a small organization, communities again had the heady experience of rival traders. The two traders were in bitter competition for months after the Hudson's Bay Company had, unannounced, bought out the upstart. Some traders have never forgiven their bosses for allowing the rivalry so long after the two companies were one.

With the closing of the South Baffin Trading Company, trading returned to normal throughout the Eastern Arctic, though conditions were sharply changed from the early years of the traders only two or three decades before. Settlement was coming fast, much too fast for those who had retreated into the last corner of the undisturbed and lonely empire of fur. The new-comers who poured into the settlements in the coming years did not encroach on fur lands as the prairie farmer had done. They were not the forerunners of industrialization or railway lines that would alter the economy. But the new-comers inevitably changed the life of the frontier. The most dramatic change of all began on a creek in the Yukon in the closing years of the nineteenth century.

5 | Gold

Skilful film-makers, through multiple exposures, represent in a few seconds of time the life-span of a flower. Suppose, for a moment, their technique had been available to record the flow of a thousand years of the history of Canada.

First, they would catch the uncertain probings of the Vikings around the north-east, then their retreat while the Canadian interior remains undisturbed. Half the film slips by before the movement at the edges starts again. Now there are two westward thrusts. To the north, men in ships batter clumsily against the ice, constantly deflected from their westward course. To the south, a line moves slowly up the St. Lawrence Basin, becoming wider and blacker as settlement follows exploration. While branches spread into the river valleys of Quebec and Ontario, the main stem goes westwards into Manitoba. Northern and southern paths come together, as the searchers for fur use both the sea lanes into Hudson Bay and the fresh-water routes through the interior. The lines move quickly west in the eighteenth century. They reach to the Pacific, but also to the north in the Mackenzie and Keewatin districts, into the arctic seas where the blinded ships still sail. But when this imaginary film reaches the late nineteenth century, the prairies are darkening with settlement, while in the North there remain only the fragile traces of those who made the maps, leaving a wilderness in their wake.

In the mid nineteenth century, the camera would catch an erratic movement in the south. It is not the lonely thrust of the explorer or the *voyageur*, for its marks are black and thick with men. The coloration spreads suddenly like a tumour, sometimes followed by the healthy growth of towns and farms, sometimes leaving nothing but decay. Then the line goes north. . . .

Here was a new age in the opening of the frontier – the search for precious metals. In Nevada and Arizona prospectors came for silver. In California, in 1849, the cry was gold. Gold moved them northwards into Canada when discoveries were made in the Fraser Valley in 1856. Gold took them to the Cariboo country. Barkerville was at its brief and gaudy height in 1860. Then, as in Leadville, Deadwood, Virginia City, Cripple Creek, and Tombstone, a city died. The thick black line moved on, to the Omineca and then into the Cassiar country.

The gold rush reached Alaska, too. For many, the natural path up the coast from California to the Cariboo led northwards to Alaska. When the last great gold rush had its climax in Dawson City, it drew its makers not just from Alaska or earlier mining-camps. Like a sudden fire, it swept in men from all the world in a compelling draft.

The fire had begun a quarter of a century before. In 1873 Arthur Harper and five companions arrived at Fort Yukon by way of the Mackenzie River, Fort McPherson, and the Porcupine River. Arriving at Fort Yukon, Harper went up to the White River area to search for the copper of which he had heard the Indians speak. Harper was an indefatigable prospector, driven on by the simple proposition that if gold stretched from Mexico to British Columbia, why should it stop in the Yukon?

Harper spent more than twenty years paddling and tramping the wilderness of the Yukon, combing the gravel of the streams and the sandbars, searching for the glint that would make him right, and rich. He explored the Stewart, the Fortymile, the Tanana, and the Klondike – all rivers that were to yield fortunes in gold before the century was out. He never found a trace. He died within months of the great discovery.

George Holt came to the Yukon from the sea. He climbed the Chilkoot Pass. Somehow his faith in the Yukon drew him past the incredible physical dangers of ice and snow, roaring torrent, crashing avalanches, inhuman slopes, and, beyond them all, the unfriendly Tlingit Indians. These were the Indians on the coast who prospered from their fur monopoly with the interior, the Indians so jealous of their rights that they drove back the Hudson's Bay Company itself. Holt got by them. In 1878, with the persuasion of an American gunboat, Chief Hole-in-the-Face opened the pass to twenty more prospectors, mostly the residue from some former rush, now drawn northwards by new rumours. The Indians charged a fee for carrying packs over the mountain, and when the human floods came over the pass to seek the Klondike the Indians found they owned the richest industry in the Yukon. Holt, who started it all, met a violent end at the hands of other Indians from the interior.

Ed Schieffelin almost made it, too. He pioneered the northern route into the Yukon, coming up the Yukon a thousand miles from the Bering Sea. He found specks of gold and was convinced that he had discovered the mineral belt he sought. But he doubted that mining would ever pay in this bleak and distant country. He went home to Oregon. Like Harper, he died in the year of the great discovery.

Many others followed. A few came by way of the Nahanni and Liard. Some came up the Chilkoot. Others drifted across the Alaska boundary from the north, restless with tales of gold, drifting with any new whisper of a find. Fortunately, not all were prospectors. Jack McQuesten, now more trader than prospector, joined forces with Al Mayo after they met Harper; together they established Fort Reliance on the Yukon River, just six miles from the mouth of the Klondike. They provisioned those who came for gold, and they were a base for other outfitters. They financed the searchers, they acted as an information centre for them, they counselled them. And they waited patiently.

In the last two decades of the century, enough was plucked from the streams to maintain high hopes among those who had fruitlessly washed a thousand pans of gold. It was enough to bring in drifters who waited with ears attuned for the sound of the newest rush. Forty miles down-stream from Fort Reliance was the Fortymile River; on it grew a town with something of the character of Dawson City, still to come. Fortymile was utterly isolated eight months of the year. Though in the Yukon, it was like an American camp. Its transportation route was through Alaska, and there was no thought of Customs. United States stamps were used on mail. The antidote to anarchy, if there was one, was not the police and the rule of law common to the gold towns of British Columbia, but the miners' meetings which dispensed a rough excuse for justice, as in the mining-camps of the United States. In 1894 Inspector Constantine of the North West Mounted Police arrived, ending the rule of the miners' meetings. When the firm hand of law arrived, many of the old non-conformist miners decided it was time to move. They shifted down to Circle, in Alaska.

Circle had its brief moment in centre stage. There was gold in the Alaskan streams: a million dollars' worth was taken in 1896 alone, and that was quite a respectable figure for a frontier town. Circle had a music-hall and two theatres, eight dance-halls and twenty-eight saloons. It had commerce and it had culture. Like many a mining town before, it had the roaring life of those briefly glittering centres that were about to die. When it did, the city that took its place made Circle's gaudiest pretensions seem dull, conventional, and conformist. But in the summer of 1896, no one had ever heard of Dawson City. It did not exist.

The prelude to discovery was in a chance conversation between a dogged Nova Scotian prospector named Robert Henderson and the descendant of an earlier gold rush, George Washington Carmack, who had been born in San Francisco in the gold rush of '49. Carmack himself was no longer much of a prospector. He was spiritually part of the easy-going Indian society of the Yukon, and his fondest wish was to be fully accepted by them. His two companions on the day of meeting were Skookum Jim and Tagish

Charlie. Henderson ran into them in a bend of the river, and told them of finding a promising prospect on a creek emptying into the Klondike. The creek was called Gold Bottom. He ended the conversation with a fateful sentence: 'There's a chance for you, George, but I don't want any damn Siwashes staking on that creek.'

A few days later, George Carmack followed up Henderson's tip. What happened on the afternoon of August 16, 1896, will never be known for sure. The likely version is that Carmack was stretched out under a tree when Skookum Jim was cleaning a pan in the creek. He stared in unbelief. There it was – rich, coarse, shining gold. A single pan yielded four dollars, a phenomenal amount where a ten-cent pan had always meant success. The next morning they staked their claim. Then they rushed to Fortymile to record it. On the way, they told everyone they met, for this was the code of the Yukon. They did not go back to tell Robert Henderson, who had spoken bitter words about Indians.

Fortymile was soon deserted. So were the rivers and the creeks. Every hopeful prospect was dropped, with the wild rumours of the find in Rabbit Creek, now renamed Bonanza. Claim-posts sprouted in confusion down the river-bank. Fortunes were at stake in the wild scramble. Even the most bullish of prospectors could not guess the extent of the riches beneath their feet.

Joseph Ladue, the trader, did not go. He staked a richer mine. He loaded a raft with all the dressed lumber he could find, then floated his sawmill to a mud flat where the Klondike joins the Yukon. He named this place Dawson City, after the head of the Geological Survey of Canada. Within two years, twenty-five thousand people had come there. It was the largest Canadian city west of Winnipeg. Lots on its main street were sold for $5,000 a foot.

With vision, one could make an easy fortune then. With shrewdness and luck, one might even hold it, though few did. By the end of August, every foot of Bonanza was taken. Eldorado was a pig in a poke staked by those too late for Bonanza, but every claim on Eldorado from One to Forty was worth at least half a million dollars, some far more. When the panning and grubbing ceased to pay, when the miners departed and the rush was over, big companies mined all of it again. Fifty years later, giant dredges still took gold from those unbelievable gravels.

Claims changed hands in wild confusion. Ownership slipped away for a pittance. Down-and-outers were to become near-millionaires overnight, though few then suspected the extent of their wealth. This was one gold rush whose riches were almost impossible to exaggerate. It was as though, for the world's last great gold rush, the Almighty had planned the greatest spree of all. And out of it He built the Yukon.

While bizarre scenes were being enacted in the first flush of un-believing excitement in the Klondike, the world just beyond was changing too. Circle quickly died. Fortymile remained the official centre of the gold rush, for here William Ogilvie, with Solomon's wisdom, presided over the mining recording-office. Dawson City had four log buildings and a growing army of tents. It lived in a vacuum. Through the long winter of 1896-7 nothing came in or went out. Ogilvie tried desperately to let Ottawa know of the explosion in this distant part of the Northwest Territories (as it then was), but the world heard of the strike from less official sources. By April there were about fifteen hundred miners in Dawson, all pulled in by rumours on the moccasin telegraph up and down the creeks of Alaska and the north-west Yukon. Another thousand were waiting to come in from the Chilkoot Pass. They were headed for Circle, for they had never heard of Dawson. They came to the Klondike and stayed.

The North American Trading Company's boat, the *Portland*, was the first out in the spring. It was laden heavily with the first eighty *nouveaux riches* and their trunks of gold-dust. With it, too, went the word of the discovery. The *Portland* arrived in Seattle on July 17 just two days after its rival, the *Excelsior*, reached San Francisco. There was no moment of unbelief, no waiting for the excitement to build to a climax and to spread. The impact was instantaneous. In their way, the cities of the Pacific seaboard were as volatile as the creeks of the Yukon.

Why did it happen that way? Why did the stories of gravels in the Klondike streams of the remote Canadian North-west have such an electric effect? Nothing before or since has so riveted the attention of the world upon Canada.

'The mining excitement of Australia, California and South Africa,' ponderously recorded the Year Book of British Columbia in 1899, 'were similar in character, but did not move the world as the Klondike moved it.' Gold had an aura about it in 1897 such as it had not had before. There was a world shortage. There was depression. It had hit especially the west coast of the United States where people had drifted on unsustained hopes. They waited in despair for some avenue out of their morass. As never before, there was transportation which could bring people quickly to the threshold of new wealth: few suspected the agonies in the last sections of the journey, or cared to dwell upon them. A new kind of newspaper was flooding the cities of North America; papers fought their circulation war with news, real if possible, contrived when necessary. The Klondike happened to have few serious competitors for the front pages until the Spanish-American War and the Boer War stole the scene.

But perhaps most of all, the Klondike rush came at a time when, psychologically, the world was waiting. The machine age had overtaken western Europe and North America. Here was a return to the individualistic qualities of the pure, raw frontier. This was excitement that any man could become a part of. The Klondike was less a concrete goal than an escape, perhaps temporary, from a confining way of life. It was the final fling of those who had come of age in the late nineteenth century. It was odd only that such a remote part of Canada should have been the back-drop.

The easy route was the long one: 2,725 miles from Seattle to St. Michael at the mouth of the Yukon, then 1,600 miles up-stream to Dawson. For people with patience, and for the gaudy freight that made this town on the mud-flats rival New York or Paris in its stylish pretensions, the Yukon River was the route. If you were impatient of distance, and could not wait for summer, you could land on the Panhandle at Dyea and go over the Chilkoot Pass, or from Skagway up the White Pass. Either could be hell. The Chilkoot was six hundred feet higher, but twenty-two thousand people ran the four-mile gauntlet up its walls from Sheep Camp to the summit. Horses were brought to pack the goods of the trail, but this was no country for horses: three thousand died in the narrow passes. The Dyea trail led straight to the base of the Chilkoot, right up the mountain almost to Lake Lindemann. The Skagway trail looked easier from the beginning, but it was a forty-five-mile switchback

over the mountains, canyons, rivers, boulders and cliffs, until finally
it opened on the path to Lake Bennett. It would be hard to say
whether Skagway at the beginning or the mountains at the end
were the worse. Skagway, in the words of Superintendent Sam
Steele of the North West Mounted Police 'was about the roughest
place in the world'. Few spoke so gently of it during the régime of
the famous boss, 'Soapy' Smith. On the other hand, human endurance was also gravely tested in the last great ascent. Before anyone
could enter the Yukon, he had to have a year's supplies, which
worked out to about a ton of goods. Each man would carry about
sixty-five pounds on his back, move it five miles, cache it, return for
more, until the whole outfit was finally up the height. This could
mean about thirty round trips, or a walking distance of 2,500
heavily-laden miles from the sea to Lake Bennett. Men succumbed
to pneumonia, grippe, or sheer fatigue One night, seventeen died
of meningitis. Others took their own lives.

At the top of the divide stood the North West Mounted Police,
establishing Canadian sovereignty by making the rule of Canadian
law immediate and direct. Of the invading forces across the passes,
or in Dawson itself, hardly a handful were Canadians. Courage,
will-power, and the mystique of the Mounties somehow managed,
not only to preserve this land as Canada, but to establish nationality
over once-uninhabited wilderness as it had never been done before.
They carried the burden alone until 1899, when the Yukon Field
Force of sixteen officers and two hundred men arrived to support
the Canadian flag. A year later, the soldiers were withdrawn and
the police carried on.

Those who reached the headwaters of the Yukon in time to sail
down the river in 1897 now faced the threat of starvation. It had
been impossible to bring anything like enough supplies up-river
to Dawson, and no one had any idea of the way that town would
suck in men from the North-west and from outside. By January
1898 there were five thousand people around Dawson City – more
than in any town in the Yukon or Northwest Territories today.

The great rush was building up over the winter at Lake Lindemann and Lake Bennett. Thirty thousand gathered there to await
the break-up of the ice, and the opening of the water route to the
gold-fields. While they waited, they built seven thousand boats,

whip-sawing the green trees and fashioning craft with hands that had never known plane or chisel. On May 29 the ice broke. On the first day, eight hundred ill-assorted craft were unleashed for the Klondike, propelled by oars or sail. Within two days 7,124 boats laden with 15,000 tons were on their way.

It was not all easy going, even then. Just south of Whitehorse – hardly a settlement at all – was Miles Canyon, a deep gorge with a menacing whirlpool at its centre. Beyond it were the Squaw Rapids and Whitehorse Rapids. In the first few days, 150 boats were wrecked. All the suffering of the endless trips over the passes, the anxious winter of waiting, the painstaking construction of boats: all these were lost in a moment amidst the fury of the black and white water. The remaining boats held back, creating a chaotic traffic jam. Superintendent Steele, a man who lived up to the legends collected about his name, saved that day as he saved so many others during the rush. He chose the boats seaworthy enough to attempt the rapids and insisted that women and children make the five-mile portage around. Thus it was that the main flotilla was saved to emerge on the relatively calm water of the Yukon River flowing towards Dawson. There were still treacherous turns, shallows, rapids, and sandbars, but after Whitehorse the worst was past. As the hot spring days slipped by, tension increased enormously.

The tension was not only among the new arrivals, the cheechakos. At Dawson City, the sourdoughs, the old-timers, traded rumours of a human avalanche to come, but none guessed its extent. The ice went out on May 8, after a threat that the town would be flooded. The first arrivals were from points nearer than Lake Lindemann and Lake Bennett. It was on June 8 that the fleet began to come into view. The same day, the first steamship of the season arrived downriver. This was the beginning of Dawson's strange year in the spotlight of the world. Within twenty-four hours, it grew by more than five thousand.

Dawson City was mostly tents in those days. At the river, the boats were so thick that all the shoreline was used up, and they tied to one another. It was hot, humid, and chaotic. It was the excitement of the state fair multiplied a hundredfold; men's emotions bubbled, simply because of the presence of the crowds. It was the excitement of countless bazaars, as veterans of the winter fought to buy the wonders the steamboats had brought, and the new-comers traded the strange collection of goods that each man, in his own peculiar definition, thought essential for a journey to the end of the known world. It was a gigantic freak-show as men and women suddenly threw over the shackles of civilized conformity in the sheer joy of having reached their goal, in the stimulation of others who had discarded their inhibitions.

Business was soon roaring. By July 1 there were two banks, two newspapers, five churches, and a telephone service. By now it was almost the size of Winnipeg, and the commonest business establishment was the bar. It is not certain how many there were, but it is reasonable to suppose that Dawson, in the next few months, set the all-Canadian record. There were gaming-houses and dance-halls There were the Monte Carlo and the Melbourne, which still stand. There were the Bank, the Aurora, the Combination, the Pavilion, the Mascot, the Floradora, and Chisholm's Saloon, which they called the Bucket of Blood. There was, above all, the Palace Grand Theatre, which Arizona Charlie Meadows is said to have built out of two old stern-wheelers. Perhaps it was most unbelievable of all – a gem of theatrical architecture, today happily restored – where the great of the entertainment world then came to perform.

Perhaps the oddest thing about Dawson City, when we look back on it, was that strange combination of sophistication and almost primeval frontier life. Across from the theatre, the latest fashions were to be seen at Madame Tremblay's salon. There was hardly anything that New York or London had to eat or drink that was not to be found in Dawson City that year. Anyone with a mind for it could buy a dance-hall, or the ladies inside. Or he could go to a church supper or listen to a reading of Dickens or Shakespeare.

It was easy to drop a fortune in the gaming-house and scarcely be noticed. Anyone could watch the passing show: Swiftwater Bill Gates or Big Alex MacDonald, the captains of commerce, Coatless Curley Munro, Two-Step Louie, Hamgrease Jimmy, Diamond Tooth Gertie, Billie the Horse, or Nellie the Pig. When it was all over, Dawson would be a tale to be told to grandchildren who would not believe it.

Bizarre eccentricity was almost normal there, but few broke the law. If ever a national stamp was placed on a bit of Canada, it was in

Dawson City then. This was unlike the old mining towns with their kangaroo courts, or Skagway with no courts worthy of the name. Dawson had the same people as those other towns, but in Canada there was the Gold Commissioner and there was the North West Mounted Police. Because of them, major crime did not exist. Anyone who locked his front door or the chest where he kept his gold would be considered odd, but one man was fined for cutting his own firewood on Sunday.

The only glitter in the creeks was gold. Here, a couple of dozen miles away from Mecca (or Gomorrah, depending on the point of view), men faced again the kind of hardship they had seen on the passes and on the route to the Klondike. When the winter came, it was agonizingly cold, but miners continued their desperate efforts to thaw the frozen ground. During the summer, a man might cut as much as thirty cords of pine, spruce, and birch. As soon as the frost dried up the creeks, the upper layer of muck was picked or thawed and shovelled out. A shaft of about four feet by six feet in cross-section would be painfully chipped into the hill-side. When it reached a depth where shovelling was too difficult, a rope windlass might be put together to bring out the dirt by bucket. Then a fire would be lit to thaw the exposed gravel. The loose stone and sand would be scooped out, the fire lit again, and the process repeated until, in this small patch, bedrock was reached: that might take a month. If the gravel yielded no gold, a cross-passage, or drift, would be dug out in the same way as the original passage. After drifting fifteen or twenty feet, there was no point in going on. A new passage would then be started from the surface.

The final stage of this process was the anxious panning of the gravel. A pan worth twenty-five cents was considered good: ten cents was bare wages. When the miners, usually working two at a time, found pay dirt, they took it to the top of their working. They could hoist about a hundred buckets a day when the gravel was loosened. With each bucket containing seven or eight pans, they would hope for a return of two hundred dollars a day. When spring came, this operation had to cease. The draft was poorer in the warmth of spring; the smoke from the fires was too choking, and the sides of the shafts unsupported by timber, began to cave. Then surface water seeped in to make fires impossible. At that stage, the miners began to collect water, in dams if they could so that they could spend the warmer months sifting their gravel in dump-boxes and sluice-boxes.

By these laborious yet ingenious means, ten million dollars' worth of gold was taken in 1898 and about sixteen million the next year. All the difficulties of acquiring it were not in the manipulation of the ground. Scurvy appeared in the spring of 1898, dysentery in June, and malaria and typhoid in July. Up to September, one or two died each day. But the stakes were high, and there were fevers more hectic than typhoid.

On January 10, 1899, the police counted 4,236 residents in Dawson City. Some of these were in Dawson because they found the mining there more profitable, as well as more comfortable, than on the creeks. The residents also included a lot of ordinary men who had faced all hell to get through four thousand miles to the Klondike, but, having arrived, didn't walk the last twenty easy miles out to the creeks because they had no claims to work. Perhaps the truth is that their great Odyssey was not in search of gold at all. They had found their place just by being a part of this gaudy sideshow. It was their protest against the dreary life they had left behind.

It has been estimated that a hundred thousand people set out on the Klondike trail, that thirty or forty thousand reached Dawson, and that not many more than half of these bothered to look for gold. Perhaps a few hundred became rich, and the number who kept their wealth was very small indeed.

No one knows how much gold was found. Tons were taken and never registered. The estimates run from a quarter of a billion dollars up, of which the greater part was taken after the rush had ended.

Thus, while most of the wealth still lay unclaimed in the gravel, Dawson's moment of glory quickly faded. It really lasted only a year at its height, from the summer of 1898 when the outsiders rushed in, until the summer of 1899 when the exodus began. All through the winter, men listened for rumours of new strikes, and raced into the wilderness to find new sources of fortune. Almost always, they failed. Others doggedly held to their faith that somewhere in those purple hills they would find the mother lode – that fabulous undiscovered pot of gold of which the grains in the Klondike streams were the merest washings. Some men and women stayed with Dawson and their faith for the rest of a lifetime, which for a few lasted another seventy years. While they were able, they went out each spring with their pans and picks to wash the gravel again, and search with misty eyes for the tell-tale flash. In the winter they would migrate back to the somnolent town, to exchange once more the tales and legends of that one great moment in their lives.

Unlike the cattle-towns or gold-camps of the west, Dawson was never swept aside by the onrush of a new layer of civilization. One by one the dance-halls and hotels were emptied. The girls from Paradise Alley followed the miners, and the miners followed new rumours of gold near Circle. Some took their possessions with them, for travel was easier than when they came. Arizona Charlie Meadows said he was going to float the Palace Grand down the river, but luckily he never did. No one took the bars, the stores, the offices, or the homes. Most burned down, and some were lost to the vandalism of modern commerce which was indifferent to the preservation of early history. Others remained as they stood on the days their owners climbed on the stern-wheelers bound for a new gold town, or for the Outside. There were famous ghosts in Dawson City, but it was no ghost town. Out of it was born the Yukon.

Dawson City was no longer a mining-camp. It was the capital of a new territory that would struggle to survive in the lean years ahead. When Front Street burned down once more, there was still the stately governor's residence, the opulent administration building, the headquarters of the police, the hospitals, the shops, and houses serving this administrative outpost. Dawson City spoke of its future, but even more of its past. Each August 17, the Yukon Order of Pioneers proudly leads the parade with brass band, flying banners, the costumes of 1898, and the fire engine that was supposed to have been stolen from Victoria. The costumes grew older, and the ranks of the pioneers grew thinner. Soon they were outnumbered by the new generation, their sons and daughters, and more cheechakos. A new Yukon was being slowly built. It never would have happened that way but for the cry of gold on Bonanza Creek, now so long ago.

6 | Whose North?

Canada's claim to its northern lands has sometimes hung by a slender thread.

Only occasionally has sovereignty in the North rested upon the outcome of diplomatic negotiation or the judgement of tribunals. More often, the rule of Canadian law has depended on the isolated actions of men carrying out their part of the nation's business in some sub-arctic or polar wilderness. Sometimes the establishment of sovereignty was a conscious act, as in the theatrical gestures of a Bernier planting flags across the Canadian Arctic in the best tradition of Cartier or Cabot. More commonly, there was someone like a Superintendent Steele standing at the top of the Chilkoot Pass, commanding the invading horde with an authority that could not have been improved upon by the Queen herself at the head of a whole army of Guards. Sovereignty was confirmed by a lonely

Mountie on patrol, by a doctor examining Eskimo throats, or by a young man walking out to make his morning observations of the northern weather.

Sovereignty in the North is no simple matter of shifting boundaries, following the fortunes of war, or protecting the practitioners of commerce. It raises questions of how a country claims or holds a land where no one lives. This is a particular problem for Canada, whose North is the most sparsely settled land on earth after Antarctica. To make matters more complicated, it is spread between mainland and islands scattered over two hundred thousand square miles. Questions of land-ownership are simple compared to the problems of the sea. Is ice to be considered water – even when it is always frozen? Are impenetrable barriers of ice really high seas? If a country claims ice, are those who sail under it it in a submarine or over it in an airplane violating sovereignty?

Before the sixteenth century, the acquisition of territory was based on papal grants. This admirably simple system carried with it the assumption that those not claiming to be Christians in good standing were undeserving of any rights to land – a proposition that sometimes required gentle persuasion in contravention of the sixth commandment. At least any disputes between right-thinking Christian people could readily be settled. Pope Alexander VI, in his bull *Inter Caetera* of May 4, 1493, divided oceans and continents between Portugal and Spain by drawing a north-south line one hundred leagues west of the Cape Verde Islands. This arrangement was inconvenient for Britain, France, and Holland, who based ownership on discovery and occupation. The planting of the national flag on new lands was the key act in adding to one's empires. By the eighteenth century the principle of effective occupation was established. No one ever really defined what effective occupation meant, but it seemed to convey two things. First, there should be a reasonable degree of occupation; that is, in lands suitable for settlement, there should be appropriate agricultural or urban development, while in remote regions scarcely fit for man or beast, there should at least be occasional visits by the power claiming ownership. Second, the claiming power should have shown more interest in the disputed lands than anyone else had done. This doctrine, couched in fitting legal terms, was enunciated by the Permanent Court of

International Justice in the East Greenland case in 1933. The court merely expressed a doctrine that had been gradually accepted for two hundred years.

Until the close of the nineteenth century, neither Canadians nor anyone else had shown much interest in questions of sovereignty. The practice among explorers of claiming land in the name of their sovereigns had been well preserved, less through anxiety about conflicting claims than because this was a neat and inexpensive act of ingratiation with the powers that were. Until well on in the Franklin search, exploration in Canadian polar regions was almost completely a British monopoly. In the second half of the nineteenth century expeditions of other nations arrived, some of them disquietingly militant. The Americans sometimes seemed particularly well stocked with flags. Peary made a point of leaving the Stars and Stripes along his way through the Arctic. The Danes and Norwegians were not conspicuous for any nationalistic designs, but they were first-rate arctic explorers whose thorough work could imply some kind of claim to real estate.

When Canada became a nation in 1867, there were no foreign clouds over the northern horizon. The British North America Act provided for the integration of Rupert's Land into Canada. First it was to be turned over to the Crown after the Canadian government had made a satisfactory settlement upon the Hudson's Bay Company. In 1870, Great Britain by Order in Council transferred Rupert's Land and the North Western Territory to Canada. A further Order in Council in 1880 transferred to Canada 'all British Territories and possessions in North America, not already included in the Dominion of Canada, and all islands adjacent to any of such territories or possessions'. The Order was given further authority by the Colonial Boundaries Act of 1895.

The new country was understandably too preoccupied with its southern regions to do much about confirming sovereignty in the North, let alone develop it. A few insistent voices cried for action, trying to persuade Ottawa that foreign whalers and journeys of exploration threatened Canadian ownership. The whalers were not openly questioning Canadian rule; they were happily ignoring it and treating whatever part of the Arctic they visited as a no-man's-land.

There was enough concern to move the cabinet, in 1904, to request the Chief Astronomer of Canada to report confidentially 'upon the title of Canada to the Islands north of the Mainland of Canada'. Dr. William King's conclusion was that 'Canada's title to some at least of the northern islands is imperfect. It may possibly best be perfected by exercise of jurisdiction where any settlement exists.' Just how imperfect were Canada's claims was illustrated by an analysis of maps of the time. All maps agreed that the mainland was British territory. Some maps did not recognize British claims to the more southern arctic islands, and many others represented Ellesmere as either United States territory or unclaimed.

Dr. King's report was bad news to cabinet ministers, but it encouraged those arctic enthusiasts who patiently awaited government support for the realization of their northern visions. The first flag-raising expedition had already set sail in the *Neptune* in 1903 under A. P. Low. In the year it spent in the Eastern Arctic, the expedition covered a great deal of territory between Ellesmere Island and Chesterfield Inlet. At Fullerton Harbour, not far from Chesterfield Inlet, it established the first police post in the Arctic, more as an instrument of sovereignty than because the citizens of that lonely cape needed protection.

Captain Joseph Bernier was one of the most persistent arctic enthusiasts, a fact to which Laurier could testify as Bernier pursued his relentless campaign in the corridors of Ottawa as well as in the press. In the winter of 1904-5 he wintered at Fullerton, and in 1906 he achieved that glittering appointment he sought. He was made a Fishery Officer. In the building of empires, that is the quiet Canadian way.

Thus authorized, Bernier sailed the Eastern Arctic in 1906-7 beyond Lancaster Sound, making many landings and a winter sled trip. The next year he returned to the Arctic for a voyage to Banks Island. He made a third voyage in 1910-11 and another in 1912-13.

Vilhjalmur Stefansson was more concerned with ethnological studies in the Western Arctic than with rolling back the frontier, but his interests coincided with the new concern over sovereignty. His first trip to the Mackenzie Delta was under private auspices in 1906-7. Between 1908 and 1912 he conducted a survey of the central arctic coast, with the support of the American Museum of Natural

History and the Geological Survey of Canada. Between 1913 and 1918 he was commander of the Canadian Arctic Expedition. Stefansson not only discovered new land north of Prince Patrick Island and west of Axel Heiberg Island, and mapped the arctic coast; he showed men a new way to live in the Arctic. Through his extensive sled trips he proved the feasibility of living off the country, even on ice-floes, without food from the outside. He helped dispel many notions about the extreme rigours of arctic living, and hence encouraged a gradual influx of southerners whose settlement would be the ultimate guarantee of sovereignty.

The Canadian government expeditions were designed to provide some basis of effective occupation to Canadian claims in the High Arctic. Just as Bernier was pushing his ship around the top of Baffin Island, Senator Pascal Poirier rose to make a memorable speech in the Canadian Senate. On February 20, 1907, he presented a motion: 'That it be resolved that the Senate is of the opinion that the time has come for Canada to make a formal declaration of possession of the lands and islands situated in the north of the Dominion, and extending to the North Pole.' While speaking to the resolution, Poirier expressed an interesting principle: 'In future partition of northern lands, a country whose possession today goes up to the Arctic regions, will have a right, or should have a right, or has a right to all the lands that are to be found in the waters between a line extending from its eastern extremity north, and another line extending from its western extremity north. All lands between the two lines up to the North Pole should belong and do belong to the country whose territory abuts up there.' This came to be known as the 'sector theory'. It would certainly be less trouble to keep arctic land by reliance on the sector theory than by occupying it.

Senator Poirier's resolution was not passed. Though his speech did not move the Canadian nation, it did move the government of Tsarist Russia. In 1917, when one might have thought it would have more pressing problems, Russia issued a declaration asserting the sector principle along the lines Senator Poirier had enunciated. In short, discovered or not, all islands between its mainland and the Pole were claimed by Russia. This was one of the few of the Tsar's enthusiasms that were shared by the new Soviet state. On April 15, 1926, a Soviet decree claimed a sector of the Arctic:

All lands and islands already discovered, as well as those which
are to be discovered in the future, which at the time of the
publication of the present decree are not recognized by the
Union of Soviet Socialist Republics as territory of any other
foreign state, and which lie in the northern frozen ocean north
of the coast of the Soviet Socialist Republic up to the North
Pole, within the limits of the meridian longitude 32° 4'35"
east from Greenland. . . . [Here follows the precise definition of
the territory enclosed.]

This decree has real importance to Canadian claims. A country
claiming lands under the sector theory must by implication recognize the application of the theory to every other country. Thus the
decree of 1926 could be considered a tacit Soviet recognition of all
Canadian claims to lands on its side of the globe. The word 'lands'
must be emphasized. Soviet views on waters and air are less clear.

Prime Minister King almost burned his fingers in a territorial
adventure in the Soviet sector. The issue was Wrangel Island, one
hundred miles off the Siberian Coast, three hundred miles from
Alaska. Stefansson was eager to appropriate it, if only to show that
the sector principle was meaningless as a basis of sovereignty; exploration and occupation were required instead. Stefansson had
many sympathetic listeners, including King. On May 12, 1922,
King told the House of Commons: 'The Government certainly
maintains the position that Wrangel Island is part of the property
of this country.' It would have been an embarrassing claim to de-
fend. Quietly, the claim was dropped three years later, when the
Minister of the Interior declared in the House: 'We have no interest
in Wrangel Island.'

Other countries have shown less enthusiasm for the sector principle. The United States has conveyed its strong opposition. Such a
viewpoint is not surprising, since there is no land between Alaska
and the Pole. Denmark and Norway have also been opposed to this
basis of sovereignty.

What, then, is Canada's view? If Canada really believed in the
sector principle, it would be hard to justify those expensive flag-
raising expeditions by a government that was not notably open-
handed. But if it did not believe in the sector principle, why have
so many government maps since 1904 shown the Canadian sector

marked by red lines along the appropriate meridians to the Pole? On June 10, 1925, the Honourable Charles Stewart, Minister of the Interior, spoke to an amendment to the Northwest Territories Act; he said that Canada claimed all territory lying between the 60th and 141st meridians. In 1953 Prime Minister St. Laurent told the House of Commons: 'We must leave no doubt about our active occupation and exercise of our sovereignty in those northern lands right up to the Pole.'

The only minister to attempt an explanation of those sector lines on government maps was the Honourable Jean Lesage. Speaking as Minister of Northern Affairs and National Resources on March 23, 1955, he gave an explanation that deserves a place in any collection of Canadian government pronouncements:

> Canada has never formally asserted a claim to the northern sector as such. Sector lines have been drawn on the map since about 1903 at which time there was no complete knowledge of the land that is in the far north and the indication was that Canada was, in effect, claiming any land within this sector line, though there was no formal statement of claim. . . . The sector lines are there, but those lines were put there only to indicate the areas within which the land was Canada.

In other words, Canada's claims were not to rest only on the sector principle. Canada had marked a sector within which it would effectively occupy lands. It was a nice Canadian kind of compromise. Unfortunately, the British hegemony over the arctic islands had been marred by the Norwegian Captain Otto Sverdrup, who was just completing a four-year voyage in the High Arctic as Dr. King was preparing his anxious report on sovereignty. Sverdrup, an accomplished arctic explorer, discovered and delineated Axel Heiberg and the Ringnes islands, to be known as the Sverdrup Islands. There was no doubt that the strongest claim to their ownership lay with Norway. This was a problem to which Prime Minister King addressed himself in a bizarre chapter of Canadian diplomacy in those days before Canada's external relations were entirely in Canadian hands.

The story opened on the south-eastern tip of Ellesmere Island in August 1907. Captain Bernier grandly laid claims to Axel Heiberg Island and all other territories discovered by Sverdrup — about

25,000 square miles which neither Bernier nor any other Canadian had ever seen. This was upsetting to Sverdrup who had all along assumed that he was adding these islands to the territorial domains of Norway. On hearing of Bernier's claim, Sverdrup pressed his government to do something about effective occupation. Fortunately for Canada, Norway was just as reluctant to spend money as was any contemporary Canadian government.

And so neither Norway nor Canada did anything about the Sverdrup Islands for fifteen years. The Canadian government contented itself with making sure that no one ever officially mentioned the Sverdrup Islands in any connection whatever. Still, the problem would not go away. In March 1925 the Norwegian Consul-General in Montreal asked the Canadian government 'how far Canada regards the areas discovered during the 1898-1902 expedition as Canadian, and on what the Canadian government bases its claim.' Canada did not reply. This ingenuous question was related to the intention, then unknown to Ottawa, of the Americans to use Axel Heiberg as a base for the MacMillan expedition. Canada then sent Staff Sergeant Joy of the R.C.M.P. to Craig Harbour on Ellesmere Island. In the spring of 1926 Joy made a patrol by dog-sled to Axel Heiberg Island. Now feeling more confident of its sovereignty, the Canadian government on June 2, 1926, asked the Norwegian government for particulars about its claim, if any. Norway did not reply.

Sverdrup continued to press his government to take action to preserve what he had won. 'Failing this,' he wrote on March 10, 1928, 'I reserve the right personally to ask the Canadian Government to refund all the expenses of my expedition of 1898-1902.' A year later, he was given permission to relinquish Norwegian rights in the Sverdrup Islands, provided he could get a refund of the cost of the expedition for himself and others who had contributed. On April 22, 1929, Sverdrup sent his bill to Prime Minister King. Mr. King, who hoped to get the islands without paying money, did not reply. Then the Norwegian Prime Minister made some ominous public mutterings about Norwegian claims. In November, Sverdrup was invited to meet in Paris with the Canadian Under-Secretary of State for External Affairs, Dr. O. D. Skelton, who had been empowered to offer Sverdrup $2,400 a year for life, or $25,000 in cash.

Sverdrup's adviser suggested $100,000 as 'a suitable and modest minimum' personal reward, a definition with which King disagreed. Then there were the costs of the expedition – $209,000. Canada made a new offer in January 1930, to which the Norwegian counter-suggestion was made: $25,000 and an annuity capitalized at $42,000, 'in view of his family's exceptionally high vital power'. There may have been a temptation in Ottawa to argue about Sverdrup's vital power, but the offer was accepted, and the niggling was at an end. Canada had some difficulty in wording the announcement of the payment and the acquisition of the Sverdrup diaries in such a way that it would not reveal any doubt about Canada's claim. The world was told of the grant on November 11, 1930. Two weeks later Sverdrup died. He had lived just long enough to provide the means of giving Canada sovereignty over the last arctic lands whose ownership was seriously in doubt. The transaction had taken Canada twenty-eight years to complete.

Canada was never involved with the United States in a dispute over the ownership of specific northern territory, but the attitudes and activities of the United States kept Ottawa officials periodically uneasy from early in the twentieth century until after the Second World War. One U.S. expedition had a close connection with the Sverdrup case. In April 1925 the United States Navy and the National Geographic Society announced an expedition under Donald MacMillan to Smith Sound, with airplanes under Lieut. Commander Richard Byrd which would be based on Axel Heiberg Island for exploration to the north and west. They hoped a new continent might be discovered. The next month, Roald Amundsen started from Spitsbergen over the North Pole in a monoplane; presumably he would conclude his flight on land claimed by Canada.

Pressed in the House of Commons, the Honourable Charles Stewart said: 'We are getting after men like MacMillan and Amundsen, men who are going in presumably for exploration purposes; but possibly there may arise a question as to the sovereignty over some land they may discover in the northern portion of Canada, and we claim all that portion.' The United States avoided the issue by saying that it would deal with territorial questions after the return of the expedition.

The American expedition set up its base at Etah, Greenland,

with the permission of the Danish authorities. On August 19 Captain Bernier dropped the anchor of the *Arctic* in the same harbour. That evening the supreme arctic nationalist and the enthusiastic young Byrd had a conversation which must have been unusually interesting. There were no witnesses or even written records. All we know is that the next day the *Arctic* sailed south, and the U.S. expedition announced that 'severe icing conditions' had forced the cancellation of plans for aerial activities. On August 23 it was further announced that the expedition was moving to Baffin Island, whose ownership was not in question, to study the home life of the blue goose.

Although a suspicion persisted that the United States War Department was pursuing a foreign policy that was cool towards recognition of all Canadian arctic claims, by the beginning of the Second World War it could be confidently and objectively stated that Canada's claim to its arctic lands was as firm as the claim to Nova Scotia or Vancouver Island. With the war there emerged a new kind of threat to Canadian sovereignty: not any overt foreign claims to Canadian land, but the risk of a *de facto* foreign administration that made Canadian rule more theoretical than real. Suddenly the North needed defences to protect 'the North American heartland'. And suddenly the United States had to build them. It was no time to quibble about legal safeguards to protect Canadian interests, for the threats to Canadian interests were infinitely greater from Germany and Japan. Besides, Canadians were too thin on the northern ground to carry out any kind of effective supervision of American activities, let alone offer to perform them.

Canada had withstood the American invasion during the Klondike gold rush through determination, bluff, and the North West Mounted Police. Again in the 1940s, the Yukon's Canadian population was greatly outnumbered by the new-comers. In March 1941 tractor trains set out to build a series of major airports at Fort St. John and Fort Nelson in British Columbia and at Watson Lake and Whitehorse in the Yukon, together with a series of flight-strips in between. In February 1942 the United States was granted permission to build a highway to link Fairbanks with the road system of southern Canada. The road was to be built and financed entirely by the Americans, but the inter-governmental agreement provided for post-war Canadian ownership. Of the fifteen thousand people in the Yukon during the year of construction, twelve thousand were Americans. U.S. military rule was sometimes more direct than diplomatic. At one point an over-zealous officer apparently attempted to control access to the territorial liquor store in Whitehorse. Yukoners can be tolerant of foreigners, but this was going too far. Though there are no published reports on the chain of events by which this crisis in Canadian sovereignty was weathered, according to hearsay the Mounted Policeman was a good deal bigger than his American military colleague. Canada was saved again.

The construction of the highway was quickly followed by the building of the Canol pipeline to supply Alaska and the Yukon with petroleum products from Norman Wells on the Mackenzie. This project led to a broadening of the friendly invasion east to the Mackenzie. The United States did everything that it reasonably could to ease the impact of its coming. For example, cautious and informal inquiries were made about whether Canada would be unhappy if a considerable proportion of Negro troops were employed in the Mackenzie. This influx gave rise to an engaging war story from the hitherto isolated Mackenzie valley. Asked what he thought of the Americans, one old-timer replied: 'Real nice fellows. Like them just fine. Them white ones is okay too.'

Deeper and deeper the American penetration went, so that Canadians formed only a minority of the population north of 60°. A staging-route was built to ferry wounded from Great Britain. The United States constructed airfields at Churchill, Coral Harbour (Southampton Island), Frobisher Bay, Fort Chimo (Quebec), and Goose Bay (Labrador). Weather observation stations were set up at many points across the North. Such was the urgency of the moment and the looseness of Canadian control that the Canadian government was unaware that some of these posts existed until they had been established. There even seem to have been some short-lived U.S. installations in the North that Canada never officially knew about.

After the war came the job of what Fiorello LaGuardia, U.S. Chairman of the Permanent Joint Board on Defence, was to call 'unscrambling the eggs'. There was a large military investment in northern Canada, particularly an investment in airfields. Articulate

Americans, including voices in Congress, were talking disquietingly about the 'special rights' to which the United States was
thereby entitled. Canada decided it would be prudent to avoid such
risks to its birthright by buying the mess of war-time pottage. The
time was propitious, for heavy military buying in Canada had left
the country with a comfortable balance of U.S. funds. The figure
agreed upon to transfer to the Canadian government all assets in
northern Canada except Canol was $76.8 million. Those who had
lived close to the tangled military situation thought it cheap at
the price.

The end of the war did not mark the end of U.S. interest in the
Canadian North. Early in 1946, the Help Wanted columns of some
American newspapers carried advertisements for young men to man
new weather stations in the Canadian Arctic. Canadian officials got
wind of the advertisements and waited incredulously. It appeared
that in the summer of 1946 the United States was ready to establish
a chain of permanent weather stations across the Canadian arctic
archipelago. With American thoroughness, close attention had been
paid to every detail – except one: no one had thought of asking
Canada's permission.

Eventually a group of U.S. officials came to Ottawa to present
their plans. Canada refused to approve, but agreed to a joint study
of weather-reporting requirements, out of which eventually grew a
plan for joint arctic weather stations. To this the Canadian government gave prompt permission, on condition that the commanding
officer and half the staff of each be Canadians. The operation was
entirely successful. At first, the supply of these five distant outposts
was dependent in part upon U.S. ships and planes. By 1951 the
R.C.A.F. was able to take over the air supply of these installations,
and by 1954 the Department of Transport was carrying their sea-
borne cargo. Thus, by the mid 1950s, Canada no longer needed to
rely on any other country to keep its arctic outposts in operation.

After the episode of the weather stations, Washington better
understood Canada's changing attitude towards sovereignty in its
Far North. When Newfoundland joined Canada, Ottawa inherited
American bases with ninety-nine-year leases under terms unaccept-
able to modern Canadian independence. The agreements were
laboriously re-negotiated through the Permanent Joint Board on

Defence. Although to the layman the new terms were not startlingly different from the old, the re-negotiation was an indication of Canada's increasingly firm attitude. The U.S. State Department was punctilious in seeking Canadian permission for every U.S. military activity in the Canadian North – when it heard of them. But there were occasional incidents, or rumours of incidents, that escaped public notice.

A Canadian military plane photographing Canada was ordered to cease immediately and go to Thule, Greenland, for further U.S. orders. The Canadian crew smiled and carried on. There were occasions when the U.S. military was told it could not establish a base without prior permission through diplomatic channels – and then established it anyway. One misguided American tried to prevent the Canadian Government Ship *C. D. Howe*, carrying the annual Eastern Arctic patrol, from dropping anchor at a Canadian port; and another ordered a Canadian military plane not to land at a Canadian airfield. These excesses of the military were, fortunately, regarded by the U.S. State Department with despair, and by most Canadians who knew about them with toleration. The U.S. government sympathized with Canadian determination to put an end to the situation that produced them. Canadian leaders felt a certain identification with a U.S. Coast Guard captain who was completing his first arctic summer operation about this time: 'Bloody ice, hellish cold, damned fog. We should give this godforsaken country back to the Canadians.'

When the United States decided to build the Distant Early Warning Line of radar stations, the exchange of notes of May 5, 1955, indicated a Canadian attitude quite different from that of a dozen years before. There were the usual clauses stipulating that all buildings and fixed property would go to the Canadian government when the line had outlived its usefulness. In addition, the notes reflected the existence of a supervisory Canadian administration in the North: all dealings with local people were to go through the Canadian Department of Northern Affairs and National Resources. Although American money paid for the line, the Canadian section was built and operated largely by Canadians. The last threat to Canada's ownership of any of its claimed arctic lands had disappeared in the early 1930s. Now there was no more fear of any foreign powers challenging the dominant rule of Canadian law. Canada's sovereignty by the early 1950s was secure from sea to sea – to the Atlantic, the Pacific, and the Arctic.

But what of the seas themselves? The situation remains far from clear. It is certain that Hudson Bay and Hudson Strait are claimed and internationally accepted as Canadian inland waters: not territorial waters, but inland waters as much as Lake Winnipeg or Great Slave Lake. Canada could openly proclaim ownership over all waters within the Canadian sector. This would carry with it an awesome responsibility of policing all traffic by submarine and air, traffic that has been completely unpoliced in the past. The likelihood of Canada's being able to do so seems remote, especially since the only arctic ship the Royal Canadian Navy ever had, H.M.C.S. *Labrador*, was de-commissioned in 1958 and transferred to civilian use. Canada could much more cheaply claim ownership of the waters in the channels among the arctic islands, even when the channels are outside the territorial limits of either shore. The polar seas beyond the islands would then be claimed by no one. A third course would be to claim the waters in all the channels among the islands, except for the main and widest channel through Lancaster and Viscount Melville sounds, which would still be high seas. There may be other courses the Canadian government could follow. Whatever claim the government eventually makes on these frozen seas will be an interesting subject for practitioners of international law.

It will be interesting partly because a policy on ownership of arctic waters and air will be breaking new ground. It will be interesting because of the attitudes of other powers, especially the U.S.S.R. and the United States. The foremost Soviet authority on arctic sovereignty has long been W. L. Lakhtine, who has clearly written with official sanction. A 1948 pamphlet published by the Commissariat for Foreign Affairs sought to prove Soviet claims to water and air within their sector. It seems unlikely that the Soviet Union would take a detached view of, for example, an American military party coasting on an ice-island to the north of the Soviet mainland. Though Soviet claims to the land in its sector seemed insurance against Soviet claims to lands in anyone else's sector, the same does not seem to hold true of air and ice. When Soviet flyers first flew over the Pole in 1937, no one asked the Canadian Department of External Affairs if it would mind. In 1954 when Soviet scientists occupied ice-islands, they were sometimes in the Canadian sector and occasionally in what was, by any definition, Canadian waters, but no one wrote to Ottawa to ask permission. Something of the extent of Soviet submarine traffic in the Canadian sector is apparent from Soviet scientific papers. It was helpful of the U.S.S.R. to let Canada know about a submerged mountain range in the Canadian sector, but it seemed almost provocative for the visitors to name it the Lomonosov Ridge on both sides of the Pole. Perhaps the Canadian government wishes to know in advance of such journeys. Undoubtedly it would like to learn a little more of the theory behind the apparent inconsistency in Soviet attitudes towards behaviour in two sectors of the Arctic that meet at the Pole.

The U.S. attitude towards ice, at least as indicated by its policy on occupation of ice-islands, is consistent with its view on the sector theory. The United States recognizes only lands that are effectively occupied. It regards the islands of the archipelago as effectively occupied, but nothing could be less occupied than a vacant, floating ice-island. The United States therefore felt free to occupy it without consulting the Canadian government. Similarly, it sailed its submarines in the vicinity of the Pole without notifying Canada first.

If Canada is concerned, no spokesman for the government has ever indicated it. To arctic residents, the immediate means of survival are of more concern.

7 | The Settlers

The Whalers. The original residents of the North were left long in peace before any new-comers came to share their land. The Vikings may well have wintered in the Canadian Arctic, or settled for a longer time in their pursuit of falcons and polar bears. They left no permanent trace, and their visiting touched only the outermost fringe of the North.

Until late in the eighteenth century, none of the British who came by sea had much effect on the original inhabitants. By this time the flow of settlement had edged deep across southern Canada, but in the North the new-comers were impatiently on the way to somewhere else. When they stayed in the Canadian Arctic, they made an island of themselves. They lived in, or from, their ships, and they remained in every way an extension of the Old World. Not until the mid nineteenth century were any explorers prepared to become a part of the North for even a brief time. Then their numbers were so small as to leave scarcely a ripple on the new land.

Those who first changed the lives of northern people were the whalers, who generally came before the fur-traders. The Basques had arrived in Greenland and Labrador as early as 1575. In 1594 the English fitted an expedition to Labrador in search of white whale and walrus, which they called sea-horse. Oddly enough, it was Henry Hudson who helped shift this industry away from the Canadian Arctic. His discovery, or rediscovery, of Spitsbergen in 1607 led to a rapid growth in the whaleries in northern Europe. The Dutch and north Germans, who were the main participants, sent four or five hundred ships a year in the 1660s, but the whale population could not long sustain such exploitation. By 1700 there was such a marked decrease that interest was again focused on North American waters. If Hudson had not gone to Spitsbergen, perhaps the Canadian Eastern Arctic would have been opened up a hundred years earlier. The course of exploration would almost certainly have been different, and perhaps the lives of the Eskimos as well.

The Dutch sent their first ships to Davis Strait in 1719. Within two years, there were 350 ships each summer in these waters. The British were slow to enter the trade. In the spring of 1725 a bold start was made by an English flotilla of twelve ships. It brought back twenty-five and a half whales, which leads one to wonder what happened to the half that got away. That was hardly sufficient 'to pay the expenses incurred by the fitments and the hire of foreign harpooners'. For some years the results grew worse rather than better. After the British government, in order to reduce the dependence on imported whalebone, began to provide bounties for British whalers, the fleets increased in size and profit. In 1752 forty English and Scottish ships went to Davis Strait; in 1755 eighty-two. By the end of the century, well over 250 ships a year went out, and many more of other nationalities.

The whaling-captains were themselves explorers, but for sound commercial reasons their explorations were never known. Their logs were jealously guarded, secret documents. Quite probably the whalers were in Baffin Bay well before Ross went there in 1818. The profits were high. By late in the nineteenth century a single bowhead whale was worth from eight to ten thousand dollars. Just

before the collapse of the industry in 1906, headbone was worth
fifty dollars a pound; then it dropped to forty cents. The large
rewards were offset by huge risks. Between 1772 and 1852, eighty
of the 194 ships sent out from Hull were lost. In 1830 twenty whaling-ships were sunk in Melville Bay.

By the second half of the nineteenth century, the Eastern Arctic
whaleries were a well-established industry. The Scots, who had
staked out Baffin Bay, operated a shore headquarters at Pond Inlet.
New England whalers worked much farther south, in Foxe Basin
and around Southampton Island. The first shore whaling-station
had been set up by Captain William Penny near the mouth of Cumberland Sound in 1840. Small shore stations continued to be maintained there by both Scots and Americans and to draw a large local
population. About five hundred Eskimos were in close contact with
the whalers in Cumberland Sound alone.

The Scottish whalers came in steamships for the summer season,
then went home. Although there was casual trading with the
Eskimos, in general the contact was slight. Eskimos did not serve on
the Scottish crews. The New Englanders, on the other hand, went
north in sailing-ships to stay until their holds were full. Usually
filling the hold required spending one winter in the Canadian
Arctic, sometimes more. The Americans employed Eskimos to help
man the small boats and search out whales, using the mother ship
as a shore station. They continued to employ the Eskimos throughout the winter: the men to hunt, the women to make fur clothing.
Eskimos were also employed in the shore stations all year, large
numbers being taken on at the height of the season.

This contact had a lasting influence on Eskimo lives. In some
ways, the whalers tried to mitigate the effect of change. They insisted
that the Eskimos hunt seals and narwhals as before, to reduce their
dependence on the provisions the ship gave to each local employee's
family. The whalers taught the Eskimos something of the arts of
the sea. Though they had always lived on the coast, and had been
dependent upon sea mammals for much of their food and clothing,
Eskimos had not been mariners. The kayak was used only for hunting; and even in the large umiak they did not usually venture far.
With new techniques of navigation taught by whalers, the Eskimo
could travel farther along the coasts or in Hudson Bay. The largest

population movements were dictated by the whalers who took families from Baffin Island, first to Southampton Island and later to Repulse Bay, to ensure a good labour supply.

The manner of Eskimo life changed irrevocably. As in the St. Lawrence valley in the sixteenth and seventeenth centuries, the fur trade began to supplement the harvesting of the sea. Steel traps were introduced, and the white fox took on a value it had never had before. A fox skin, at the turn of this century, was worth as little as a dollar, but it was enough of a supplement to income to introduce the vocation of trapping. A whaling-vessel might expect to return to New England with well over a thousand pelts. The white man's tastes were introduced – tobacco, tea, and other foods, metal utensils instead of stone, woven garments instead of fur, canvas tents instead of skin, wooden boats to replace the umiaks. The red-headed Eskimos in the Eastern Arctic are an indication that not all the activities of the whaling-crews were economic. The whalers also brought disease, which was sometimes to prove terrifying in its uncomprehended impact.

In the Western Arctic, contact between the whalers and the Eskimos was limited in space and time. It was none the less an almost unrelieved disaster. The ships did not arrive until 1889. The whaling-ship *Grampus*, out of San Francisco, ignored the warnings of the experts who said there were no whales in the Beaufort Sea. On its first trip it brought back twenty-two bowhead whales, worth in all not much less than a quarter of a million dollars. Within six years, fifteen vessels a year were spending the winter at Herschel Island in the Mackenzie Delta. They generally completed their five-thousand-mile voyage from San Francisco in early August. Before the whaling began, there was a week of unrelieved orgy with the full participation of the delta Eskimos. From then until late September, while the ships were at sea, there was no local contact. Then the whalers returned to winter at Herschel Island or Baillie Island. Many Eskimos were employed to gather driftwood for fuel, and to hunt caribou as fresh food for the crews. The crews lived aboard the ships, though some stayed in huts on shore or with Eskimo families. Eskimo women were brought on board for duty with the senior officers of the ships. The western whalers showed none of the restraint of their eastern counterparts. Large quantities of spirits were brought from the United States and freely distributed among the Eskimos. The major skill imparted to the native people seems to have been in the manufacture of home brew and spirits, an art preserved from generation to generation in the Western Arctic, with a vigorous assist from traders who have always kept the ingredients in stock. Disease struck with devastating speed, particularly measles and syphilis. Of the two thousand Eskimos Franklin had found in the area, scarcely a dozen descendants remained a hundred years later.

Memories of these whaling years are still vividly retained by some people of the Mackenzie Delta. At the time there were a few voices to cry loudly at the disaster, and Ottawa was under considerable pressure to do something about it. At last, on August 7, 1903, two North West Mounted Police arrived to establish a post at Herschel. This decision may have indicated genuine anxiety for the Eskimo people; or was it concern about sovereignty? The post was opened fourteen years after the whaling began – a few months after Dr. King embarked upon his troubled report on sovereignty in the Canadian Arctic.

The instructions of the two policemen were to inspect the cargoes of the whaling-ships, to collect taxes, and to confiscate illicit liquor. By flying the flag, invoking the law, or quoting the authority of the King, the police managed to create the illusion of an active and effective Canadian occupation. This was not surprising in the light of their earlier exploits on the northern frontier. They ensured the rule of Canadian law (which they were sometimes obliged to write from hour to hour), but they could scarcely raise relations between the whalers and the community to that state of mutual uplift to which men of goodwill might aspire. Nothing, indeed, was further from the terms of reference which the government gave its distant representatives. The problem of racial contact was solved partly by death and partly by the market-place. After taking a million dollars a year, the whalery suddenly collapsed. Its demise was due to the invention in 1906 of a cheap substitute for whalebone as a means of keeping women in their places. The whaling-ships came no more, but the Mackenzie Delta was left with the deep scars of their former presence. Economically, nothing was left but the fur trade.

The Church. The first written record of Christian exhortation in the Canadian North was on Frobisher's third expedition.

Master Wolfall, a learned man, appointed by Her Majesty's Council to be their Minister and Preacher, made unto them a godly sermon. . . . The only care he had was to save souls, and to reform those Infidels if it were possible to Christianity, and also partly for the great desire he had that this notable voyage so well begun might be brought to perfection: and therefore he was contented to stay there the whole year if occasion had served.

Although Master Wolfall performed services on behalf of Frobisher's crew, it appears that he had no opportunity for proselytization. The North remained untouched by representatives of the Christian churches for nearly two hundred years.

In the summer of 1752 a Moravian missionary came to Labrador. On September 13 of that same year he and his five companions were murdered at Davis Inlet. Though this was a discouragement to the spread of Christianity in the Arctic, the Moravians established a permanent mission at Nain in 1771.

In the Mackenzie District, the missionary followed the trader. The 'almost pioneer' was a Methodist named James Evans, who was to have a lasting influence throughout the North that he never saw. In 1842 he went as far as the Hudson's Bay Company trading-post at Chipewyan on Lake Athabasca. In three years he returned to go northwards impelled in part by solicitude for the Indians and in part by stories that Roman Catholic rivals were going to get there first. On the way, his Indian guide was accidentally killed by the discharge of a gun in Evans's hands. Evans did not go on, and the mission field was left almost entirely to the Roman Catholic and Anglican churches until recent years. It was Evans, though, who was responsible for adapting a form of Pitman shorthand to give the Crees a simple method of writing their language. Years later it was modified for use by the Eskimos. It became the main written language of many, though not all, Indians and Eskimos. While the syllabic writing was extremely useful as a temporary means of communication, or as a vehicle for putting religious writings in the hands of the Indians and Eskimos, it was later to have a divisive influence. The residents of the Eastern Arctic who came to depend on this syllabic system of writing were unable to communicate with other Eskimos or Indians who used Roman characters.

Two years after Evans's abortive trip, Father Henry Joseph Faraud followed in his footsteps and built a mission at Fort Chipewyan. It was not until 1852 that the first missionaries crossed the sixtieth parallel into the Northwest Territories. Fathers Faraud and Grandin went as far as Great Slave Lake, but did not stay. The first permanent mission was built by Father Peter Henry Grolier at Fort Resolution in 1852. Within three weeks an Anglican representative was in vigorous pursuit. Archdeacon Hunter by-passed Resolution to go down-river to Fort Simpson. Father Grolier set out from Resolution after Archdeacon Hunter, but his only means of travel was the Hudson's Bay Company barge his rival was already aboard. The staff undoubtedly tried unsuccessfully to discourage the project. Their reluctance probably arose less through anti-Catholic bias (as has been alleged) than through sheer embarrassment at being involved in the unseemly contest. It was a difficult situation, but the company was to become accustomed to it. Father Grolier returned to Fort Resolution, while Archdeacon Hunter established his mission at Fort Simpson. Later, the archdeacon's successor, the Reverend W. W. Kirby, was to find himself joined by Father Grolier on a north-bound barge. Father Grolier now started missions at Fort Providence, Fort Norman, and Fort Good Hope. Archdeacon Hunter had reached this far north earlier the same year, but had not established a permanent mission. Father Grolier did, and he secured the people of Fort Good Hope for his church. The next year, Father Grolier went on to Fort McPherson, again the farthest reach of any Christian church. Here Father Grolier did not establish a permanent outpost, but returned to Fort Good Hope where he died in 1864. This remarkable priest was then only thirty-eight.

The Anglicans continued to be active – in a variety of ways. Mr. Kirby opened a mission at Fort McPherson. According to Father Duchaussois, historian of the Roman Catholic Church in the Mackenzie, Mr. Kirby alleged that Father Grolier was married and that Father Séguin and Bishop Grandin had numerous wives. 'If you do not give me tea, and tobacco, and clothes,' Indians were alleged to have said, 'I must go to the Protestant minister for them: he gives me all I want.' The official Anglican history is silent on this charge, but it does record successes in combating primitive beliefs: 'Murder, infanticide and polygamy were publicly confessed and solemnly abandoned.' Kirby and his family journeyed by the recognized trading route into the Yukon, and established the Anglican Church in Fort Yukon. Thus the Church of England was established on the edge of the Russian empire.

In 1874 the Church of England created the Diocese of the Mackenzie with Bishop W. C. Bompas as its head. When he held his first Diocesan Synod two years later, he had three clergy. Despite the undoubted vigour of his predecessors and himself, by 1887 he had to report that he 'estimated the whole population of the diocese at 10,000, of whom one half were more or less under Romanist influence, while of the other half the Church of England had won 3,000, and 2,000 were still unreached.'

The Roman Catholic Church entered the centre of Anglican power when the Oblates opened a mission in Fort Simpson. In 1867 the Grey Nuns arrived in the north, establishing themselves first in Fort Providence. The next year, the Abbé Emile Petitot travelled extensively in the Mackenzie Delta. The Roman Catholic Church established the Vicariate of the Mackenzie in 1901. Bishop Breynat made his residence in Fort Resolution, but the headquarters was moved to Fort Smith in 1927.

The pattern of church expansion in the Yukon followed a familiar course. A year after Mr. Kirby's entry in 1861, a young catechist from Red River, Robert McDonald, went to stay at Fort Yukon. He was not an ordained minister, and the post was not in the Yukon itself, but his stay is usually considered to be the beginning of the permanent Christian church in the Yukon. Fort Yukon that winter was like the barge shared by Father Grolier and Archdeacon Hunter, for the small community included also a Roman Catholic priest, Father Séguin, who had been active in the Mackenzie. Father Séguin's trip was not immediately followed up. While the Roman Catholic Church turned towards Alaska, the Yukon received relatively brief visits until prospecting for gold became active. The northern Yukon, now separated from the Mackenzie jurisdiction, had one of the most famous priests ever to serve in the North. Father Judge of the Jesuit Order first established his mission at Fortymile, then moved with the miners into Dawson City. He became spiritual leader of the community, with the strong support of all faiths for his good works, particularly in the building of St. Mary's Hospital. Father Judge died at the height of the gold rush. His work was already being pursued by the Oblates, who opened the first school in the Yukon in 1899. By the turn of the century, the Roman Catholic Church was also active in the new town of Whitehorse which was being built at the terminus of the White Pass and Yukon Railway. With the end of the gold rush, the Roman Catholic Church moved its headquarters out of Dawson City and directed its Yukon affairs from Prince Rupert. During the war-time boom of the 1940s a new and separate vicariate was established in Whitehorse under Bishop Coudert, who served there until his death in 1965.

The Church of England, unencumbered by responsibilities in Alaska, continued in the nineteenth century to administer its Yukon affairs from the Mackenzie. The Reverend Mr. Bompas went to Fort Yukon in 1869, just in time for the U.S. take-over from Russia on August 9. He stayed there four years until he was made a bishop. Then the Roman Catholic clergy also left Fort Yukon. There was no ordained minister in the Yukon until 1881 when the Anglicans decided to send a man to Fortymile, which Bishop Bompas later made his home. The move into Dawson City and Whitehorse paralleled the expansion of the Roman Catholic Church, though the Anglicans also established missions in a number of smaller communities. The Yukon was established in 1907 as a separate diocese.

Understandably, the churches came into the Arctic later. The first efforts of the Roman Catholic Church working from the Mackenzie ended in disaster. In the autumn of 1913 Fathers Rouvier and LeRoux moved out from Fort Norman into the barrens. As they travelled towards Coronation Gulf they encountered many Eskimos, most of whom had met Stefansson or the free trader Captain Joseph Bernard. White men were not yet readily accepted and communications were difficult. As the consequence of a misunderstanding, the two priests were murdered on the Coppermine River, but this did not stop the spread of the Roman Catholic Church.

The Church of England established its first arctic mission at Churchill, Manitoba, where the Reverend J. Lofthouse built a church in 1883. In 1898 an Anglican missionary went north to

Chesterfield Inlet where he stayed a year, then withdrew. In the Keewatin District of the Northwest Territories, the first permanent mission was established in 1912 by Father Arsène Turquetil, the lasting effects of whose work can be seen in the strength of his church in that area. In most parts of the Arctic, Roman Catholic adherents have always been in a minority. Since the Eskimos rarely came to Churchill after the Hudson's Bay Company opened posts in Keewatin, the Church of England established missions alongside the trading-posts. The first were at Eskimo Point in 1926 and on Baker Lake the following year.

The Anglican Church had been more successful than the Roman Catholic in approaching the Arctic from the west. The Reverend Isaac O. Stringer lived on Herschel Island from 1892 to 1902 when the whaling industry was at its height. During the First World War the Reverend H. Girling moved eastwards as far as Dolphin and Union Strait, and won the allegiance of most Eskimos in that area. In 1894 Dr. E. J. Peck opened the most south-easterly of all arctic missions in Little Whale River, Quebec, and extended his teaching as far north as Ungava. The first mission in Baffin Island was opened at Cumberland Sound, near Pangnirtung, in 1894. The second was opened by the Reverend A. L. Fleming at Lake Harbour. Most of the expansion of missionary activities came in the 1920s, with renewed work after the Second World War in the wake of new settlements.

The coming of the missionary was important to the changing patterns of northern settlements as well as to the means of livelihood and the customs of everyone he met. There is little point in weighing the good and bad influence of either the trader or the missionary. The people of the North had once been an island, little touched by the waves of economic expansion to the south, or of exploration to the north. While even today some wish that the people of the North might be left untouched as noble savages, the wish, whatever its merit, is as futile as commanding the waves to be still.

The purpose of the traders was to make money. To many of them, the welfare of the people may have been a secondary objective but it was none the less important, for the human resources of the North were vital to commercial prosperity. The missionary saw the people of the North as the first consideration. There is no doubting the sincerity, the patience, or the heroism of most of those who chose a career in these distant mission fields. There is also no doubting their tremendous influence, though even now it may be too early to judge their imprint in perspective and with objectivity.

The blessings of Christianity itself will be evaluated according to the personal beliefs of the individual. Even those who do not accept the Christian faith have acknowledged some benefits of the Christian ethic in social relations. In the simplest terms, the teaching of the missionaries has had a large part in making the North safe for the travel of all men. On the other hand, the nature of Eskimo relations before and after Christian teaching was more than a contrast between 'telling lies, committing murder, and killing babies' beforehand, and a Christian peace afterwards. Ethnologists doubt that the coming of the missionary or of any other white man has significantly changed the Eskimos in respect to the first two alleged practices, and it required the economic revolution of the family allowance to end the third.

Sometimes the conflict between old and new beliefs proved too great, or the new beliefs proved too hard to grasp – with disastrous consequences. Religious fanaticism was a factor in a series of slayings at Home Bay on eastern Baffin Island in 1922. Neakoteah was seized with the idea that he was the Messiah and had so convinced the community. In Belcher Island in 1941, Charlie Ouyerack proclaimed himself Christ, and murdered three who refused to believe. When his followers were told the world was coming to an end and they must remove their clothing and walk over the sea-ice to meet God, six children died. Some Eskimos, strong in the profession of their new faith, have risked starvation rather than hunt on Sunday, or have denied themselves and their families the chance for medical care if the only day when the doctor or dentist could reach their community was the Sabbath. A religious group active in post-war years in the Mackenzie Delta urged its followers to have nothing to do with any secular doctors, but to put all faith in the healing power of God.

It would certainly be wrong to blame the church as a whole for the unreasonable action of a few of its representatives, or for the irresponsible interpretations of some of its flock. In the conflict between any old beliefs and new learning, each man has to make his own reconciliations.

In general, the influence of the missionaries was conservative,

not only because of the conservatism of the church, but because of
the background of the missionaries themselves. Few came from
Canada or had ever lived in Canada before their northern ministry,
and few understood Canada or Canadians. This fact seemed unimportant in the early frontier days, but it mattered a great deal when
the missionary had to guide his flock through the turmoils of a
changing life. When Canadians of South and North began meeting
more frequently, the missionary often understood the new-comers
from southern Canada as little as did native people of the North. It
was therefore difficult for missionaries to guide their people through
the trials of impact. Not understanding the character of the new
life, often they simply resisted it and romanticized the olden days.
The Church of England traditionally recruited its arctic missionaries direct from England. There have been few 'country brethren',
as Canadians are called by Anglican historians. The Roman Catholic Church recruited from Belgium and France, though in recent
years more of its priests have come from the French-speaking population of Canada. At the same time, it will be remembered that
most of the traders were brought from Britain and pre-Confedera-
tion Newfoundland. The North American outlook was dimly
understood by many who manned these northern outposts, secular
or spiritual. The outposts often became bastions of an Old World
point of view that both resisted Canadian attitudes and attracted
others who were also unsympathetic with Canadian life. Perhaps
this partly explains the high proportion of non-Canadians still
found in the North. Canadians may be less anxious than Europeans
to move from their comfortable living-rooms, and the early arrivals
in the North had created the kind of atmosphere where Europeans
could feel particularly at home.

Until the mid twentieth century Canadians left their social conscience for others to exercise. The churches provided almost the
only education the North knew until the 1950s. Few of the teachers
were trained. There was no curriculum related to the needs of the
people, and the nature of instruction was left to the judgement of
those who taught. Sometimes it was from school-books of southern
Canada, sometimes from materials familiar from the instructor's
own upbringing, sometimes from religious tracts. Children were
taught in large residential schools, of which there were three Angli-

can and three Roman Catholic, all in the Mackenzie District, by the mid twentieth century. Children were taught in mission houses across the North, or in camps during the fleeting visits of priests and ministers. Always the missionaries seemed to have forty-eight hours' work for each twenty-four hours in the day.

Most of the missionaries became quickly and thoroughly proficient in the language of their flock. Religious literature was available in the vernacular. While some English and French was taught, language instruction was not generally effective outside the residential schools. Later, when the government took over the school system, great emphasis was placed on English as a vehicle for learning, as the key to a world literature to supplement a local language that had no literature of its own. The emphasis of the missionary was, not unnaturally, on religious rather than on secular horizons. As long as the main religious literature was available in a local language, concentration on English would take too much time. Knowledge of English might also open unwanted doors to competitive or undesirable reading material for which the Eskimo still seemed unprepared.

The missionaries worked hard to strengthen and preserve local language. They wrote dictionaries and grammars and toiled patiently to widen the scope of the religious books available to their congregations in their own language. Other aspects of the cultural heritage of the North did not fare so well. Among people who lacked a written literature, the heritage of the old passed tenuously from generation to generation in tales or songs. Very often these old stories were bound up with beliefs in non-Christian spirits. It was therefore common for missionaries to equate all the old stories with paganism, and to do everything possible to banish them from native memory. When modern ethnologists have tried to preserve the last vestiges of this old culture by tape-recording reminiscences, the old people have sometimes shown an almost mortal fear in recalling tales they now believe pagan. Yet the old spirits creep into conversation rather as non-Christian superstition permeates the culture of all Christian peoples.

A particular target of arctic missionaries was the Eskimo drum dance. The Eskimos' only form of musical creativity and the most popular outlet for group expression, the drum dance was the occasion for telling the old tales and keeping them alive. Sometimes the drums were smashed publicly by the white men. At least one missionary asked the government to ban the drum dance by law because it was non-Christian. (There were occasions when government inactivity was a blessing.) In place of the drum dance, the Eskimos, or at least the four-fifths of them who were Anglican, were encouraged to memorize nineteenth-century hymns from the Church of England hymnbook. No native literary or musical impulses in support of the new Christianity seem to have developed. The words of these familiar Victorian refrains were translated into Eskimo in the idiom, the music, and the culture of another world. The preservation of Eskimo culture, in the minds of many white men, meant the preservation, not of the Eskimos' own cultural heritage, but of Eskimo translations of white man's religious instruction.

Christianity has not always displaced the traditional culture of a native people quite as effectively as it has in the Canadian North. In southern Canada, the adaptation of the Nativity to the Huron way of life has provided more than a meaningful Christmas carol for the Indians of Ontario: it is an enrichment of Huron and Canadian culture. In Greenland, the expression of Christian feeling takes forms that are partly Danish, partly Eskimo; and the popular traditions are preserved through modern religious expression. In Greenland, the old-time dress is respected and worn with pride on important occasions. It has been elaborated and modified with the passage of time, but the sealskin trousers of ancient times are still a basic part of the women's costume. In northern Canada women were taught by missionaries that the wearing of trousers was pagan and immoral, at a time when women in the rest of the world were learning emancipation from the skirt for such activities as riding horses, skiing, and other sports. Eskimo women therefore had to outfit themselves from the trader, who welcomed their trade. Only the outer wear, especially the parka and boots, remains traditional in style, and even it is often sewn from the trader's merchandise.

Missionary activity in Arctic Canada and Greenland shows other contrasts. In Greenland, until contemporary times, only the state church was allowed to proselytize. This prohibition may not have been fair to other churches, but it did avoid the fervent, often acrimonious, competition among Christian denominations that has often split Eskimo communities and families. When the state took over the Greenland schools it integrated all students without regard to race or creed. The result was a more efficient and economical school system than would otherwise have been possible with classes divided by religion. But whether these advantages of integration are outweighed by the value of specific religious environments is a question that only the various religious adherents can decide.

When the only settlers were the traders and the missionaries, each had many roles beyond his nominal calling. The traders were, for a long time, doctors, nurses, engineers, agriculturalists — the whole administration, and even the law. The missionary was teacher and minister to the sick as far as his pitifully small physical resources allowed. Both Roman Catholic and Anglican churches started hospitals, though in the absence of any doctors most could more properly be described as nursing stations. The missionaries with their 'ham radios' were often the vital communication link before radio became common, and radio had no more important use than to send rapid medical advice to places beyond the reach of doctors. Where there were no traders, the missionaries often held trading licences, receiving and selling fur given to the Church, or on behalf of Eskimos who had no post near by. These many tasks were reduced or simplified as other professions came to live in the north.

Men of the Law. With the addition of each new-comer to the small white population in the settlement, each could follow more precisely his calling, each was less of all things to all men. The arrival of the second or third or fourth man in each community may have been viewed with mixed feelings. Performing as doctor or social worker could be a nuisance to many a trader, but it was part of an old and simple world which was now penetrated by new complications, by new opinions, by new tempos, by new judgements. Generally, the third man was the policeman. Almost the least of his duties were those generally associated with police work. His objective at first was simply to exist. He was to occupy effectively, to raise and lower a flag each day in some lonely solitude, to ensure that the political maps of the world could clearly state the extent of Canada's northern reaches. His second job was usually administration of one kind and another: census-taker, administrator of relief (a job often shared with the trader), licence-issuer, customs and immigration officer. He was, in short, the representative of whatever arm of government might be called upon to assert itself or render service in the North.

The Royal Canadian Mounted Police began as the North West Mounted Police in 1873, specifically to maintain law in the Northwest Territories and the remainder of Rupert's Land that Canada had just acquired. Its work spread rapidly across the prairies. The northern fame of the police began with the celebrated work of Steele and Constantine in the Yukon in 1895. The police asserted sovereignty. They were, at many times and in many places, the only administration. In the larger new communities such as Dawson City they performed more conventional police duties efficiently.

After several years of patrols from below the sixtieth parallel into the Mackenzie District, a detachment of N.W.M.P. was posted permanently in Fort McPherson in 1903, and one on Herschel Island the next year. (Though it is legally in the Yukon, Herschel Island has been treated administratively as part of the Mackenzie District by private agencies and government alike.) Before the end of the First World War, other Mackenzie posts were opened at Fort Resolution, Fort Simpson, and Fort Norman. The work of these widely scattered detachments was greatly reinforced by the remarkable patrols outward from the Mackenzie as far as Dawson City in the west, and Baker Lake in the east.

Patrols now had to do much more than show the flag over thinly occupied Canada. As settlements in the Mackenzie grew, the police were given a good deal of business through the increasing competition of private traders. In 1907 Hyslop and Nagle entered the field in opposition to the Hudson's Bay Company and acquired seven posts as well as a steamer. Captain Klengenberg and Captain Bernard were so active along the arctic coast that the police decided to open a post at Tree River, east of the Coppermine River, from which they could supervise trading and, through patrols, extend their area of effective occupation to Victoria Island.

The first police post in the Eastern Arctic was established in 1903, the same year as was the one in Fort McPherson. The place chosen was Fullerton Harbour, a whaling-station on the west coast of Hudson Bay about sixty miles north-east of Chesterfield Inlet. Fort

Churchill got a detachment three years later, and Baker Lake in 1915. Another nine posts were established in the Eastern Arctic between the wars. By 1950 there were twenty detachments in the Northwest Territories, eight in the Yukon, and three in arctic Quebec.

The Royal Canadian Mounted Police (as they were called after 1920) were much more than a police force. They were the administration of the North. They had widespread power and influence extending from the community level to the senior levels of government. Between 1905 and 1919 the Commissioner of the R.C.M.P. was the Commissioner of the Northwest Territories. When this function was turned over to civil authority, commissioners continued to sit on the Council of the Northwest Territories until 1960. The Commissioner of the R.C.M.P. still has the authority of a stipendiary magistrate whenever he is in the Northwest Territories, though it is a power rarely used today. Every commissioned officer of the force is a justice of the peace. This also is an authority only cautiously invoked, for the police are reluctant to be criticized for acting as prosecutor, judge, and jury; an R.C.M.P. officer taking a case as a justice of the peace would normally be judging a charge laid by a member of his own staff, a situation which, as the force is keenly aware, has its drawbacks.

When the police upheld the law on lonely passes or in distant arctic wastes, it was an advance beyond those days when the trader himself was the sole, if unofficial, representative of the law. The R.C.M.P. applied justice with a striving for impartiality which was divorced from any self-interest or desire to protect any entrenched class within local society. In applying justice, before the days of modern courts or any communications beyond an annual visitation, the young constable was faced with a staggering problem which no one learned in the law has yet solved. He was applying Canadian law to a people who were not only totally ignorant of the principles of the Canadian criminal code, but who possessed their own informal codes not necessarily in line with it. Canada, desiring one criminal law under which all its citizens may live, has resisted the temptation to write a special law for any race or special group. Instead, the law of the land has been tempered for those who live at its fringes.

The introduction of law to the settlement could make an enormous, if subtle, difference to the lives of those who lived there. The law, as administered by young members of the force who were almost invariably Canadian in upbringing, training, and outlook, was the first sharp reminder to many northern residents that the North was not an island separated by distance from the mainland of Canada. Those who criticize the sway of the R.C.M.P. over the North and deplore a 'police state' set in a modern western democracy overlook the root of the situation. The role was not sought by the police and it was often discharged with reluctance. But the people of Canada, through parsimony, were unprepared to invest the large sums of money necessary to provide a broad administration for a thinly settled land, and the R.C.M.P. therefore carried out the administration for a third of Canada. The wonder, to paraphrase Dr. Johnson, is not how well they did it, but that they did it at all.

The police went to enormous lengths to provide not only justice, but the appearance of justice. It now seems incredible that there were many cases — of which the Home Bay murder was one — when word of a major crime was sent back to Ottawa, a judicial party was assembled with judge, prosecutor, defence counsel, and court staff, the long trip was made by ship deep into the North, a court went into session with all the dignity and panoply the tiny settlement could command, and then after a few hours the party retraced its lengthy steps, returning home perhaps six months after it had left. Ironically, the Eskimos present did not really know what was happening. But something important was being done, and some day they might understand.

In the handling of local problems, and in the settlement of cases before formal courts, there was leniency and toleration in the application of the law, though sometimes convictions in major crimes led to hangings. Frequently there were jail sentences. For short sentences jail meant the hut of the local police detachment. For more severe penalties, the miscreant was sent to one of the larger northern guard-houses or to a penitentiary in the South. Such incarceration, with good food, warm clothes, shelter, and a rest from the problems of survival, may have been less of a deterrent for arctic residents than for southern Canadians. The local constable had to become adept at turning a blind eye to many minor deviations from the law.

Sometimes such difficulties were best handled by local social action. Sometimes pressure from white settlers forced the police into literal interpretation of the law, which did not always make sense on the frontier. Dawson City once had the best-run brothels in Canada, and no man, woman, or child could have been ignorant of their discreet though illegal activities. Then someone lodged a formal complaint. With heavy heart amid popular mourning, the R.C.M.P. marched into Paradise Alley to do their duty. The predictable result was uncontrolled prostitution and the spread of venereal disease.

The making of home brew is considered by some to be one of mankind's essential freedoms. Few in the Northwest Territories even knew that it was illegal. The most respectable moonshiners were caught in the net when complaints from teetotallers obliged the R.C.M.P. to move in, and people turned to much more lethal spirits until home brew was legalized in 1962.

Members of a typical northern police detachment usually spent a good deal of time on patrols — distant safaris on which they undertook all manner of duties. At first, their major concern was to carry the flag, whether or not anyone was there to see it. Later it became more and more important to show scattered people that they had some contact with the nation of which they were dimly a part. What a single policeman with his interpreter and dog-sled or canoe could do in a camp was necessarily limited, but it was a kind of tenuous connection with national reality, a connection whose significance increased as the settlements grew, and as the administration was gradually given the resources for more effective service.

The policeman took the census. He registered births and deaths. He filled in applications for old-age pensions and enmeshed himself in the long struggles to prove old age in a country that had no written records when the old were young. He might be a commissioner of oaths, a notary public, a coroner, a dog officer, a fur-export officer, an issuer of licences, a postmaster, an inspector of weights and measures, a fisheries inspector, a game officer, an inspector of customs, and an immigration officer. In his spare time, he might help a scientist by collecting rock samples or local flora and fauna. This brief catalogue leaves aside such miscellaneous duties as dispenser of drugs, medical practitioner, and midwife.

The typical headquarters for these activities was a small white building with a red roof, identified readily by the flagpole in front. As more married men were posted to the North, the detachment building might be flanked by the houses of the permanent members of the force and by the special constable locally hired from the Eskimo, Indian, or Métis population. In the detachment building was the office and its near-by steel lock-up which was not big enough for much of a crime wave, especially one that involved both sexes. This was a modest assertion of Canada's responsibility over its lands and people, but until Canada was prepared to do more the R.C.M.P. bore the burden well.

Men of the Rock. Though the geologists, the prospectors, and the bush pilots were rarely part of the neat little settlement at the edge of the river or the sea, they were builders of the new community of the North.

Joseph Burr Tyrrell was a member of the Geological Survey of Canada, and responsible for some of the first serious geological exploration in the North. As important as the extensive information he recorded was the new direction he gave to the mining industry of Canada, which slowly began to consider the possibilities in the northern third of Canada.

His first trip into the Northwest Territories was made in 1893. On the way, he stopped to examine oil seepage near Edmonton. Wells were dug there the next year, though not in the pattern he suggested. One can only guess whether, if his directions had been followed, the Edmonton oil-fields would have been exploited fifty years earlier. That trip took him from Lake Athabasca to Hudson Bay via the Dubawnt and Thelon rivers, Baker Lake, and Chesterfield Inlet. He then paddled down to Churchill. In eight months he covered 3,200 miles, nearly half of it over previously unexplored country. He made another trip in the barrens the following year; after extensive work in northern Manitoba, he found himself in Dawson City at the height of the gold rush. Then he returned to Ottawa, where his situation was familiar to civil servants; after making enormous contributions to the development of Canada and its mineral industry, he was being paid $1,800 a year. The desire to eat led him away from government service and into the business of mining engineering, first in Dawson City, later in many parts of

Canada and abroad. He lived long and contributed greatly to the Canadian mining industry, but his great talents and energies were lost to the North.

Robert Bell, on the other hand, worked for the Geological Survey from 1856 to 1908, except for four years of teaching. He spent his last years as its director. Much of his high reputation was built on his work in the North, where he explored vast areas of unknown country and gave names to three thousand geographical features. James Mackintosh Bell, his nephew, and Charles Camsell were two other names left on the rocks of the north. Camsell gained a special fame as the first home-grown hero of the Mackenzie. He was born in Fort Liard in 1876, the son of a Hudson's Bay Company post manager. As a young man, he accompanied Bell on one of his field trips between Great Bear and Great Slave lakes. He later joined Bell as a member of the Geological Survey. Apart from some work between Great Slave Lake and Lake Athabasca, most of his later work was in southern Canada. After the First World War, he became Deputy Minister of Mines, and he headed this department under its different titles until after the Second World War.

The bold and painstaking work of Bell around Great Bear Lake had its sequel twenty-nine years later, when Gilbert LaBine read the report of cobalt-bloom and copper green at Echo Bay. LaBine followed it up and found the enormously rich deposits of pitchblende on which he built the Eldorado mine. Charles Camsell was among those able to celebrate the production of the first ounce of radium in 1936, when radium was worth about two and a half million dollars an ounce.

Eldorado illustrated the partnership of the explorer-geologist with the prospector and developer. Its opening was a revolutionary event in Canadian mining. No one before had seriously thought of the economic possibilities of the Mackenzie Precambrian Shield, so discouragingly far from the national transportation networks. Later, the mine was to have its own air service, for the value of the ore in relation to its weight justified air freight. In the early days shipping it out was formidably complicated. The ore in bags went by boat from LaBine Point, across Great Bear Lake to Great Bear River. The ninety-mile river trip included eight miles of cataracts which required the cargo to be off-loaded, carried on trucks over a rough road, then reloaded for the 500-mile trip up the Mackenzie River, across Great Slave Lake to the Slave River. There was another portage at Fort Smith for sixteen miles, then the reloading for the final 382 miles to the railhead at Waterways. There were still 2,500 rail miles to go before delivery at Port Hope, Ontario.

The value of the ore justified the trip, and LaBine was to prove that the climate on the edge of the barrens provided no insuperable obstacle to mineral development. When this operation proved profitable, the rocks around Great Slave Lake took on a new meaning in the board rooms of Bay Street and St. James Street, or wherever northern prospectors met. They were equally important for members of a new profession that was being born in Canada — bush pilots.

Men of the Air. During the First World War the accomplishments of Canadian aviators were out of all proportion to the size of Canada. A quarter of the flyers in the Royal Flying Corps were Canadians. By the end of the war, Canada had about thirteen thousand combat flyers, only a few of whom could be absorbed into the new Canadian Air Force or in the limited civilian operations of the Canadian Air Board. War-surplus planes were cheap. For the unemployed flyer, the flying circus or the aerial stunt man was an interesting if insecure occupation. A few flyers cherished a dream of putting the airplane to new commercial uses as a means of transport where other methods were lacking, and they looked north.

The first chance came during the oil rush down the Mackenzie. In 1920 the Imperial Oil Company brought in a well fifty miles down-river from Fort Norman on the spot where Alexander Mackenzie had noticed seepages 131 years before. The well prompted a rush of prospectors eager to stake claims around the new bonanza. It started from Edmonton and gathered mass en route as traders and trappers in settlements from northern Alberta to the Mackenzie joined in the trek. Imperial Oil itself could not get its men in until break-up the next spring, by which time the company's interests would be seriously prejudiced. The company ordered two Junkers planes flown from New York. On March 28, 1921 the aircraft 'Vic' and 'Rene' reached Fort Simpson, piloted by G. W. Gorman and E. G. Fullerton. In a series of mishaps there, propellers of both planes were smashed. A local Hudson's Bay Company carpenter was able to fashion a new propeller, an extraordinary feat with the materials and tools available, and one of the planes completed the flight to Great Bear Lake.

Though this pioneer venture was a success, no plane went north again for seven years. In that buoyant, bullish period of the Roaring Twenties, money could be found for all kinds of unlikely ventures – even flying into the North. 'Doc' Oaks organized the Northern Aerial Minerals Exploration Company for prospecting, and its first venture was in the Nahanni Valley. It was formidable country for pioneering the airplane. The Nahanni Mountains lie about sixty miles west of Fort Simpson. The Nahanni country is rugged and inaccessible, with some of the most spectacular scenery in Canada. It has also spawned more legends than any part of Canada, though the airplane dispelled most of the myths. Northerners told tales of a deep valley that had mysteriously escaped the Ice Age; a semi-tropical land inhabited by monsters of another age. Everyone who had ventured in was said to have died a violent death, sometimes by decapitation. The Nahanni also generated stories of ore with the richness of the Klondike. There was even a gold mine which had once been worked by the McLeod brothers before they were killed – and decapitated. Oaks took in a party to find the lost McLeod mine, and was to pick it up in the autumn. They didn't find the gold, and Oaks couldn't find the party (which made its way back on foot), but the project marked another milestone in the developing North.

During that same autumn of 1928 another famous bush pilot entered the North. 'Punch' Dickins landed in Fort Smith on September 6 after a 3,000-mile flight from Winnipeg, north to Chesterfield Inlet, west to the Thelon River, across the barrens, and south to Fort Smith. His passengers were two American mining men. His flying time was twenty-seven hours for a trip that, before the airplane, would have taken a year.

The Northern Aerial Minerals Exploration Company ventured deep into the North. John McDonogh was the first to pilot a plane into the Yukon. 'Pat' Reid pioneered the coasts of Hudson Bay. The first flyers to cross the Arctic Circle in Canada were Americans – Byrd and other members of the MacMillan Expedition who flew over Ellesmere Island on August 8, 1925, and landed there four days later. Western Canada Airways, which made the first flight over the barrens to Churchill in 1927, began an airmail service into the North in 1928. On March 6 Dickins crossed the Arctic Circle; on July 1 he set down in Aklavik. Later he made the 1,500-mile Edmonton-Aklavik flight in seventeen hours. Next summer LaBine went on to Aklavik, then across the mountains on the first flight to Dawson City.

The airplane began to come into its own for mercy flights in the late twenties, and the biggest mercy flight of all was in search of lost flyers. When Colonel C. D. H. MacAlpine of Dominion Explorers was lost in the barrens on the way from Churchill to Coppermine, the search for his party recalled the search for Franklin in the previous century. This time the vast search used aircraft. Directed from Winnipeg, it prompted more flying that autumn than had been done in all the years up till then. MacAlpine, Tommy Thompson, and Stan McMillan, flying a Fokker and a Fairchild, lost their way after leaving Baker Lake. The aicraft ran out of fuel, but the three men survived with the help of friendly Eskimos and reached Cambridge Bay on foot.

In 1930 'Wop' May, flying for Commercial Airways with three Bellancas and a Lockheed Vega, pioneered the first government airmail service the full length of the Mackenzie – 1,200 miles from his headquarters in Fort McMurray, in northern Alberta, to Aklavik; the round trip took four days. It was the longest airmail route in the world. The coming of the mail service meant more to the settlers in the North, to the missionary, to the policeman, to the trader and his wife, than any previous exploits of the air. For the old-timer it was one more attack on the security and isolation of the world he had built far from civilization.

Aviation became less a novelty and more a part of northern commercial life during the thirties. Though the depression had hit the air transport industry especially hard in the Mackenzie District, aircraft became commoner. LaBine's finds at Great Bear Lake touched off an aerial stampede, and the development of Port Radium in itself generated a continuing air traffic deep into the North. Canada's northern bush pilots were becoming something of a legend in the outside world. There was big news in the flight of the Lindberghs in July 1931 from Ottawa to the Orient via Moose Factory and Churchill, over the barrens to Aklavik, then to Nome. Northern flying drew attention again that winter when 'Wop' May in a Bellanca took part in the pursuit of Albert Johnson, 'the mad trapper of Rat River', one of Canada's few rivals to the senior villains of the American West. The gunmen of the banana belt were not pursued by Mounties or bush pilots. If only there had been a few more mad trappers in the Mackenzie, the North might have spawned a national television industry!

The North did become an appendage of the American entertainment industry when a celebrated fan dancer called Faye Baker headed north from Winnipeg, presumably for a little sociological research into the impact of such a traveller on single young northerners in danger of being bushed. She got only as far as The Pas. On the way back, she and her pilot made a forced landing in the middle of nowhere which miraculously turned out to be beside a well-stocked cabin. That was lucky, for Miss Baker's fans would not have kept her very warm. They were marooned for three days before coming south to hit the headlines as hard as the traffic would bear. Miss Baker was, in her way, a pioneer of the North. Among the North's less numerous but most persistent settlers was a long line of breathless publicists who calculated (usually correctly) that doing routine things far enough away is the stuff of which publicity is made. The airplane contributed greatly to this activity, for what fashion model would have travelled two years by sailing-ship to be pictured in semi-dress beside an ice-floe or an igloo? The old northerners claim to hate this sort of thing. That is doubtless why they talk in excruciating detail of such exploits during the long winter nights.

While the Mackenzie and the Eastern Arctic were being newly opened by the bush pilot, the Yukon was experiencing the birth of its own air industry. Clyde Wann and Jim Finnegan started commercial flying there. Andy Cruickshank was the pioneer pilot, and Ted Field surveyed the air route from Grande Prairie in northern Alberta through northern British Columbia to Watson Lake and Whitehorse. Planes of his Yukon Southern Line flew this route for years without airports or hangars, while Grant McConachie pioneered the radio compass. By 1939 McConachie was running a weekly service to Whitehorse. In the days of war he was to see the fragile chain of airstrips grow into the vital Northwest Staging Route. Later, as President of Canadian Pacific Airlines, McConachie still used that route, now serviced by enormous aircraft and modern facilities which no bush pilot of the thirties could have dreamed of.

Though the Second World War caused a sudden expansion of transportation facilities, the long conflict in Europe drained the North of pilots and called a temporary halt to the fulfilment of its newly awakened commercial hope. Prospectors and developers turned away to more immediate enterprises, and so did those who might have built the settlements around them. The North returned to economic cold storage, but the patrols, the patient trips by sled to Indian camps, the lonely life in trading outposts, the mapping, the chipping of rocks, the advent of flying – all had opened a frontier of knowledge for later generations. After the war, the North would be invaded by waves of a new kind of settler, bringing what was called civilization. On the tongues of many, civilization was a term of abuse.

8 | The Quiet Years

On New Year's Day, 1900, there was almost no one in the whole of the Eastern Arctic who realized that a new century, or a new year, was beginning. The heyday of the Eastern Arctic whalers was over; the resident trader, the missionary, and the policeman had not come into their own. There was little indication that anything in the coming years would change the splendid isolation of the past. In the Mackenzie, glasses were raised to the new year and the new century. There was no doubt many a reminiscence of home across the seas, for few of the whites could regard this northern bush as more than a temporary lodging. To the whalers near the mouth of the Mackenzie River, the signs were propitious for continuing prosperity. They were in a well-established and extremely lucrative industry whose suddenly impending doom they could not foresee. It was a doom in which others would have rejoiced, had they but known of it: there were already voices raised in horror over the social consequences of the activities of the itinerant whaling-captains and their crews.

Up-river, it looked like a century for the fur-trader. The Hudson's Bay Company had an entrenched position from which no one seriously thought it might be dislodged, but there was keen and not always scrupulous competition. Had the Indians and Métis been asked their opinion, they might have applauded the new régime by which they were released from the whims of one company. Whether they benefited most from the fur wars or from the paternalism of the Hudson's Bay Company would have been difficult for them – and for us – to answer.

There were hints of the character of the new northern century, but almost no one recognized them. Prospectors on the way to the Klondike camped at Pine Point on the south shore of Great Slave Lake. They identified ore that was apparently rich in lead and zinc; but they sought gold, and considered this dross. A prospector on the lake's northern shore, near the mouth of the Yellowknife River, submitted ore samples to the Geological Survey of Canada: one contained 2.158 ounces of gold per ton. Another sample had 38.86 ounces of silver. This was not dross, but still the Klondike seemed brighter.

The glory of the Klondike was about to fade. Nowhere else in the North, perhaps nowhere else west of Upper Canada, was the new year so handsomely ushered in. The highest industrial achievements of the Victorian age were available on this frozen mud-flat for the benefit of the *nouveaux riches* of the gold-fields and those content to watch them. Dawson City was now the capital of the Yukon, no longer an uncertain outpost of uncertain lands nominally the Northwest Territories. Some citizens had plans for fine new buildings befitting the town's status. More had plans for shipping out of Dawson in the spring. Perhaps the gold had not all gone, but miners' feet are itchy, and there were rumours of new fields. Perhaps back in Alaska, maybe near Circle, or even Nome. . . .

The North reacts more slowly than the rest of Canada to stimuli from outside. It takes longer to do big things in the North because of climate and distance. Transportation routes are long, and many stay locked for most of the year. This was so at the turn of the century, even more than now. George Carmack found gold in 1896. The height of the rush was in 1898. By the summer of 1900 the party was over. But it was just then that some of the lasting consequences of the rush began to take shape.

On July 21, 1898, construction had begun at Skagway on a narrow-gauge railway. In the first nineteen miles it climbed 3,000 feet. For the rest of its 110-mile journey, it followed the gold-rush route into British Columbia via Lake Bennett, then into the Yukon for the second half of its journey. The last spike of the White Pass and Yukon Route was solemnly hammered in place on July 30, 1900, in Whitehorse. The spike went in crooked, which reflects less on the standards of railway construction than on the natural exuberance of Yukoners celebrating a remarkable achievement.

The railway was a great boon to business. A telegraph line was started on April 28, 1899, from Bennett to Dawson. The first telegram was sent from Dawson to Skagway on September 28. The line was linked to Atlin, Telegraph Creek, and Quesnel by 1901 to permit communication with any point in Canada. A mail service, weekly in winter, semi-weekly in summer, was established between Dawson and Atlin in 1899. By 1902 there was a reasonable winter road between Dawson City and Whitehorse, a distance of 278 miles. In 1912 it was used by an automobile.

Better and cheaper transportation to and within the Klondike permitted the importation of heavy equipment by 1900, and a new phase of mining began. Properties too marginal for manual exploitation at the height of the rush now became commercially attractive. The little man with the pan was displaced by the big company with steam-powered thawing equipment, huge dredges, and, above all, sophisticated schemes for pumping and storing precious water for higher workings. Ground worth five cents a pan could be worked profitably. Though the rush was over, the gold industry continued.

A dollar spent in the development of northern Canada generally causes more ripples on the Canadian economic pond than a dollar spent anywhere else, if only because it travels farther and through more pockets. The Klondike mining industry not only gave birth to the Yukon but stimulated many industries outside. Goods manufactured in the industrial East generated traffic for the Canadian

Pacific Railway. Western Canada provided agricultural products. Horse ranches in Alberta facing a decline suddenly found new markets. Only a small proportion of the horses intended for Dawson City reached their destination, but many others remained along the various routes to develop other areas, especially in the Mackenzie.

Within the Yukon itself, prospects for the many little men who remained were uncertain or bleak. Wages dropped at least as much as the price of goods, which had been reduced by the new transportation. Even with the extended mining operations, there was bound to be a surplus of labour when a mechanized operation with five men could do a job that formerly took fifty. Some subsidiary industries needed men. The mining operations, as well as the town, voraciously consumed wood. In 1901 the Klondike used three million dollars' worth. The White Pass Railway, the steamers on the Yukon, and the local Klondike Mines Railway were such large consumers of fuel that coal mines were started. The Tantalus mine, 215 miles up-river from Dawson, was producing thirty-five carloads a day by 1905. The mines and the towns also needed food, and some local agriculture was started. It was limited by soil and climate, but in 1908 the Dawson area produced about 600 tons of vegetables from 200 acres.

The Yukon promised minerals other than gold, and these became more attractive when the gold workings were taken over by large operators. In 1910 a copper deposit was developed near Whitehorse, but it closed down in 1921 after producing ore worth $2,690,516. Two hundred men had been employed at that enterprise and they took half a million tons of ore. In 1914 silver-lead was discovered near Mayo on the Stewart River, and a concentrating plant built there in 1925 became the major mining operation in the Yukon and the largest silver operation in Canada.

After the gold-rush days the Yukon developed the beginnings of a tourist industry that took advantage of the region's relatively good transportation, its scenery, its game, and its legends. It was still too early for tourism to be a major industry or to pick up much of the slack that the gold rush had left. The Yukon would have to wait for better roads and that period of affluence that set all North America on the move after the Second World War.

1. The Yukon River around Miles Canyon near Whitehorse was a critical part of the route to the Klondike during the gold rush. A hydro development has quietened the once turbulent water.

2. In two years, a mud flat became the tinselled city of Dawson, half gaudy, half respectable, capital of the new Yukon, and gold-mining centre of the world.

3. Near the Arctic Circle, on a winter day scarcely lit by the sun, pieces of caribou meat hang from poles above the dogs.

4. 1898 – and miners by the thousand were pouring into Dawson City by steamboat up the Yukon River. The steamboats brought not only prospectors but food, fashions, girls, mail.

5. In the sub-arctic climate at Inuvik, large buildings, like the one on the left, rest on piles driven 15 to 30 feet into the permafrost. The utilidor, in the left distance, carries water, heat, and sewage.

6. At Pelly Bay in the central Arctic, an Eskimo family in traditional clothing rests after a day's fishing for arctic char. Once food
for dogs, char is now an important arctic product.

7. Bright orange lichens, red saxifrage, white arctic cotton, or mountain avens spring to life in southern Baffin Island in July.

8. In Arctic Quebec, Eskimos now catch char in nylon nets, and then flash-freeze and package them for market.

9. Pelly Bay Eskimos still live in summer tents of sealskin, wear
clothing made from the skin of caribou, and eat raw fish.

10. Fishermen of Pelly Bay spear char trapped by receding tides
in a stone enclosure.

11. Seemingly unchanging, the glaciers are in fact moving slowly downwards to the sea.

12. Old Crow is one of the North's most picturesque Indian villages. The frame in the foreground is used to stow a canoe safely out of reach of the dogs.

13. Between two generations of Eskimo, a revolution: only the aged now are tattooed, and the young may never have seen a caribou parka or snow house.

14. Eskimo children now find doors being opened for them by the same kinds of books that schoolchildren everywhere else in Canada are using.

15. Young Eskimos train as riggers so that they can help search for oil in the Mackenzie basin and the high Arctic. Rig 22 was set up at Winter Harbour on Melville Island.

16. No single Eskimo print has surpassed the fame and popularity of 'The Enchanted Owl', drawn by Kenojuak, woman artist of Cape Dorset.

17. Kenojuak's imaginative print combines arctic birds and human forms.

18. Eskimo graphic art is the combined creation of the artist who draws the original design on paper and the craftsman who carves it with knife and chisel on soapstone.

19. At round-up time
on the federal reindeer station
in late summer, hundreds
of animals are
close-herded for
inspection and treatment,
although it is commoner now
for biologists to
fly out to the
herds on the range.

22. These three young bears were caught in a shallow stream on Baffin Island as they crouched to escape the noisy aircraft.

20. In the face of danger
musk-oxen quickly
form a square,
the bulls ready
to repel the
enemy with their
sharp horns.

21. This hunting
expedition heads
for the floe-edge
where the seals
should be.
Before long,
the young people
now on the sled
will run beside,
especially where the
ice is rough.

23. Mould Bay, a weather and research station at 75° North, was set up in 1948 and has been maintained since then entirely with material flown from the south to the mud airstrip. The cliffs on the western (right) side of the frozen bay are five miles distant.

24. The Selwyn Mountains
near Mayo rise between
the southern Yukon
and the potentially rich oil
and gas fields
of the Peel Plateau.

25. At midnight on June 15,
in northern Baffin Island,
the sun still shines
bright on rocks
newly free of snow.

26. Cambridge Bay, in the central Arctic, is one of the biggest stations on the Distant Early Warning Line, a reliable network communicating weather and radar information to central North America.

27. Travel between southern Canada and the Queen Elizabeth Islands is by large aircraft. Local transportation is by single-engine bush plane and by helicopter, such as this one at Isachsen in latitude 79°N.

28. The Mackenzie River system is still the only highway for heavy freight from Great Slave Lake to the Arctic Ocean. Barges are lashed together and pushed for greater control.

29. Annual ship-time is still an event for arctic settlements. As the ice-breaker *C. D. Howe* drops anchor in the fiord at Pangnirtung, all available boats converge on her.

30. Much of the interior of St. David's Anglican church, built in 1858 at Fort Simpson, dates back to early fur-trading days.

And so, between 1900 and the Second World War, the Yukon lived through a time of decline. The population of 27,219 in 1901 slipped to 8,512 in 1911 and to 4,157 in 1921. It remained at about that level until war broke out. Whitehorse had only 342 people in 1931.

The Northwest Territories had not reached any pinnacles from which to fall. The collapse of the whaling industry affected only a limited region and a few northerners. Until the 1920s the character of the settlements of the Mackenzie valley was little changed. They were typical fur-trading posts, the larger ones having also a mission, sometimes a mission school and nursing station, sometimes an R.C.M.P. detachment. The only change from the nineteenth century was the arrival of new fur-traders to challenge the monopoly of the Hudson's Bay Company.

It was not until the twenties and the thirties that the shape of the future was discernible to those who looked for a changing role of the North in Canada at large. The tocsin of the old order was in the sound of airplanes in 1921, but it sounded only faintly and briefly. It was in the sound, too, of the oil rush to Norman Wells. Three leases had been staked in 1914. In 1920 drilling was started and oil was established in commercial quantities. In 1921 Imperial Oil built a small still to produce gasoline and diesel fuel, but it was not until LaBine established his radium mine at Great Bear Lake, so fortunately near, that production at Norman Wells had any importance.

By 1925 the end of steel advanced farther through Alberta from Athabasca Landing to Waterways. This line was not to move north again until the mid 1960s. The Northwest Territories had neither railway nor permanent road until after the Second World War. It was also in 1925 that the Royal Canadian Corps of Signals established a wireless communication system from Fort Smith through Fort Simpson to Aklavik. The Hudson's Bay Company and the Northern Trading Company had established themselves in Aklavik in 1912. The Church of England came in 1919 and the Roman Catholic Church in 1926. The R.C.M.P. opened a detachment there in 1922. With the coming of the signals unit, Aklavik was confirmed as the commercial and administrative centre of the Northwest. Northern prospectors entered the air age in 1928. The first dramatic result was the Eldorado Mine at Port Radium. In 1932 nearly 300 men were in the area, and by the end of the year 3,000 claims were recorded. Production began in December 1933.

Meanwhile, the omnipresent Geological Survey of Canada was at work around Yellowknife Bay to the north of Great Slave Lake, where the first interesting ore had been discovered thirty-three years before. The publication of the Survey's report was followed by the North's next gold rush. A few claims were staked in 1933, but the first important finds were recorded in September 1934. The next year, visible gold was discovered on the west side of the bay. Yellowknife soon became an established gold camp. In September 1938 the first gold brick was poured in the Northwest Territories. This achievement by Con Mine was soon followed by Negus which first recovered gold in February 1939. Within four years there were six producing mines in the area. By 1942 annual production of Yellowknife mines reached about four million dollars.

When the Klondike prospectors sampled the ore at Pine Point, they precipitated a small staking-rush from near-by Fort Resolution. A few local people filed their claims, then forgot them. In 1921 Mackintosh Bell visited the site on behalf of a group of Boston business men who formed a company that proved up half a million tons of ore by 1929. There was brave talk of a railway north to Great Slave Lake, and the Edmonton *Journal* predicted that 'within eighteen months a huge oil-burning smelter will be going full blast on the south-east corner of Great Slave Lake', but nothing more happened at Pine Point before the Second World War.

The pre-war years brought promise in other parts of the Northwest Territories. The development of Churchill, Manitoba, as a harbour for grain ships and the completion of a railway terminus there in 1931 sparked interest in the Precambrian Shield to the north, now no longer so remote. Intensive prospecting by four major companies began in Keewatin in 1928. The Cyril Knight Prospecting Company, after a season of diamond-drilling, concluded that a profitable mine could be established at Rankin Inlet. The depression delayed their plans; they resumed work in 1937, but finally decided not to go ahead.

Since 1916 interest had been expressed in the iron ore of the Belcher Islands, a part of the Northwest Territories about sixty miles off the east coast of Hudson Bay. In 1928 some surface work and drilling was done and it was followed up from time to time until war-time conditions made it too difficult to continue.

There had been some mining in Baffin Island even in whaling days. In 1876 an American took $120,000 worth of mica from Cumberland Inlet, and after the turn of the century the Hudson's Bay Company did some mining there. In 1904 a private operator shipped thirteen tons of graphite of excellent quality from Lake Harbour on the south coast of Baffin Island, together with some garnet. Towards the end of the First World War and just afterwards, the Hudson's Bay Company shipped mica and garnet from Lake Harbour to England, then dropped the project.

Captain Bernier found, and made immediate use of, coal deposits near Pond Inlet on northern Baffin Island. He took 155 tons in 1910 to burn in the C.G.S. *Arctic*. Captain Henry Toke Munn, the private trader, used the coal at Pond Inlet in 1920, and the Hudson's Bay Company began to mine it in 1924. The coal is chemically of good quality, but it crumbles so badly that it is not in favour if fuel oil is available. The market was too limited to warrant manufacture into briquettes.

According to J. F. Tibbett, a geologist who prospected around Arctic Bay and northern Baffin Island in 1937, 'there is plenty of mineralization and unusual rock formation, and conditions are favourable for prospecting'. But Baffin Island seemed then most distant of all as a prospect for economic awakening.

The Second World War struck first and hardest at the Yukon, but it struck in a way that the Yukoners could generally applaud. For more than forty years they had campaigned for better transportation. It was a hopeless, almost wistful campaign, for the Yukon lacked people and proven resources to justify the enormous cost of northern road-building after the gold rush was over. A short-lived attempt at a road to the outside had been made in 1897, and an equally ill-advised effort was made in 1905. Now the war brought reasons for improved transportation which would sweep aside the question of cost. The defence of the Pacific North-west was at stake.

First came the Northwest Staging Route, a series of airports to be built along the line that McConachie had pioneered for nearly twenty years. Seven months before the attack on Pearl Harbor, tractor-trains set out to build airports at Fort St. John and Fort Nelson in British Columbia, and at Watson Lake and Whitehorse in the Yukon. Later, that line was to be filled in with smaller landing-strips so that planes could fly from Edmonton to Fairbanks and never be more than a hundred miles from landing facilities. Towards the end of the war, this route carried an almost steady procession of aircraft bound for Alaska or beyond. The airport high on the bluff above Whitehorse became the busiest cross-roads of all, a link not only on the way to Alaska but on the lifeline to the U.S.S.R.

Then came the road. The exchange of notes between Canada and the United States of March 1942 gave the United States permission to build the highway, on condition that it be turned over to Canada at the conclusion of hostilities. Within a month of the agreement, the first crews of the United States Army Engineers were on the ground, starting from both ends. The total length of the Alaska Highway was to be 1,523 miles, of which 1,221 were in Canada. It was, even by Yukon standards, quite an undertaking.

To those who remembered, it was like the gold rush again, but only because of the numbers who came. This was not the carefree atmosphere of escape from the cloying civilization of the South. There was an immediacy and a sense of incomprehensible order as the unlikely mechanical giants churned into the muskeg and bush.

No road like it had ever been built before. Most of the route was underlain by permafrost. Everywhere there was muskeg – frozen, marshy land on which men said no road could be built. Sometimes the road had to detour along ridges, sometimes huge trenches had to be dug and filled with rock and gravel. In places, brush five feet thick was piled on the ground, and gravel put on top to serve as insulation in order to prevent the permafrost from melting and heaving the road-bed into an impassable condition. So many rivers had to be bridged that all the bridges, put end to end, would have stretched seven miles. There were seventy miles of culverts. Streams that were mere trickles in the autumn became wild torrents in the spring. There were glaciers and rock-falls. Countless rivulets seeped from the hills to freeze as they crossed the road, and make impenetrable barriers of ice. In winter the temperatures dropped lower than −45°. In summer, clouds of vicious mosquitoes rose from the bush to torture the road-makers. And there were forest fires.

Ten thousand U.S. troops, five thousand civilians, and seven thousand trucks clawed this passage through the Yukon. The population of Whitehorse jumped overnight from four hundred to nearly fifteen thousand, eighty per cent of them Americans. In June 1942 Japanese bombers made their first attack on Alaska. North America awaited invasion.

In September 1942 bulldozers working from north and south crashed through the bush to meet. In November the road was officially opened. The task, originally estimated at five years, was completed in just over seven months. This was, of course, only a pioneer road, still too rough to be called a military highway. Still, it was there, to the immense relief of those responsible for the defence of the North-west. On April 1, 1946, it was turned over to Canada. Again there was much rebuilding, but at last the Yukon had a good gravel highway leading south-east and north-west.

The next war-time project met with less enthusiasm. The United States had strong advocates for a fuel-supply system based on a pipeline from Norman Wells to serve Alaska and the Yukon. Its opponents, though they recognized the advantages of a safe inland route for oil to Alaska, argued that before such a gigantic project could come into operation, the north Pacific naval war would be settled, one way or the other. The Canadian government was cool to the plan, but offered no barriers to the United States if it should decide to go ahead. The $137 million project was approved, and sixty-one wells at Norman Wells went into production. Sixteen hundred miles of pipe went through the mountains to Whitehorse, then north to Fairbanks, and south to Watson Lake and Skagway. A refinery was built at Whitehorse. A road had to flank the pipeline for its maintenance. The Canol line was finished before the end of the war, but too late to be of any use. It was soon abandoned and scrapped. Scarcely a million dollars was realized from all its assets.

The building of Canol affected the Mackenzie District as well as the Yukon. Twenty-five thousand men – soldiers and civilians – were employed on the project between 1942 and 1944. So many trucks were taken down the Mackenzie River that they had to be stood on end on the barges. Fort Smith was inundated with the newcomers, for here they had to wait, sometimes for weeks, to get passage down-river.

Less spectacular than the pipeline but of more importance for the future were the many airfields built across the North during the war. Landing-fields were made at the main communities down the Mackenzie. Far larger facilities were constructed in the east, as a staging-route to evacuate war casualties. The airports at The Pas, Churchill, Coral Harbour, Frobisher Bay, Fort Chimo, and Goose Bay date from the war. In times of peace they were to have a continuing use, but they were also an unfortunate legacy.

Fort Chimo probably created the most difficult problem of all because it was the centre of a relatively populous Eskimo area. In those war-time days, the Canadian government had little time, inclination, or knowledge to consider the effects of the impact of defence construction on the native population. The base became a magnet for those who were finding the living on the land already thin. Jobs requiring no skill were easy to find. Apart from the jobs, there was the open-hearted generosity of the American troops and civilians. Fort Chimo became a community of great but transitory affluence. When the boom suddenly ended, the Eskimos could neither continue in the new life nor go back to the old. The results were painful. It was years before Fort Chimo could begin to pull itself up by its own boot-straps and belated assistance from other Canadians.

There were radio stations and weather stations dotted across the northern map. Even before the Second World War, there were stations at Resolution Island, Cape Hope's Advance, Chesterfield Inlet, and Churchill. Most caused little ripple, except among the very few who chanced to live in the neighbourhood. They were, nevertheless, the forerunners of a peace-time technology that opened up the North.

When the war ended, the North felt a special uncertainty. The free-spending Americans went home, leaving a sudden hiatus in many a northern community which was beginning to depend upon the artificial prosperity they brought. It was too soon to judge how many of the ventures interrupted by war would be resumed, or how much effect the new communications would have on the future building of the North. Canada in general had too many national problems of readjustment to be able to spare a thought for the underpopulated North. Industry was anxiously converting from its war-time strength to its uncertain but hopeful peace-time program. Materials for any new venture were in short supply.

Still, things began to happen.

The war years were not auspicious for the Northwest Territories mining industry. In June 1940 Eldorado closed. Two years later, it was reopened with as little publicity as possible. As the world entered the nuclear age, Eldorado became the major North American source of uranium. Materials from the shores of Great Bear Lake were in the bombs dropped on Japan, and the sudden demand for fissionable materials gave a new significance to Canada's most remote mine. Because of its importance to the Allied war effort, it was taken over by a Crown corporation in whose ownership it remained until the mine was closed in 1960.

War had a very different effect on the Mackenzie District's new gold mines. As gold took a distinct second place to strategic minerals, markets became uncertain and there were growing shortages of labour and supplies. The industry around Yellowknife continued to expand until 1942; then it declined until all production ceased during the last year of the war. Surprisingly, there was another minor gold rush in 1944. In January of that year, the Frobisher Exploration Company started a large drilling program on the Giant property at Yellowknife and soon concluded that this was the most important gold deposit ever found in the Northwest Territories. By 1945 about two hundred mining companies or syndicates had interests in mineral claims in the district, and active exploration had spread 150 miles beyond Yellowknife. Before the year was out gold production was resumed at the Negus Mine. Not long afterwards Con Mine started up again. The Giant Mine was begun, although it was not until 1948 that its first gold brick was poured.

The Yukon had no such war-time flurry in mining activity. Production continued on a reduced scale near Dawson City and in the Elsa-Keno area. It was not until the post-war years that prospecting and production became active.

The fur industry of the North suffered from war-time labour shortages, but not from low prices. The white fox reflected the usual four-year cycle, unchanged in peace or war, but the take of most other furs declined after 1940 although there were still many traders in the country. After the war, the Hudson's Bay Company had forty-one stores in the Northwest Territories, and nine in Quebec. In the Northwest Territories there were just over a hundred free traders, each operating on a small scale. Unlike the miners, the fur-traders looked forward to the post-war years with some apprehension. In the Arctic there were all the risks of a one-crop economy. The economic future depended on the market for one single fur which did in fact decline disastrously. In the sub-Arctic there was a variety of pelts to cushion the effect of price changes, but there was also over-trapping in some of the best areas within reach of the towns. There were also disquieting rumours about the effects of the new technology which might soon be producing cheap synthetic fur.

In the first half of the century the government started the only new industry in the Mackenzie organized specifically to help the native people. Following up a recommendation of a royal commission on reindeer and musk-oxen, Dr. Porsild of the National Museum studied the Mackenzie Delta as a grazing-range. He reported favourably on the conditions there and on the practicability of moving a herd from northern Alaska. In 1929 the Minister of the Interior signed a contract with the Lomen Brothers of Nome to deliver up to 3,000 reindeer to a range on the east side of the Mackenzie Delta. The epic migration ended in March 1935, when 2,370 animals were delivered to the new reindeer station. At first the project prospered. By 1941 the total herd had grown to 8,000, of which 5,000 were on the original reserve. The remainder were in two herds under the management of Eskimos who had been trained by Laplanders. The Eskimos were given animals to start their own herd on condition that, as the animals multiplied, the government would receive back its original loan in order to start new private herds. By this means it hoped to spread the industry far beyond the delta where the caribou herds were showing the destructive effects of the rifle. But the scheme failed because Eskimos found trapping was more lucrative and less confining than reindeer-herding. When opportunities for wage employment increased, herding could not compete with the bright lights of the town. The reindeer industry survived, but it did not prosper. Today, about 6,000 reindeer remain, all in government herds.

Administration. Slow as the growth of the economy was in the first half of the twentieth century, the growth of administrative services was slower. Most administration was in the hands of the police, and education was left to the churches; the few social services were shared among the police, the churches, and the traders. In all respects the Yukon was more advanced than the Northwest Territories. In 1937 the Yukon member of the House of Commons, George Black, estimated that the Yukon had produced in total $225 million in minerals and through customs duties (an interesting combination of extractive industries), against about $32 million in federal expenditure. If the figures were designed to show that Canada was living off the fat of the Yukon, they were less than convincing, for there is a painful gap between value of production and revenue to the Crown. At the time George Black was speaking, the federal government was earning each year from the Yukon about half the $300,000 it spent annually. This did not represent a bold national investment in the development of frontier areas. During the war, federal revenues and expenditures in the Yukon came close to equality.

With money from Ottawa and the revenue it raised locally ($154,000 in 1939, $865,000 in 1950), the elected Yukon Council provided funds for a local administration. Before 1950 the only major trunk road was the Alaska Highway maintained by the federal government since the take-over from the Americans in 1946. The Yukon Council built and maintained many local mining roads. The R.C.M.P. provided law and order, as well as administrative services, though their numbers had dwindled to about a quarter of the force of 227 men who had been on strength at the height of the gold rush. State schools were operated in Dawson, Whitehorse, Carcross, and Mayo. Hospitals were maintained at Dawson, Whitehorse, and Mayo, largely through public funds. Separate from the territorial administration, the federal government provided staff for such specific federal functions as land disposal, mining recording, and forest conservation. These were part of the job of the Lands, Parks and Forest Branch of the federal Department of Mines and Resources which succeeded the Department of the Interior in an economy wave of 1930. Under yet another name, Resources and Development, the department in 1950 maintained a staff of twenty-one in the Yukon and about a hundred in the Northwest Territories. Its budget for 1950-1 was five million dollars.

In the Territories there was no separate territorial civil service, such as the Yukon had possessed since the turn of the century. Those few field officers of the Resources Department, together with the R.C.M.P., were responsible for virtually all the tasks of administration from the municipal to the federal level, from garbage collection to the grand designs of manifest destiny. What they could do was understandably limited.

The core of the administration was the police. Its arctic posts dropped from thirteen to seven during the war, but in 1950 there were thirty-two posts in all, half of them in the Mackenzie valley. There was little attempt at local economic development, measures for local industry being largely confined to the enforcement of game regulations and the maintenance of the ill-starred reindeer herds. The Hudson's Bay Company opened a development branch in the hope of fostering new local industry. One of its projects was the publication in English and Eskimo (Roman orthography) of an *Eskimo Book of Knowledge* about the Eskimo's place in the scheme of things from the King and Queen down to more local powers. The branch experimented with small local factories to reclaim oil from sea mammals, so often left to waste. Perhaps its most picturesque, though not most successful, project was a machine to simulate the traditional method of cleaning sealskin in preparation for sewing. Unfortunately the experimenters found that nothing chews like teeth.

By mid century there were eight doctors at work in the whole of the Northwest Territories. Hospitals at Aklavik, Fort Simpson, Hay River, Chesterfield Inlet, Pangnirtung, Rae, and Fort Smith were operated by religious denominations. Though they were called hospitals, not all had resident doctors. The only non-denominational and secular hospital in the north was at Yellowknife.

A listing of medical institutions gives no real indication of the medical situation in the North at the turn of the century. For too many years, the white man had spread diseases that he did not pause to cure. The resources of the local laymen who cared were inadequate for much more than first aid. Tuberculosis found fertile ground among an undernourished people never before exposed to it. In areas where Eskimos met many white men, venereal disease took firm root. Devastating epidemics often were not even chronicled. In 1944 forty-eight Eskimos died of diphtheria in the small community of Eskimo Point. The next year, forty-five died of typhoid at Cape Dorset. In 1948 poliomyelitis spread on the west side of Hudson Bay, attacking ninety Eskimos by March of the following year. A year later, measles hit three hundred in the Western Arctic, and fourteen died. Famine and pestilence, familiar enough to Eskimos, took new forms in these years.

Underlying all this suffering were malnutrition and wretched housing. The laws of the Northwest Territories prescribe a minimum standard of space for human habitation. No one knows what percentage of northern homes reached this standard in 1950. It seems a reasonable estimate that of the Eskimo population of Canada not one per cent were then housed at the minimum standard laid down by law. This was a problem so gigantic that it called for a revolution in northern society, a revolution that still has far to go.

The problems of education seemed in their way no less infinite. There were church-operated residential schools at four Mackenzie communities, and mission teaching in many other places. Few of the pupils in these institutions progressed to the higher academic grades, and none ever achieved matriculation. Before the war, the residents of Yellowknife began the first non-sectarian school in the Northwest Territories; in 1941 it had two teachers looking after seventy-five pupils. Fort Smith was next, but throughout the war it had only one teacher. Both schools were almost entirely concerned with white children. The first government-built school in the Arctic was opened at Tuktoyaktuk in 1947. In 1949 four followed at Coral Harbour, Lake Harbour, Fort Chimo, and Port Harrison. In the spring of 1950 the federal teaching staff in the Northwest Territories and Arctic Quebec was thirty-two.

In the post-war years there was a growing sense of Canada's responsibilities towards its northern peoples. In the context of the years and centuries before, the new efforts in health and education were bold, almost dramatic. In terms of the need, they were hopelessly inadequate. Those concerned intimately with the North – administrators in Ottawa, northern residents of many callings – knew the situation. Unfortunately for them and for the underprivileged people of the North, private anxiety was slow to touch the public conscience. The era of awakening opened in the early 1950s. It was proclaimed in the House of Commons in the closing days of 1953.

9 | Change

On the afternoon of December 8, 1953, Prime Minister St. Laurent rose in the House of Commons to move second reading of Bill No. 6 'respecting the Department of Northern Affairs and National Resources'. The effect of the bill, he explained, would be 'to give a new emphasis and scope to work already being done, and to indicate that the government and Parliament wish to see such greater emphasis made a continuing feature of the operation of government'. He used the occasion for a national stock-taking. Of the North he said:

Apparently we have administered these vast territories of the north in an almost continuing state of absence of mind. I think all honourable members now feel that the territories are vastly important to Canada and that it is time that more attention was focused upon their possibilities and what they will

mean to this Canadian nation. We in the southern part of
Canada have been so busy in recent years that we have given
little close attention to the north country. In the thirties we
were concerned with economic problems; then during the war
years there was little that we could devote ourselves to but to
the tasks of war. Since the war the growth and development in
every province and the problems of the cold war have absorbed
practically the whole of our attention.

The Prime Minister spoke of the North in the national context,
of its size and rapid growth. In 1941 the population of the Yukon
was about 5,000; by 1951 it had grown to 9,000 and its largest town
had expanded from 754 to 2,500. In the Northwest Territories the
population in the same period had climbed from 12,000 to 16,000.
The white population – the new-comers – had risen from 2,300 to
5,300. He referred to the production and potential of northern
mining, to fisheries, to the possibilities of water power. He briefly
mentioned sovereignty and defence in the North, and ended with a
reference to the needs of the Eskimo population.

None of the members who spoke in that debate questioned the
words of the Prime Minister or the intent of Bill No. 6. Their
comments ranged far from the Canadian North, but in total they
gave northern development a new respectability like other national
institutions beyond the range of attack by prudent men. The bill
passed without dissent. Thus the Department of Northern Affairs
and National Resources came into being, and the minister's broad
responsibility for northern administration and development was
set forth.

The government had undertaken its symbolic act, an act that
might reshape the map of Canada as no single deed had done since
Confederation. The Prime Minister commented:

> This will be the first time that this designation 'northern
> affairs' will have appeared in the name of a department of the
> government of Canada. I hope it will be felt, as we felt, that it
> is desirable that this be done as one of the indications of the
> growing interest in the importance of these northern terri-
> tories. The functions of the department will remain essentially
> the same as those of the department of resources, except that
> hereinafter responsibilities in relation to the north will be

more fully and clearly spelled out. The minister will have the specific duty to co-ordinate the activities of all government departments in the Northwest Territories and the Yukon. It will also be his responsibility to promote measures for further economic and political development in the Northwest Territories and the Yukon and to develop knowledge of the problems in the north and the means of dealing with them through scientific investigations and technological research.

The new Department of Northern Affairs and National Resources had a confusing lineage. On July 1, 1873, the Department of the Interior came into being as a consequence of an Act of Parliament passed without controversy. Its responsibilities included the affairs of the Northwest Territories (then including Saskatchewan, Alberta, and the Yukon), Indian affairs, Crown lands, and the Geological Survey. The functions of that department changed greatly over the years as the administration of the young country grew and as various responsibilities were split off. The creation of the provinces of Alberta and Saskatchewan in 1905 changed both the nature and the outlook of the Department of the Interior, though still it looked anywhere but north. The transfer of ownership of their natural resources to the western provinces in 1930 lightened the departmental load. Lands, forests, and rights to minerals had until then been owned and managed by Ottawa. Then depression, after first curtailing virtually every government program, led to a consolidation of departments; the Department of the Interior gave way to the Department of Mines and Resources, which combined such assorted offices as Mines, Interior, Indian Affairs, Immigration, and Hydrographic Survey. The whole northern administration was buried in a corner of the Lands, Parks, and Forests Branch of the new department.

The Department of Mines and Resources lived thirteen years. At the beginning of 1950 this unwieldy agglomeration was divided up. Forestry, the Trans-Canada Highway, Water Resources, National Parks, the Canadian Government Travel Bureau, and Northern Administration now became neighbours within the Department of Resources and Development. The Northern Administration and Lands Branch had two divisions, one embracing the administration of the northern third of Canada, the other administering federal lands and northern forestry. Vast enterprises were brought together within the compass of a single office, a reasonable organization when Canada's role in the North was still so passive. Perhaps the most picturesque office in those days was headed 'Liquor and Reindeer', a combination whose rationale is lost in the memories of administrators now gone.

The Department of Resources and Development was soon succeeded by the new Department of Northern Affairs and National Resources – on December 16, 1953. (It continued under that name until a federal reorganization in 1966 which split off certain resource responsibilities and added Indian Affairs. The title of the department was then altered to 'Indian Affairs and Northern Development'.) Canada had at last decided to move in earnest towards its third sea. It was to seize the opportunities that lay in 700,-000 square miles of Precambrian Shield, in a million cubic miles of potentially oil-bearing sedimentary rock. It was to ease the conscience of a nation towards the neglected citizens of its fringe. But, when the oratory faded, the new department had more hopes than resources for nation-building.

Then as now, many government agencies were concerned with the North. The Department of Transport operated airfields, radio stations, and weather stations from the sixtieth parallel to the islands of the High Arctic, and its ice-breakers threaded their way each summer from Montreal to the archipelago. The Department of Mines and Technical Surveys carried on the traditions of the Geological Survey and Hydrographic Survey, gradually filling in the white spaces on northern maps. Like the National Research Council and the Defence Research Board of the Department of National Defence, these agencies sponsored scientific projects on subjects ranging from cosmic rays to permafrost. The Department of Fisheries and the Fisheries Research Board investigated marine resources and set quotas for the northern fishing industry, notably on Great Slave Lake. The Department of Agriculture established experimental farms in the Yukon and Northwest Territories. The Department of Health and Welfare had already addressed itself to the desperate medical problems of the North. The Royal Canadian Mounted Police enforced the law and provided the administration.

A host of other agencies carried on such functions as paying pensions and family allowances, delivering the mail, and collecting income tax. The sale of Canada Savings Bonds or the collection of customs duties differed only in detail between Halifax and Aklavik. Such departments were concerned with providing a national service in all parts of the country, though they might have to adapt their methods region by region. The North was an incident in their duties, and the opening of the frontier was beyond their concern.

Some agencies were active in the North because it *was* the North. Ice-breakers moved in summer to the ice-fields. Glaciology was studied among the glaciers. Other scientific work – for example, in the upper atmosphere – was not specific to the North, but the North for technical reasons provided useful conditions for such work. Northern weather observations were important to forecasters across the continent. Agencies engaged on scientific projects worked largely apart from any program of economic or social development, though some of their work might have a long-term influence on the North. The expansion of these scientific and technical frontiers needed to go on independently of any new plans to help the people of the North, or to promote their industry. Even if there had not been a single permanent resident north of sixty degrees, this considerable staff and money were required for purposes of importance to the country as a whole, or to the broader scientific community.

A third group of agencies at work in the North provided services to residents and encouraged the development of resources. These were the doctors and nurses, teachers, collectors of garbage, social workers, liquor vendors, police, architects, and operators of power stations. These were also the economists, industrial promotion specialists, oil geologists, resource experts, and staff officers to advise the minister in developing new policies, and to assist him in reporting to Parliament and the public on the affairs of the northern third of Canada.

In 1953 most of these administrators did not exist. To undertake the ambitious role Parliament had granted it, the government had two sharply different courses to choose from. On the one hand, it could set up a single control agency which would be a super-government of the North. The North could, in effect, be declared a special area in the way that Greenland had been made a special area by Denmark. Not only would special laws be passed in recognition of the North's peculiar physical and human problems, but the principles of Canadian government and administration (of southern Canadians) would be largely set aside. Such a course had some obvious advantages. A new criminal code for Eskimos could free officers of the law from the worrisome anomalies in applying principles of justice to a people who had different sets of values. Special incentives could be offered to resource industries to encourage massive private investment and rapid exploitation of the frontier. Controls could be established in retail trade so that northern peoples would not be exposed to the worst excesses of Canadian diet for which they were ill prepared, whether alcohol or chocolate bars. There could be rigid centralization among all departments working in the North so that all would conform to plans for community and national development. The plan would simplify administration but it would in effect mean creating a special colonial régime for a third of Canada, and no federal government seriously contemplated it.

The alternative was untidy, fraught with inconsistencies and frustrations and often confusing to the outsider. This approach was simply to treat the North as Canadian and to encourage the most rapid growth possible of private and government institutions, without converting the North into a special compound where it might superficially progress while sliding away from the mainstream of Canadian life. On the human side, the highest ideal was that the citizens of the North should enjoy the same rights and responsibilities as other Canadians, the same standards of physical well-being, the same intellectual, spiritual, and material potential, the same political duties and privileges. It was to be neither a land of forgotten squalor, nor Plato's modern republic. It was to be Canadian, because that is what history made it. On the physical side, northern resources would be developed when they attracted capital in competition with other investment fields at home and abroad. The North was not to be an experiment in costly autarchy which could survive only in the hot-house of special subsidies; on the other hand, it would no longer be forgotten. It would receive a sharply increased degree of federal government support, notably in transportation, that would permit northern resources to compete with southern resources similarly aided by public funds.

While succeeding governments have proposed differing approaches to northern development, and succeeding oppositions have performed their duty of criticism, this fundamental understanding about the future of the North remained a consistent and bipartisan foundation of northern policy.

Still, it was confusing, especially to those many northerners, old and new, who had little acquaintance with the Canadian way. Europeans often understood little better than Eskimos or northern Indians the nature of Canadian federalism. To them it seemed odd to have territorial and federal laws and government side by side, sometimes with municipal administrations as well. Naturally, to such people a single northern agency seemed simple and attractive. It is easy to forget that a citizen of southern Canada may find himself dealing simultaneously with a municipal regulation, a provincial office, and a federal department of the same name. He may not know when to turn to the city health department, the health ministry in his provincial capital, or the federal Department of National Health and Welfare. This may not seem to be the most efficient form of government in the world, but the price of Canadian federalism is paid in part by inefficiency.

The North, while adhering to the fundamental constitution of Canada in the division of powers and duties, can ill afford duplication of service. The civil service at each level of government has therefore had to achieve more inter-governmental joint action than in any other part of the country. The Yukon built its own civil service from the beginning, and maintained it through good times and poor to administer the functions that are provincial under the Canadian constitution. The federal government is also present in the Yukon, as in any province, to administer such federal functions as weather reporting, mail carrying, defence, and broadcasting. Since ownership of natural resources such as minerals and oil remains vested in the federal government (as it was in the West until 1930), the federal government pays for their administration too. In addition, the territorial administration may from time to time call upon the specialized services of the federal government for advice, rather than setting up a separate agency whose cost would be out of proportion at this stage of development, and the territorial service performs some federal duties on contract to avoid the cost of parallel offices.

In the Northwest Territories, the cost of Canadian federalism was further reduced by the almost complete consolidation of federal and territorial administration. Since one service looked after both realms of government responsibility, an individual officer would find himself acting first in his territorial and then in his federal capacity on the same day. In the long run, all northerners should have their own administration. In a sparsely settled land with an exceedingly low tax base, the temporary consolidation of services made sense, for money could better be spent on desperately needed services than on proliferating the bureaucracy to create parallel administrations.

Untidy it may have been for those accustomed to the central systems of government in Europe, or to the simple line of authority from the whaler, the trader, or the missionary. But at least northerners did not have to debate which of three levels of government to consult when they had a problem; they simply approached a local administrator wearing three hats, and let him worry about the implications of the British North America Act for the collection of their sewage. The separation of administrations and governments would emerge as the needs of the local population required.

Having rejected a central agency to operate the North under special laws and regulations, the government still had to decide how fast and how far to exercise the co-ordinating functions that Parliament had assigned to the Minister of Northern Affairs. The decision was on the side of caution, since the resources of the new department were unequal to anything else.

The administration of the North had suffered bitterly from the depression. The curtailment of finances for programs was tragic enough when northern efforts were already so modest: the curtailment of staff was even more damaging. Small though the administrative agency was, it had many knowledgeable and devoted employees. It was no fault of theirs that they had never been given the resources to do a real job. In the shuffle and consolidation of the 1930s many of the experienced old hands disappeared. On those who remained was almost indelibly stamped the mark of retrenchment which lasted through both depression and war.

When the Department of Northern Affairs and National Resources was formed in 1953, the total staff of its Northern Administration and Lands Branch was 376. Of these people, 150 were in Ottawa, the rest thinly scattered in the larger settlements of the Yukon and the Mackenzie. There were only twenty-six teachers. Game and forestry and the administration of Wood Buffalo National Park were the main concerns of the field staff. There were four administrative officers in all the Northwest Territories, all junior, not one of them beyond the tree-line, not one in Arctic Quebec. The Commissioner of the Yukon had one junior administrator to assist him. There was one junior engineer in all the North. Not a single social worker concerned with the North was employed in the North or in Ottawa. The entire northern budget for capital and operating expenses in that first year of the new department was four million dollars.

Just before the department came into being, the cabinet gave new life to the Advisory Committee on Northern Development, a senior inter-departmental group that had fallen into disuse soon after its founding in 1948. Under the chairmanship of the Deputy Minister of Northern Affairs, it brought together the administrative heads of all agencies with substantial operations in the north, assisted by a permanent secretariat. It acted as a clearing-house for information and a forum for discussion of major northern policy. Especially through its sub-committees, it consolidated federal activities that had formerly gone their separate ways. The kind of simple but effective reform it effected was to ensure that only one government department generated electric power in each community and that all sizeable construction programs in a community would normally be brought together in one program and one contract. The day was still distant when anyone might claim completely effective co-ordination of government effort in the North: when there would be total planning in the location of services and buildings, and complete consistency among all government agencies in their internal policies or in their relations with the people of the North.

The Northern Administration and Lands Branch underwent rapid reorganization and expansion. A Territorial Division was created to administer all parts of the North where there were trees. An Arctic Division would look after the roughly one million square miles mostly farther north. The organization of schooling was put into an Education Division whose activities crossed the tree-line. An Engineering Division also served both the Arctic and the sub-Arctic.

The newly organized branch was not intended to create revolutions, but to react to change that had taken place silently in the North during the years of national indifference. The first minister of the new department, Jean Lesage, enunciated a policy that was to remain the foundation of government effort on behalf of northern people:

> The objective of government policy is relatively easy to define. It is to give the Eskimos the same rights, privileges, opportunities, and responsibilities as all other Canadians; in short, to enable them to share fully the national life of Canada.
>
> The broader needs – and they are immediate needs – are health, education and a sound economy. They are not separate problems, each is related to the other. It is not enough to cure disease, the cause of disease must be removed and this is largely a matter of education and improvement of economic conditions. Education must be provided, but this depends on good health and the needs of the economy. A sound economy means a diversified economy not based on the white fox alone; but for new occupations, both health and education are required. In providing health, education and the broad economy the complications are infinite.

To launch this campaign for equality of opportunity and responsibility across the North, the branch recruited six field men whom it called northern service officers. In retrospect, it was a brave but pathetic attempt to meet the problems of destitution and despair that left few northern communities untouched. The objectives of these new pioneers were clearly set forth, but the means of achievement were still distant and uncertain. There was no organization to help the Eskimos, the Indians, and the Métis to organize local resources as a substitute for the decaying caribou economy and the ailing fur trade. The school system, where it existed, was in an infancy that could yield little immediate help in preparing native people for new avenues of endeavour. One Eskimo in seven was already in a southern hospital or in transit; those who remained in the North found the present brutal, the future unknown. Life expectancy at birth was less than a third of Canada's national average, and the infant mortality rate was five times as high.

The pressures for action were so immediate that the six new officers, all with some previous northern experience, were sent northwards to their tasks with no training. They had the broad objective of introducing community-development principles to alleviate poverty and help stricken people to develop new avenues of useful activity. They had the advantage of coming late on the scene and of being able to profit from the errors of earlier administrations around the world. They knew some of the pitfalls of social programs implemented so slowly that they would create zombie societies, neither of the old native way, nor of modern mainstreams: programs that merely created a new 'native problem' by shaping a society robbed of its past, but unable to share the future of its contemporary neighbours.

What the new northern service lacked was the means to give effect to a policy based on the consensus of modern anthropology. It also lacked experience, for it was breaking new ground in social and economic development. Costly failures still lay ahead. Of the original half dozen northern service officers, two had to be spared from community development before they started, as a new cataclysm hit the Arctic. The Distant Early Warning line brought sudden inter-racial contact requiring careful supervision.

Canada had learned from the consequences of earlier defence projects of the North when troops or southern civilians were thrown against native peoples ill equipped to meet them. The 1954 Canada–United States agreement permitting construction of a major part of the DEW Line on Canadian soil required that all questions regarding Eskimo affairs be referred to the Department of Northern Affairs. In this way the Canadian government hoped to avoid conscious or unconscious exploitation in trading or in sex, and to be spared the ill effects of misguided acts of intended kindness.

Canada wanted to use the DEW Line as a means of giving Eskimos

badly needed income, but it came before the needed training programs were started. By coping with immediate problems arising
from Eskimo employment on the DEW Line, the Arctic Division
spread its meagre resources hopelessly thin.

Northern service officers went to arctic communities to help in
repair and building. The repair – in the form of relief – was often
the more urgent and time-consuming need. The government had
delegated the traders or police to issue relief in most places. It might
seem a questionable principle to ask a trader to judge how much of
his goods should in effect be sold to the government for use by
destitute Eskimos, but in practice this power was rarely if ever
abused. The traders tended towards conservatism in the volume of
supplies they issued. But the trader could be expected to do no
more than look after the needs of the local community, or send out
supplies if he heard of trouble in some remote camp. Each winter
still brought cases of starvation in its wake. The cases of malnutrition were harder to count, and the instances of premature death
through general debilitation would never be known.

The building of a new economy was to be started by seeking
opportunities for wage employment for those Eskimos inclined to
experiment with a new life. The new schools were too late for the
older generation, but adult courses were organized in a variety of
skills, notably the operation of heavy equipment. The new administrator had to choose the candidates. He was unofficial mayor of the
town. He was to be the originator of small industries to diversify
the economy. Above all, he tried to reverse the trend of exclusive
white rule, and to foster the fragile institutions of local government, through community councils.

The policeman or the trader was usually happy to be freed from
administrative burdens which he had assumed only of necessity.
But, as the most recent new-comer always does, the new administrator disturbed the equilibrium of white society. Anyone who
shook the isolation of the past, or who seemed to be doing so, could
be in for a difficult time from the old-timer and his wife. He would
be the whipping-boy for the real or imagined ills of the community,
for the true or apparent inadequacies of government. The job of
the new administrator took more than usual patience, persistence,
and sense of mission.

Gradually Eskimos found doors open to them that had not been opened before: at first to unskilled jobs previously denied them, later to increasingly responsible jobs as their new training permitted. There was not an inevitability about poverty, about the menial life of hewing wood and drawing ice, about being always the doer of the white man's bidding. Many Eskimos remained the servants of the white man, but there was at last a chance for them to raise their sights. For their children there was now a bigger chance, even though the how and where of the future generation was still dimly comprehended.

There were failures. Sometimes the Eskimo new-comer failed on the job because the adjustment was too sudden and too great. He failed less often than might have been expected, for the adaptability of the Eskimo to new situations was remarkable, and the social attitudes of fellow workmen across a racial barrier were positive. Eskimos did not suffer from the prejudices fixed in many white minds towards the Negro and the Indian. Sometimes the job broke down because of the unaccustomed labour discipline in sharp contrast to the freedom of one of the most independent occupations in the world, the arctic hunter. More often the strains were in the family; it was difficult for the wife at home to move into the new society as quickly as the bread-winner on the job. These domestic tensions, too, were problems on the desk of the northern service officer.

Sometimes the failures were worse. The awakening of government had come too late in the chronicle of human misery of the people of inland Keewatin. They had been hit worst of all by the erosion of the old ways, for they had been almost totally dependent upon the disappearing caribou. They lived far from the seal and other sea mammals that could have provided substitute food and clothing: they knew no more of the arts of the sea than a white man. When the herds of caribou did not come, the people died.

When coal or uranium mines close down, or textile mills shut their doors, there is never an easy solution for a community suddenly losing its livelihood. The crisis in the Arctic was most acute of all, for the people had been so little equipped to seek other opportunities. Years later, there would at least be well-proven techniques to apply to such disaster areas: the intensive survey to make accurate inventories of resources, pilot projects to exploit them, forms of consultation to discover Eskimo thinking about possible solutions, retraining, and market development. All these were unheard of in the Arctic of the early 1950s, when starvation spread across inland Keewatin. The immediate reaction was to help a people move from the place that had failed them. With memories of earlier arctic migrations, there were attempts to ask the Eskimos their wishes, using as intermediaries people who knew the Eskimos and their language well. But it could not be a fruitful dialogue when the only real question was whether to stay and face an almost certain death, or move to an area whose future was unknown. On the basis of local advice, but without any opportunity for objective resource surveys, the people were taken from Ennadai Lake northwards, to live around Padlei. It was no use. The suffering continued. Means of supervision over the dispersed people were almost totally lacking. Disaster struck more quickly than news could travel. The tragedies of pursuing a hunting life where there could be no hunting were once more repeated. Many deaths were needed to break down the old myths about the noble savage whose life would continue to be happy and carefree if only the new-comer would go away.

Eventually the scattered survivors had to be brought to the coast of Hudson Bay to start a new community. The roots were more successfully put down, though some were still to face inroads of disease born of the long thin years and the still miserable housing. The war against want had to be fought on so many fronts all at once that many campaigns and lives were lost before victory was in sight. Inland Keewatin was evacuated: a hundred thousand square miles from the Manitoba border almost to Baker Lake were left empty, except for the unmarked graves of those who died while Canada remained detached from its northern problems.

The administrative task force grew slowly. In small communities the trader's store had a minimum staff of two and sometimes more, plus local employees; the police detachment was the same size. The Northern Affairs administrator was expected to manage the services of the town. He was to see that the power, water, and garbage services worked, to act as a municipal works department, to co-ordinate federal activities among the agencies in the town, and to perform tasks on behalf of others. He had to meet immediate human needs across perhaps a thousand square miles of tributary barrens, finding jobs, nominating trainees, issuing relief, and organizing emergency evacuation. He was to help build the new society; perhaps encouraging a local council, explaining the principles of co-operation, or acting as adviser in personal and community problems. All this was accomplished by a staff of one, plus an Eskimo interpreter-assistant. The northern service officer was the federal administration, the provincial administration, and the municipal administration. Like the R.C.M.P. before, he had a wide variety of duties: unlike his predecessors, he was also charged with helping to shape a new society that southern Canada now impatiently awaited from its North.

At the beginning of 1959 the Northern Administration Branch underwent a major reorganization. The immediately apparent effect was to break down some of the expanded agencies into smaller units and to create two new divisions, one for welfare and one for local economic development. The 1959 reorganization began a process of decentralization with far-reaching consequences to northern development. The objective was to remove all day-to-day administration from Ottawa and to place it in the North. The Ottawa staff would advise the deputy minister and the minister and give broad professional help and supervision to the field. They would help in the designing of the school curriculum, in plans for human rehabilitation or for buildings. The administration itself would be carried on in the field under three senior field officers – the Commissioner of the Yukon, the Administrator of the Mackenzie, and the Administrator of the Arctic. A transfer of administrative functions from Ottawa to the North had begun.

Eventually, the new organization produced one of the most decentralized services in the Canadian government. As decentralization took effect and decisions in the North could be made more quickly, without time-consuming reference to Ottawa, the administration became closer and more sensitive to the northerners it served. The transition to full local government was eased and hastened. Decentralization must, however, always be limited by the needs of ultimate parliamentary control over the expenditure of public funds. While most of the money for northern development is being voted by the Parliament of Canada, the appropriate minister has to remain accountable for it. This accountability necessarily acts as a brake on delegation of public spending by local bodies in the North. It also requires that the minister know at all times exactly how his own staff is using public money. By 1967 the annual budget of the Northern Administration Branch stood at just over $50 million, of which nearly $19 million was for capital expenses. The authorized staff was about 1,700, almost three-quarters of them in the field.

The economic difficulties in which Canada found itself in the early summer of 1962 led to an austerity program for all government departments. One of its measures was, in effect, a 15 per-cent cut in staff. Government budgeting is planned a year and a half in advance, and current needs are generally met only after that lapse of time. A new agency growing at the rate of 10 per cent a year would therefore generally have a staff which, without austerity, was 15 per cent below its proven needs. With austerity, the moratorium on new staff together with the 15 per-cent cut proved crippling to the administration of the North. During the period of just over two years when austerity was in full force, almost no programs of development were dropped, for the governments concerned were committed to the principle of northern development, but the resources to carry out those programs were seriously curtailed and their efficiency critically affected. Maintenance of physical facilities slipped far behind, bills were left unpaid and revenues uncollected; much more important, social services were withdrawn from much of the North, rehabilitation programs were suspended, adoption of children virtually ceased, the co-operative movement was halted, administrative posts were closed, new local industry had to be shelved. The strain upon the morale of those who had made a heavy personal investment in the tasks of the North was serious, but the northern program was never abandoned or submerged as it had been in the 1930s.

10 | The Modern North: Transportation and Communications

Northerners do not often talk about the weather. They are more likely to discuss the last plane – and the next.

However remarkable the weather may be to the outsider, in the North it is something to be taken for granted, to be provided against. For the man on the street, for the man in the igloo, and for the management of industry, weather is a problem, but the northerner learns to live with it. Mostly it requires money. Transportation has always been a far bigger problem than climate itself, and it has been solved only in some places for some purposes.

To meet the cold, more money obviously has to be spent on fuel. Relative costs can be measured by using 'degree days', which reflect the amount of heat needed to maintain a building at a temperature of 65° throughout the year. For Ottawa, the figure is 9,000 units. Kapuskasing, Ontario, and the southern Yukon need 12,000 units.

179

This means that if a given house is built in the southern Yukon with no extra insulation, snow porch, or other protection from the cold, it will take one-third more fuel oil than the identical house in Ottawa. Churchill and Port Radium need 17,000 units, Aklavik needs 24,000 units, more than three times as much as Toronto. In practice, there is not quite so great a variation in heating costs, for in the extremes of temperature northern residents reduce heat loss by means of added insulation, triple windows, and smaller windows. Snow porches are built around outside doors, and sometimes snow walls are built part way up the wall that faces the prevailing wind. But whatever the defences against winter, northern heating costs are higher. It is also more expensive to run machines in the extremes of cold.

Commercial enterprise must have an added margin of profit to pay higher staff costs – pay incentives to compensate for higher costs of food, and for isolation – factors more of distance than of climate.

The really serious problem of northern operations, whether simply living or producing, is that the North is far away from centres of population. Almost everything costs more because it must be carried farther, and many things cannot reasonably be carried at all because of the limitations of northern transportation. Billions of tons of mineral ore lie fallow because they are too far from practical routes of transportation. This simple statement of the northern economic problem carries both frustration and hope.

The North is not going to be much nearer to its markets and sources of supply for a long time to come. Not even the most enthusiastic advocates of northern development foresee major population centres north of sixty degrees. Many towns will grow, but they will be small towns to serve a local resource industry. Between them will be wide and expensive spaces.

The towns themselves, when they grow to a thousand or more, will provide some market for local services and local industries. Here lies a paradox: the very improvement in transportation which has made possible those resource industries and the population centres around them is at the same time a discouragement to local endeavour. A hundred years ago there were more local industries in the Mackenzie District than will probably ever be seen in the present century. They were industries that grew because settlers had either to make for themselves or do without. The same story has been told throughout eastern Canada where many a crossroad village with its blacksmith and its general store has left a ghostly presence as modern roads and vehicles bring remote residents closer to better sources of supply. Dawson City had some agriculture at the time of the gold rush, but few will risk the experiment now. When crops succeed, they must be sold at prices held down by the availability of trucked produce from Alberta; there is no bonanza of profits to tide the producer over bad times. Aklavik once had cows; it probably never will again, because processed milk can be bought relatively cheaply, and fresh milk can be flown in for those with expensive tastes.

On the other hand, the fact that the present problems of distance can be drastically reduced by conventional methods of transportation is encouraging. Before the highway reached Yellowknife in 1961, articles of freight that had to be carried by plane cost $25 per hundredweight. After the road arrived, many could be brought by truck, and the cost dropped to something like $2 a hundredweight. A railway that would pay for itself at last made it possible to derive returns from the enormous deposits of base metals at Pine Point.

Modern technology can be counted upon to bring unconventional answers to transportation problems. Forty years ago even the airplane was an unconventional tool in resource development. In the future, new types of freighter aircraft may replace surface transportation in some conditions. Much nearer, short-take-off or vertical-take-off aircraft can operate far beyond the last conventional airfield. Modern ice-breakers, especially those powered by nuclear energy, can convert sea passage from experiment and adventure into commercial routine, as in the Soviet North. Where surface ships are stopped by ice, nuclear submarine freighters may be able to move with ease, surfacing in harbours kept open by artificial means. On land, the so-called ground-effect machines travelling on a cushion of air a few inches above the surface may give ready access to places now hazardous or difficult to reach. Sleds driven by air propellers can move on water, ice, or snow. By land or sea, pipelines can carry liquids or solids.

The whole history of the North has been bound up with the solution of the transportation problem. The Eskimo solved it within a limited range. He could never move easily by land in summer, or by sea at any time, and so his whole life was governed by these restrictions in mobility. Travel by dog-team is uncomfortable, and recommended only for the able-bodied. Dogs may die of disease, or starve in times of scarcity, adding to their owner's plight by reducing his mobility. Still, the Eskimo made the best of the only means of land travel available to him by ingeniously devising harnesses and sleds. No one could have done more than the Eskimo to solve winter transportation problems with the resources at hand.

In the modern North, the dog-team in many places is giving way to the small tracked vehicle which is much faster and more convenient to keep, especially near a settlement. It is more comfortable and cheaper to maintain, except in districts where there is enough local food to keep a dog-team fed. When dog feed must be bought, the internal-combustion engine, which needs feeding only when being used, is cheaper to run. Since a mechanical vehicle can break down on the trail, safety requires their use in pairs. These small, open, tracked vehicles cost around a thousand dollars in the North. Enclosed vehicles able to carry passengers and freight cost about seven thousand.

The kayak has almost disappeared from the Canadian North, though there are still a few in Greenland. For those skilled in their manufacture – and few today still are – the kayak could give speed and manoeuvrability, but not range, cargo capacity, or safety. The Eskimo today prefers the heavy canoe powered by an outboard motor, and so does the northern Indian. The umiak is to be seen only in museums. For heavier use, the common sea-going boats are the trap-boat and the long-liner which generally are replacing the whale-boat and the Peterhead. The trap-boat is an open vessel from twenty-six to thirty-five feet long, used mainly in fisheries. It is powered with an engine of the order of twelve horsepower. The long-liner is from forty to forty-five feet long with engine below deck and a small cabin. It usually has an engine generating from sixty-five to eighty horsepower. It is similar in size to the Peterhead, but is usually of somewhat broader beam.

The oldest and still the cheapest means of moving men and supplies in the North is by water, despite the shortness of the shipping season and the scarcity of navigable waterways. Ships bound for the Eastern Arctic leave Montreal in early July with the expectation that the waters of Hudson Strait, south Baffin Island, and Hudson Bay will be free enough of ice by mid July to ensure reasonably safe passage. Churchill, at the end of a 510-mile railway from The Pas, is generally receiving vessels from eastern Canada and abroad between July 20 and October 1; then approaching winter sends insurance rates up so sharply that commercial traffic stops. The hazards have been decreased and the season lengthened by the provision of ten well-equipped government ice-breakers and by air patrols to forecast the movement of ice. There are no wharfing facilities anywhere in the Eastern Arctic, except at Churchill and Frobisher Bay. Hence, in the cost of shipping must be reckoned the expense of landing-barges, trucks, or tractors, and manpower for unloading. There is almost no backhaul. A ton of freight carried by Department of Transport vessel from Montreal to the west coast of Hudson Bay costs $87.50, to Hudson Strait, $70.

In the Western Arctic, there are two routes: through the Bering Strait, and down the Mackenzie River Waterway. The latter has proved much more reliable despite attempts to develop the 4,000-mile salt-water route from Vancouver to Tuktoyaktuk. The cost per ton from the end of steel at Hay River to Inuvik is about $49. (The rail cost from Edmonton to Hay River is about $50.) The most expensive communities to supply (apart from remote outposts in the Queen Elizabeth Islands) are in the central Arctic. Freight from Edmonton into Cambridge Bay costs $219 a ton, into Spence Bay $251. The margin between sea- and air-freight costs at these points is often small, especially when one takes into consideration the greater flexibility of air freight, the avoidance of big inventories, and the smaller risk of damage in transit.

Canada is unlucky in its northern rivers. The Yukon River was an important transportation route during the gold rush, and until roads made it obsolete. After the Second World War, river boats once more went up and down the river, though only to serve the tourist industry. The experiment was unsuccessful, and now bridges bar the passage. None of the other Yukon rivers, so important in the early exploration of the territory, is of any economic importance for transportation today.

In the Northwest Territories, only the Mackenzie River is

navigable. It is part of an extensive system, 1,680 miles from the railhead at Waterways to Tuktoyaktuk on the Arctic Ocean. Before the coming of the Mackenzie Highway after the Second World War, and the railway in 1965, it was in every sense the lifeline of the Mackenzie District, despite the disadvantages of a short navigation season. The first trip leaves Hay River about May 25, and the last leaves about August 10. The season at Tuktoyaktuk is only fourteen weeks. The route has two obstacles: shallow water and shifting channels in the delta of the Mackenzie River, and a sixteen-mile portage between Fort Fitzgerald and Fort Smith. The latter, of course, is circumvented if goods travel between Great Slave Lake and the South by road or rail. Vessels on the Mackenzie River must be of very shallow draft for they cannot work on more than four feet of water. To achieve greater control, tugs commonly push their three or four barges. The waterway is also subject to sudden and violent storms. Since shallow-draft river vessels cannot safely sail the ocean, goods shipped to destinations along the arctic coast must be trans-shipped from Tuktoyaktuk. Nevertheless, the river is there where the road leaves off. It will long be the only way to fill the big gap between the end of the road network and the Arctic Ocean.

The Yukon gained its major highway through the accident of war, rather than in response to local needs alone. In 1946, as the Canada–United States war-time agreement had provided, Canada took over the Alaska Highway. Under the maintenance of the Canadian Army until 1963, it became known as the Northwest Highway System and was much improved over the hurriedly built war-time road. It is an immensely important artery right through the populated Yukon, with an access road leading to Haines on the Alaskan panhandle. Apart from local Yukon travel, it annually serves more than fifty thousand tourists travelling between the mainland United States and Alaska. Still, since it is only a gravel road, it can be almost lost in clouds of dust in summer when travel is heaviest. The Yukoners and Alaskans want it paved; the cost has been estimated at $167,651,000 over twenty years.

The other main roads in the Yukon are from Whitehorse to Mayo-Keno, and to Dawson City; the latter is in fulfilment of a promise made when the capital was moved out of Dawson City in 1952. More recently, a road was built from Watson Lake in the south-west to Ross River and Carmacks, partly to serve the tungsten mine in the Selwyn Mountains. A road circles from Dawson north into the Alaska Highway, and the Dempster Highway takes off from Flat Creek just south of Dawson in a bold thrust towards the Peel Plateau and the Mackenzie valley. Though it was started in 1958, progress has been slow because of the high cost (about $45,000 a mile) in relation to established need.

The Northwest Territories has only one highway, from the Alberta border to Hay River, with one arm reaching around the west end of Great Slave Lake, across the Mackenzie River by ferry or ice-bridge, then to just beyond Yellowknife. The other arm takes off to the south of the lake heading for Pine Point and Fort Smith. Fort Smith has a road that reaches southwards through the Wood Buffalo Park into Alberta, but does not yet lead into the Alberta highways system.

These all-weather routes are supplemented by winter roads that reach suddenly to some new resource exploration, then revert to bush, and by trails that are opened to trucks each winter as the only land link for long-established communities. One of the most ambitious of the winter roads was cut 380 miles north from Mayo to the Bell River area west of Fort McPherson. Built in the search for oil in 1959, it was Canada's first road north of the Arctic Circle. Less spectacular, but none the less important, is the winter road that each winter connects Fort Simpson to the Mackenzie Highway, until an all-weather route is built. During the war, winter roads and trails were laid out down the Mackenzie to Norman Wells and westwards along the Canol route to the Yukon.

The building of northern roads confronts any government with a dilemma. There is a vicious circle between resources and the means to get them out. Should roads be built to encourage prospecting and development? Bad guesses cost millions. This is not the most expensive country in all of Canada for road-building – roads through the Rockies cost several times as much per mile – but northern roads are costly, and they have no alternative community use if resources do not prove out. The slow devouring of a painfully constructed road by the encroaching bush and flooding freshets is a depressing sight, and it was seen in the post-war years. On the other hand, building no roads until resources are ready to come into production may mean building no roads at all. Transportation is the government's chief way of providing a climate conducive to private enterprise. Few resources in southern Canada would have been exploited if the public treasury had not paid for a transportation network.

Road-building has therefore been a major part of northern resource policy since 1954. Some critics have regarded its scope as extravagant, preferring improved and subsidized air facilities. Others have been equally unhappy because roads have grown so slowly. The submissions made by the commissioners of the two territories to Canada's Royal Commission on Economic Prospects (the Gordon Commission) in 1955 projected transportation routes to 1975. By the mid-way point in that projected period, less than an eighth of the anticipated roads had been built. Annual expenditures on all northern road-building in the early 1960s were about $8.7 million a year. This investment on roads in the costly northern third of Canada represented under 1 per cent of the national expenditure on road-building across Canada.

Succeeding governments experimented with various formulas to set the financial responsibilities of the federal, territorial, and municipal governments, and private enterprise. On major communications roads to join communities in the North or to give access to airports, the federal government pays the whole cost of construction and the major share of maintenance; the rest is paid by the territorial government. Roads into resource areas giving promise of new mines are financed the same way. Two-thirds of the cost of a road from a public highway into a mine property is paid by the federal government; maintenance is paid by the mining company.

The Yukon got its railway in 1900, long before there was a good highway in the whole territory. It leaves Skagway on the Alaskan panhandle to cross a corner of British Columbia. For the second half of its journey it is in the Yukon. It is a scenic railway *par excellence*. Passengers can look out at more than spectacular views of the coastal range: this was the cradle of the Yukon's history where men stormed the hills on the road to gold. It is strange enough today to pass in peace the scenes of all that human travail;

it is stranger still to think that the railway was laid so early in the assault on the north-west frontier.

Today, the Yukon railway is far more than a passenger route for a tourist industry. It is the path along which the wealth of the Yukon's mines is carried to the sea. The ore from United Keno Hill Mines is loaded in sealed containers which are carried on trucks to the railway terminus at Whitehorse, shifted onto railway cars, hoisted from the railway to the company's ocean-going motor vessel for the journey to Vancouver, then moved again to railway for the final run to Trail. The use of these containers has been an effective answer to the problem of constant shifts of cargo on the way from the mine to the refinery.

Only a major new mineral development would be likely to cause more railway-building in the Yukon. If the extensive iron-ore properties at Snake River were to come into production, there might well be another railway to the sea or there might be a pipeline.

The Northwest Territories had a long wait and a harder struggle for its railway. It, too, was the product of mining, but it was sixty-seven years after Pine Point ore was found that the railway reached the property. Its immediate purpose was to make it possible to open a mine at Pine Point by linking the site with the rail network 420 miles to the south. It was also a public investment of $86 million to bring the whole Mackenzie District closer to its markets and sources of supply. It is two or three times more expensive per mile to build a railway than to construct a development road, but one mine alone would eventually pay for the railway. Its advocates confidently predicted that it would act as a spur to other mining enterprises that seemed hopelessly distant when only a highway served the North.

The railway short-circuited the Mackenzie River system by bringing steel to Hay River, almost at the entrance to the Mackenzie River itself. The Great Slave Lake Railway was completed only in 1965 and its full effect cannot yet be assessed. Rumours of future railway-building centre on distant parts, such as a line to bring the ore from another iron mine to the coast of Baffin Island. In either territory, if more railways are not built soon, modern technology might make trains obsolete. Pipelines may be the best way of transporting ores as they have already transported oil in the north. The war-time Canol project was largely abandoned, though the four-inch pipe to Skagway was kept for commercial use. A new eight-inch pipe was brought in from Haines, Alaska, to Haines Junction in the Yukon. The new lines, originally built to satisfy military demand in Alaska, have since acquired real commercial value for the Yukon. The Northwest Territories, on the other hand, has no pipelines at all.

In the North, more than in any other part of Canada, the airplane has brought an economic and social revolution. In summer, every lake is a landing-place. The Yukon has far less water than the Northwest Territories and it has mountains to add hazards to light aircraft; but even here one can travel far deeper and far faster by air than by any other means. The lakes can make smooth landing-places in summer, but they have serious limitations. Planes equipped with floats have much less carrying capacity and speed. Frozen lakes are much better for emergency landings than are rocks or treetops, but they are not to be recommended unless landing-strips are regularly cleared and marked. For reliable air access, the North needs permanent landing-strips, available every month of the year, cleared, preferably lighted, and equipped with beacons. One of life's more sinking feelings is the realization from the cold comfort of a small airplane that the only settlement for a few hundred miles is lost somewhere below in a blizzard. It is an experience that those who work in the North will have to accept for a long time to come, but the hazards are being reduced and the reliability of air links is improving.

The scheduled mainline to the Yukon from Vancouver and Edmonton runs through Watson Lake into Whitehorse, with connections for Alaska and regular service into Mayo and Dawson. Most of the war-time airstrips that followed the route of the Alaska Highway are no longer in use. Areas off the mainline have to be reached by bush plane landing on frozen or unfrozen water, save where a mine has opened a temporary airstrip for its development work.

The mainline into the Mackenzie District runs from Edmonton to Fort Smith, Yellowknife, and down-river to Inuvik, with flights to Hay River. Coppermine and Cambridge Bay have a semi-monthly schedule, mostly with light planes. From Churchill there is a scheduled run twice a month into the main communities of Keewatin. Larger aircraft operate three times a week from Montreal to Fort Chimo and Frobisher Bay, with weekly flights as far as Resolute on Cornwallis Island, and Hall Beach on Melville Peninsula. The east coast of Hudson Bay is served by weekly planes out of Moosonee.

Fares to the North are high, far higher than in southern Canada even on a per-mile basis, and there are many miles between stops. Edmonton to Whitehorse costs $75; to Yellowknife is $56; to Inuvik is $137. Montreal to Frobisher Bay costs $125. If the traveller wants to visit smaller communities the costs mount quickly, for he must charter. A single-engine Otter with a 1,500-pound payload in high-cost areas can run well over $150 an hour, and they cruise at only 100 miles an hour.

These are pioneer routes, whose volume of traffic does not justify purchase of the most recent types of airplanes. The enormous distances with few stops would make jet planes ideal, but there are few runways suitable for jets, and too little traffic to make them pay. As northerners become gradually accustomed to enjoying the sort of facilities southern Canadians take for granted instead of the primitive accoutrements of the frontier, airlines come in for a good deal of passenger abuse. Schedules are missed, services sometimes exasperate the passenger accustomed to southern routes. When an engine fails in the North – not a rare occurrence on older aircraft with limited local maintenance shops – a substitute cannot be wheeled into place in half an hour. Even so, the remoteness of northern communities has been shattered with astonishing rapidity, and the quality of service has improved gratifyingly in most regions.

Part of the reason for the remarkable growth of the northern air industry is the explosion of government activity. The government has also given a good deal of direct support to airlines, primarily through the creation of physical facilities such as airfields and communications. The government pays the cost of public airports, and shares the cost of company-built fields. No one has accused the government of extravagance or haste in the improvement of passenger facilities in the North, but most of the larger centres now have reasonable air terminals. Mail contracts have made possible schedules to smaller communities whose own traffic would never justify regular air links. The government has, by and large, kept out of airline operations itself. The Department of Northern Affairs, biggest northern user of aircraft, has never had any planes of its own and buys all its services as a means of building the air industry. The R.C.A.F., which flew its own service into Resolute Bay until 1964, now uses a commercial carrier. Commercial airlines also serve the DEW Line. The only government aircraft still operating continuously in the North belong to the R.C.M.P.

The continued government support of the airline industry, with the added traffic that new resource industries produce, can be expected to bring improvements in equipment, service, and fares. The government may well take some part in supporting the development of new types of aircraft that will change transportation patterns. Any northern operator would like to be emancipated from the need for airstrips, not only because they are relatively scarce, but because everyone is reluctant to invest in new strips until there is some reasonable certainty of their continuing need. Helicopters have had military value in parts of the North, but they have been too expensive to attract widespread civilian use by government or industry. Scientific parties working in the arctic archipelago have successfully used light aircraft equipped with over-sized, under-inflated tires that permit landing where no craft except a helicopter would once have ventured. This is the cheapest solution ever found to summer operations without floats beyond the limit of airfields, but the terrain on which it can be used is obviously limited, and so is the payload. The vertical-take-off plane is a dream that will some day be workable, but too expensive for many uses. The so-called ground-effect machines such as the Hovercraft (are they airplanes at all?) could be extremely useful in the North for getting people to out-of-the-way places. They can carry up to twelve tons, but it will be a long time before their use will be significant in northern freight operations.

The bush planes of the sixties are still conventional single-engine machines. The Junkers and the Anson have long since gone, the canvas-covered Norseman is disappearing, and the commonest types are the Otter and the Beaver. Any single-engine plane has, in remote and rugged places, the disadvantage of creating nervousness in its passengers and the more practical drawback that it cannot be used over open water, unless equipped with floats – which in winter no plane is. A second engine gives a precious margin of safety in case of trouble. While some small twin-engine planes have made their appearance, nothing has yet touched the Otter for sheer reliability in country that can be cruel to engines and airframes alike. Under ordinary conditions it needs a runway of no more than a thousand feet. The next-larger work-horse is the DC-3 which has proved adaptable in arctic conditions, but only where there are runways over twice the length that the Otter needs.

The major importance of defence to the North has been in transportation and communications. The construction of defence installations during and since the war has provided employment and, at least in the more populated areas, a stimulus to the local economy. This is especially true in the Yukon where the maintenance of the Alaska Highway has long been an important industry. The change-over of the highway from military to civil management in 1963 gave rise to serious concern about the effect on the economy, for the army had a large organization with a welcome payroll, but the change proved less serious than feared. The decrease in the labour force took place at the beginning of an upswing in mining activity, and it was accompanied by an increase in local purchasing.

The Northwest Territories saw much less war-time military activity than the Yukon. Projects such as Canol and the staging-routes had little lasting effect on the local economy. In the immediate post-war period the military did relatively little. The Americans extended the airfield at Frobisher Bay and kept detachments there until 1963. When they moved out, they left the Canadian government an immense building that had cost over $20 million just a few years before. They built two communications stations in east Baffin Island and soon abandoned one. These activities provided little employment, though the costly runway extension at Frobisher Bay, which only defence needs could have justified, proved most useful to later civil operations. The R.C.A.F. long maintained a small detachment to manage the airfield at Resolute Bay on Cornwallis Island, but turned this over to civilian management in 1963, while still running a survival school near by for a few weeks each winter. The navy maintains radio stations in Inuvik and Frobisher Bay. This is the extent of permanent military establishments in the North, apart from the DEW Line.

The DEW Line cost the taxpayers of the United States about one billion dollars. For their money they got one of the best alarm and communication systems ever devised for military use. Along roughly the seventieth parallel for three thousand miles, from Alaska to Greenland, there were originally seventy manned stations, some now closed down. It supplemented two other lines, the Mid-Canada Line, about the fifty-fifth parallel, paid for and manned by Canada, and the Pine Tree Line, built by the Americans farther south with Canadian participation in financing and operation. Oddly enough, the final link in the Pine Tree Line was at Frobisher Bay, far north of the Mid-Canada Line, and not far south of the DEW Line; it was closed soon after the DEW Line came into operation.

Canada has benefited from the DEW Line; though paid for by Americans, most of the construction in Canada was done by Canadian firms which employed many Eskimos. Some of the equipment was made in Canada. The line is manned largely by Canadians working for an American civilian contractor. It does not now provide very many jobs for local people – across its two thousand Canadian miles there are fewer Eskimos employed than in the town of Frobisher Bay. Only an infinitesimal fraction of the construction cost was spent in the North.

The North does, however, benefit from the communications network of the DEW Line and the associated Ballistic Missile Early Warning System (BMEWS) that came into operation in 1960. The DEW Line has given the Arctic a series of landing-fields across the seventieth parallel, and a communications network available for civilian use. It provides a vital weather-reporting system of immense use to arctic flyers in country where normal meteorological stations are few and very far between. If the DEW Line should outlive its military usefulness, undoubtedly the major airfields would continue to operate under civil control, a process of turn-over that has begun. The question of manning the smaller stations for airstrips, radio communication, and weather will face the government of the day with some difficult balancing between costs and benefits.

The civilian communications network has increased enormously in scope and efficiency since the Second World War. Before the war, the only commercial communications were provided by the Dominion Government Telegraphs and by radio circuits mainly operated by the Royal Canadian Corps of Signals down the Mackenzie. A land-line was laid along the Alaska Highway and operated by the Department of Transport until it was taken over by the Canadian National Telegraphs in 1958.

Throughout the rest of the Northwest Territories the only communication until the fifties was by means of the radios operated by the Hudson's Bay Company, the missions, the police, and enthusiastic amateurs. As a communications network it had its limitations, but it made of the North – and especially the Arctic – a village with a party line. People in the North knew one another astonishingly well, in spite of the distances. They tended to move from settlement to settlement within the North, and the exchange of personal news was naturally a hobby bordering upon a passion. In the evening exchanges of gossip, even those who had never met became fast friends who might years later resolve to rendezvous face to face in Winnipeg or Montreal. (Conversely, it must be added, there were monumental feuds and manifestations of more than usual eccentricity which led next-door neighbours to refuse to exchange a word over the years.) Radio regulation and licensing was loose in the Far North and the communications traffic was heavy.

The old-timers would spend the evenings on the polar net with the gossip about Constable Smith's new baby in Cambridge Bay, or the transfer of the store manager at Pangnirtung, or news of a medical emergency, or a message about an administrator's overdue quarterly report. On a good evening, a lonely bachelor might propose marriage to his boyhood sweetheart in the South, with willing intermediaries to relay tender sentiments through the static. The administration used a code for its more confidential communications, but it was a code easily broken; any government message in the familiar garble was the signal for everyone available to tune in on the administration's private affairs. It provided a change from breaking the trader's commercial code on his groceries and ladies' lingerie. It was a sad day for the North when the new administration equipped itself with an unbreakable cipher, so complicated that it was hardly ever used.

Even when every self-respecting northern community was connected to the outside by telephone, the Northern Messenger service of the Canadian Broadcasting Corporation continued to have
its faithful followers. The Northern Messenger was a pleasant
anachronism: a weekly potpourri of personal messages – some
highly personal – solemnly sent out one night each week across the
airwaves from the South. Hundreds of people who had never been
near the sixtieth parallel remained devoted fans of this service and
became a vicarious part of the tight-knit community of the North.
It was the party line *par excellence* which defied technology, convenience, and privacy.

The efficient networks that spread through the North in the
fifties and sixties were a wonder of the receding frontier. In the
east, the Bell Telephone Company operates a radio-telephone network based on a scatter system. While still vulnerable to changing
radio reception, it dramatically ended the isolation of the North.
The new northerner can pick up his dial phone in his Igloolik
living-room (with a coloured extension in his bedroom or kitchen,
if he has a mind for it) and talk to Whitehorse, Montreal, or
Baghdad. In the West, the size of the population justified Canadian
National Telecommunications' operating a more sophisticated
system. From the Peace River to the southern Mackenzie, voice was
carried by microwave. A tropospheric multi-channel radio system
connected with the High Arctic. For the Mackenzie itself, a land-
line was boldly constructed along the lonely 900-mile stretch from
Hay River to Inuvik, and around Great Slave Lake to Yellowknife.
The service approximates the standard of southern Canada and
emancipates the people along its route from the frustrating and
sometimes dangerous radio blackouts of old.

These are not easy links to build or to maintain. High-tensile-
strength steel wire with a copper or an aluminum conductor is
needed where the line is subject to the onslaught of weather far
from maintenance crews. Between Hay River and Aklavik, Canadian National Telegraphs used wire with polyethylene covering,
mostly carried on tripods. On a microwave system, unattended
stations are needed every twenty-five or thirty miles with reasonable
access for maintenance. The tropospheric scatter system needs
stations only every 150 or 200 miles. Between Hay River and Lady

Franklin Point on the Arctic Ocean, there are two repeater stations. Access for maintenance must be by air. The Hay River terminal site had to be put on seventy-foot piles, sunk into the permafrost. Each uninhabited station needs its own power supply created by diesel generators. Oddly enough, winter temperatures are less of a problem than summer ones: heat from the generators is used to warm the buildings, but in summer the difficulty is in keeping the installation cool enough.

The completion of these telephone links to most communities of the North does not end the need for better communications. Each new survey party or remote camp-site creates a new problem of simple and reliable connection with the main commercial system. Air-to-ground communications and beacon systems to make northern flying safer are still being improved. And there are those who agitate for circuits to bring television into the remote places of the North.

There are more television sets in the North than a stranger might imagine. Whitehorse has a closed-circuit system, and Yellowknife, in 1967, became the first town to get the C.B.C.'s new 'frontier' television – a small transmitter unit to reach the local area. Gamblers have occasionally brought sets to such unlikely places as Baffin Island in the hope of picking up southern programs through a freak 'skip'. Occasionally they find something, though the chances of getting a reasonable picture and recognizable sound at the same time are not high.

When the Canadian Broadcasting Corporation addressed itself to the task of providing service to the North in the mid 1950s, it did not have television in mind. The problem was to link the northern population by short- and long-wave radio with the rest of Canada, and it was not an easy one to solve. There were a few community-operated stations using Army Signals Corps equipment, but they had no real links with the South and their program content was, to say the least, limited. The objective was to provide the North with current news and network programs, though not necessarily on the day of original broadcast. Christmas carols had an unappreciative audience in February.

One proposal was to provide one or more high-powered transmitters in southern Canada to blanket the North. No one could be sure that such a technique would be successful, for the behaviour of radio waves in the auroral zone creates transmission complications of a degree found nowhere else in Canada, perhaps in the world. The government decided not to risk huge expenditures that might not be fully effective.

Instead, the C.B.C. built a number of northern transmitting stations with power of up to 1,000 watts; low-power repeater stations brought the signal into smaller places. The Yukon is thus served from Whitehorse, the Mackenzie from Yellowknife and Inuvik, and a small section of south Baffin Island from Frobisher Bay. The Churchill station serves the lonely places in Keewatin. All of these transmissions together reach 80 per cent of the population of the North listening with inexpensive long-wave receivers. In addition, the C.B.C.'s short-wave transmitters in Sackville are beamed for seven hours a day to the North to send the news to the local stations and to give short-wave programs to those who have short-wave receivers and who live beyond the reach of the medium-wave broadcasts.

The Northern Service of the C.B.C., which began in 1958, provides a good selection of national network programs, but it goes much further. Special programs in Eskimo are carried by short-wave and by the arctic long-wave stations. The stations employ a good many local people, and broadcasts in local languages are a regular feature. CHAK in Inuvik has long been managed with great competence by an Eskimo. The Northern Service also produces special programs about the North for use locally and on the national network. Fort Simpson, lacking C.B.C. service, obtained a licence for its own community station in 1961, in order to keep in touch with itself and the world.

Of course, there are many who quietly miss the isolation, even the loneliness of the early days when there were no radio programs, no telephones – only an infinite peace. Thanks to the development of transportation and communications, economic development has been encouraged and the private citizen's life has become easier, more varied, and richer. The wide open spaces of the North where men could go to escape the world are rapidly narrowing. The North is becoming a part of Canada.

A lot of people think that worth while.

11 | The Modern North:
An Inventory of Resources

The population of the world is growing by about four thousand an hour. The increase of the past two dozen years has been greater than the total human population at the beginning of the last century. The population of the world, now just under three and a half billion, will double by 1999.

During the final third of this century, therefore, man will have to find new resources equal to all now known in the world. This definition of the task assumes no depletion of present resources, and no improvement in living standards: hardly safe assumptions.

It has been estimated in the 1963 annual report of Resources for the Future that world demand by the end of the century will increase three times for food, five times for power, five times for iron ore and ferrous alloys, five times for copper, and more than five times for aluminum.

This soaring expansion of human consumption is one reason for the potential importance of the resources of the Canadian North. Another reason is the extent of those northern resources. Geology gives evidence to suppose that in the northern third of Canada there can be more mineral resources, both in hard-rock minerals and oil, than in all the rest of the country. There is little doubt, therefore, about the supply and the demand. If the resources can be developed and delivered economically, Canada can live handsomely on its northern inheritance. The question is development.

The Mining Industry. No one can say with certainty what minerals, in what locations, in what concentrations, in what quantities, lie in the North, or in any other part of Canada. One can speak with confidence of what has been extracted, or developed, or at least clearly delineated. In the North this is relatively little, for the northern mining industry is in its infancy. One can also reach reasonable conclusions by comparing the nature of the northern ground with the surface and the sub-surface of the rest of Canada whose industrial potential is known.

The Yukon lies in the same geological region as British Columbia – the Cordilleran. British Columbia accounts for one-sixth by value of all Canadian metals production, including four-fifths of the lead and two-fifths of the zinc. The comparison, which is supported by other points of reference, suggests that the Yukon could be a major producer of minerals.

Twenty-five minerals have been discovered in the Yukon, and ten have been produced: gold, silver, lead, zinc, cadmium, copper, coal, tungsten, platinum, and antimony. The placer gold of the Klondike creeks has a more colourful past than future, though it has sustained an industry for nearly seventy years. During that time it has produced gold to a value of something like $261 million. Those gravels will not produce much more gold, though the nature of the industry in the past will help to draw tourists.

Not far from Mayo, United Keno Hill Mines Ltd. has been the largest producer of silver in Canada and the fourth largest in the world. It also mines lead and zinc. In 1964, production of silver was valued at nearly $6 million, of lead at $2.5 million, and of zinc at $2 million. The company also operates the Tantalus Butte Coal

Mines near Carmacks, mainly to supply fuel for its operation at Elsa-Keno.

The rough mineral potential of the Northwest Territories can be measured in a comparison with Ontario. Over 700,000 square miles of the Northwest Territories (about half of it) is underlain by Precambrian formations favourable for hard-rock mining. Ontario, with one-third the area of such rock, has an annual mineral production of a billion dollars a year.

For obvious reasons of transportation, exploration has been much less extensive in the Northwest Territories than in the Yukon. There was simply no point in investing time in the search for minerals that lay hundreds of miles beyond any reasonable transportation route. Radium ore justified the high cost of distance and was therefore mined from 1931 until the Eldorado Mine closed down in 1960. The gold of the Yellowknife area was rich enough to be economically attractive long before there was a mile of road or rail in the Northwest Territories. Gold-mining has a continuing future around Yellowknife. In 1966 the value of production was nearly $16 million. The industry is gradually spreading north and north-east: the Giant and Con Mines at Yellowknife, Discovery, sixty-five miles to the north, and Tundra, 150 miles north-east.

North Rankin Inlet Nickel Mines Limited reflected the delicate balance between resources and transportation economics. The claims were first staked in 1928 and limited work was done from time to time in the 1930s. The mine was at last brought into production in the summer of 1957. The ore body was limited, but it was a reasonable mining proposition because the deposit lay on the west coast of Hudson Bay, within easy summer reach of Churchill and Montreal. Rankin Inlet was a bold venture, for it was the first mining enterprise of consequence in the true Arctic. All the workings were in permafrost. It was also the first northern mine to make extensive use of native labour. A few Eskimos worked underground; on the surface they were about half the labour force. The life of the mine was short. While much of the Keewatin coast was explored, not enough ore was found near the Rankin Inlet Mine itself to justify its operation after the summer of 1962.

The Rankin Inlet Mine had an importance out of proportion to its production. It proved that mining in the Arctic presented no insuperable obstacles. The management of this mine worked against unusual difficulties in its employment of Eskimos, for almost none of them could speak English, let alone read, write, or do simple arithmetic. Within these educational limitations – which would largely disappear in a generation – the Eskimos proved adaptable, productive, and interested. This break-through gave promise of an answer to the problem of costly labour turn-over in remote mining operations. Undoubtedly the experience of the Rankin Inlet Mine encouraged exploration in more distant arctic regions.

The base-metal deposits at Pine Point on the south shore of Great Slave Lake are possibly the largest and richest in North America. The mineralized area stretches thirty-six miles, and the potential is claimed to be in the order of eighteen million tons, most of it available by open-cut mining methods, all of it relatively easy to refine. The annual production is expected to be about 1,825,000 tons.

In the Selwyn Mountains, close to the Yukon boundary, the Canada Tungsten Company opened a tungsten mine in 1961. Falling world prices caused it to close before it reached full production. It reopened in 1964 with much more favourable prospects. Tungsten reserves in the area amount to two million tons, and annual production is likely to run to about 100,000 tons.

All these are producing mines in the Northwest Territories. The preliminary results of exploration give an optimistic picture of the mining potential. Near Great Slave Lake, with its rapidly improving transportation system, deposits have long been known. Base metals and lithium occur at the east end of Great Slave Lake, and a mineral belt has been identified right from Lake Athabasca to Rankin Inlet. Radioactive ores of high quality remain unworked because of weak markets.

The Belcher Islands in Hudson Bay have extensive deposits of iron ore, but since their discovery the spotlight on iron has been taken by the Snake River deposits on the N.W.T.–Yukon border and the Milne Inlet development at the north of Baffin Island. The latter ore is of a spectacular grade, 68 per cent, warranting substantial private investment despite its extremely remote location. And it is not alone. Work has been done on base-metal deposits near

Strathcona Sound, not far away. The metal development farthest north is on Little Cornwallis Island, latitude 75°, site of other base metals. As interesting as these remote deposits themselves is the confidence of the mining industry that they are worth examining. Private investment so far north in the Arctic reflects a belief that resources of the North can be extracted at almost any latitude, and that there is at least a reasonable chance of working out favourable economic equations.

Oil and Gas. Although to bring in a producing oil well is no easier – perhaps even more difficult – than to start a producing mine, it is simpler to estimate the oil potential of a region. It is generally assumed that 50,000 barrels of oil will come from every cubic mile of sedimentary rock. By this rule, the mainland of the Yukon and Northwest Territories has reserves of about ten billion barrels of oil and sixty to ninety trillion cubic feet of gas; this is about equal to the reserves in Alberta. In the arctic islands less is known about the thickness of the sedimentary formations. On the reasonable assumption of thicknesses of 10,000 feet, the reserves would be about twenty-one billion barrels of oil and 150 trillion cubic feet of gas, double the Alberta reserves.

The only producing oil wells in the North are at Norman Wells. Although the capacity of the field is far greater, production is held to 1,700 barrels of crude oil a day because of the limited local market. The oil is refined locally. From the opening of that field just after the First World War until the early 1950s there was little apparent interest in seeking new northern oil and gas. With gas discovered in north-eastern British Columbia in 1952, a lively interest was expressed in the Liard Valley just to the north. It was beginning to peter out when, in 1957, there was a sudden demand for oil permits not only around Fort Liard, but in the Eagle Plain and Peel Plateau in the north-eastern Yukon and the Mackenzie Delta. From there the interest spread to the Queen Elizabeth Islands.

Hopes for oil were encouraged in 1960 when the second well sunk into the north-eastern Yukon showed a trace of oil and gas in volume which would have been commercially practical had there been a pipeline close at hand. Between then and the end of 1965, ninety-three wells were sunk in the North. Thirty-five of them were in the Arctic where it can cost $2.5 million for a single well. Privately sponsored oil exploration represents an average investment of $20 million each year. The failure to achieve a producing well is hardly surprising in the context of the odds in the oil industry. Before Imperial Oil found Leduc in southern Alberta, that company alone drilled 133 dry holes in a relatively small area. Each new well in the North lowers the odds against success, and provides valuable information about the substructure for the guidance of the next year's drillers.

Explorers of the arctic archipelago have found oil and gas seeps and bitumen residues in many places. On Melville Island, oil sands have been discovered. They are not of immediate commercial importance, but they are a further encouragement in the far-off search for oil.

The northern oil industry seems to face a difficult situation. The world now has a surplus of oil which may last until the 1980s. By the beginning of the next century, oil could be obsolete, displaced by other sources of energy. Oil on the scale of the northern reserves must, therefore, be exploited during the next few decades, or Canada will lose this impressive asset for all time.

But how could arctic oil compete in price with oil from the centre of the continent? It is largely a matter of how it is developed. A high proportion of the final price of a barrel of oil is the cost of extraction. It has been estimated that in Alberta's Redwater field twenty wells were drilled for every one that was really needed for efficient extraction; 95 per cent of the development costs might, therefore, have been avoided had there been a different pattern of oil leases and, consequently, of oil-wells. Regulations to increase the spacing of wells and to keep drilling costs to a minimum could reduce costs enough to compensate for the longer hauls to market and the added cost of operation in low temperatures. No overwhelming physical problems are foreseen in transportation. Oil from the arctic islands could be delivered by pipeline and tanker to the Atlantic seaboard at prices competitive with oil from any other source. Oil from the Yukon could be brought by pipeline to the Pacific for sale at no higher cost than any other oil on the west coast of North America. The arithmetic of the situation has obviously appealed to the oil industry which has invested so heavily in the northern search.

The Renewable Resources: Forestry. Even though most of the Northwest Territories is too cold, and much of the Yukon is too high, for forests, there is a sizeable forested area in the north. The Northwest Territories has an estimated fourteen billion cubic feet of marketable timber, which puts it between Manitoba and New Brunswick in potential. The Yukon has about nine billion cubic feet, just under that of Manitoba. The North, though, has a far slower rate of growth and therefore of replacement. Trees may reach maturity only after 150 or 200 years. Near the tree-line, a mature tree may be an inch or two in diameter, a few feet high.

Farther south, trees grow to a respectable size. White spruce, the main source of the northern lumber industry, reaches over twenty-four inches across and is a hundred feet high. Balsam and poplar, half as thick again, have potential for plywood manufacture. Jack pine, while growing to a diameter of only fourteen inches, covers such vast areas that, commercially, it may well be the most important of all; it is used for pulp, especially from the southern Yukon. Diamond willow will never be of major economic importance, but it has a specialty use for furniture and small, hand-crafted objects.

One of the big users of forest products is the Yukon mining industry which consumes a great deal of timber to shore up underground workings in the unstable ground. In an average year, anything from five to ten million board feet of lumber and over two million feet of round timber may be used in the Yukon. Somewhat less is cut in the Northwest Territories. In each territory about four thousand cords of wood are burned for fuel each year.

The local construction industry has been using more and more northern timber: in 1965 over a million and a half cubic feet were cut for all purposes. Most of the twenty thousand piles on which the larger buildings of Inuvik are placed came from northern trees. Power and telephone poles are often cut from the forests of the territories. There have been many small sawmills both in the Yukon and the Mackenzie, some operated by mines for their own needs. In Wood Buffalo Park, just south of the sixtieth parallel, a commercially successful lumber company has long been exporting its products north and south. Near Aklavik, a government-sponsored logging project has provided much-needed local employment as well as logs and cut lumber for piles and local construction. Logs have been taken from just south of the tree-line about forty miles up the Coppermine River and floated down to the arctic community of Coppermine for housing: even there, a small mill might be justified. Even deeper in the Arctic, wood is found: driftwood, carried down the Mackenzie River during spring flood when the current pulls up the trees lining the banks, together with their shallow roots. They float to the Arctic Ocean and then through the arctic seas. For centuries, Eskimos who have never seen a tree growing have depended upon wood for small objects such as drum frames and parts of harpoons.

Northern forests, because of their direct commercial potential, and their importance to game conservation and in some places to tourism, require protection from fire. The federal government, which owns the forest resources, operates a forest service in each territory. The fire season is shorter than it is farther south, but it can be more dangerous. In these dry regions, fires do not cool down and die during a night which may be only an hour or two long. Not only trees, but reindeer moss along the edge of the bush or on the tundra need protection. If it burns, the void will not be filled for dozens of years; meanwhile the caribou and the people who depend upon them suffer, sometimes disastrously. The small forest service cannot protect all the areas over this large empty land. Top priority is given to bushland near settlements, highways, and rivers. In 1958 a forest fire started by man threatened Whitehorse. It is discouraging to any government to have to invest in forest protection so much more than the revenue to the Crown, but to let the forests burn is an alternative which the present generation cannot contemplate and which future generations might well regard as criminal.

Agriculture. At first glance there seems to be a lot of arable land in the North. Though surveys are far from complete, the Yukon apparently has about half a million acres and the Northwest Territories two or three times as much. This is only a small fraction of the North, infinitesimal compared to the arable land of the relatively soil-rich Soviet North of comparable latitudes, but it does provide the basis for an agricultural industry.

That industry is never likely to grow to real importance in the economy of Canada, or even of the North. The climate creates too many risks, especially when improving transportation makes alternative sources of food supply so much simpler. Grains have been grown at the Experimental Farms one hundred miles north of Whitehorse and at Fort Simpson, but it would be folly to look to the North for even local supplies of flour when it can be brought in and stored with relative ease and economy. Market gardens have much better possibilities because of the demand for freshly picked fruits and vegetables. Probably Baffin Island can claim the distinction of having the most northerly market gardens in Canada, if the category includes greenhouse produce. It takes determination to grow vegetables in a Baffin greenhouse, for there is unlikely to be any local soil. Enthusiasts have occasionally brought earth from the South to supplement seaweed which provides an adequate base. One intrepid botanist even let it be known that he would welcome gift parcels of soil by airmail. Those who persevere often achieve startling results, for plants grow quickly and often to great size during the summer of almost continuous sunlight.

Tuktoyaktuk claims the most northerly outside garden; it is within the Arctic Circle and on the Arctic Ocean. Market gardens were a feature of all fur-trading posts as far north as Fort Good Hope as early as 1826. The missionaries were often keen and patient gardeners, particularly those who had come from rural France. When the Grey Nuns arrived in Fort Providence in 1867 they brought cattle with them; but cattle had been introduced to Fort Simpson at least fifteen years before. Just before the Second World War, an enterprising doctor in Aklavik brought a cow from Edmonton. There was enough pasturage in summer, and hay was cut for the winter. In the cold weather the cow lived in a small shed. The milk in winter was stored in frozen blocks for delivery to his patients and friends. In 1939 bovine society in the Delta was enhanced by a bull brought from Fort Simpson. Within two years there was a herd of nine cattle living beside a flock of hens. Today there are no cattle at all in the Northwest Territories. Chickens

thrive in many places, even in the Arctic, whenever there is someone with enough patience and a yearning for fresh eggs.

The Yukon has more land under cultivation than the Northwest
Territories. Livestock is raised, as well as fruits and vegetables.
These well-run, productive farms will no doubt continue, but
experts think that the Yukon has little agricultural potential.
Anyone interested in homesteading is likely to find equally good
land and a safer agricultural climate in lower latitudes. In both
territories, low rainfall and risk of summer frosts are the greatest
of several hazards to farming. The early farmers of the Mackenzie
sometimes suffered almost total failure because of locusts and cater-
pillars. Clearing the land can be difficult, and local labour is hard
to find. There are almost no experienced farm hands; among the
unskilled, the choice of vocation is likely to be between the trap-
line and something in the town. The discipline and low pay of
farm life have little attraction in the North.

The potential of northern ranching is brighter. Both territories
have a large acreage of suitable land, and the coming of the railway
to the Mackenzie District has spurred interest in ranching. Beyond
these enterprises on the southern edge of the territories agriculture
is likely to be more of a hobby or a sideline than an important
northern resource.

Fur. Although clouded in some respects, the future for fur is still
much brighter than the future for farming. The major problem is
the uncertainty of markets. The widespread use of synthetics is an
increasing threat to the short-hair furs of the sub-Arctic. The white
fox, though never imitated in the plastics factory, has its own competition – the possibility of large-scale imports from the U.S.S.R.
Perhaps more than most skins, it must also face the violent price-
swings that reflect changing fashions. No one dares hope that any
northern fur will again command the top prices common in the
heyday of the fur trade, but the industry is far from dead. In terms
of today's dollar value, white fox has fluctuated from around $50
a skin to less than $5. Muskrat has experienced even wilder swings
– from about $4 to twenty-five cents – and there have been more
swings down than up.

Markets are not the only problem. Over-trapping has affected entire species. The musk-ox, with its extraordinary quality of wool, was just saved from extinction through vigorous conservation measures, and it is not likely to be commercially significant again. Attempts to domesticate the musk-ox were to be a preliminary to musk-ox ranching in the North, but the results were not encouraging enough to prompt such a major enterprise. The polar bear has had to be protected from hunting, particularly since the construction of the DEW Line. Near some communities, there are no longer enough of any kind of fur-bearing animals to make trapping commercially attractive. As the animal population drops through long pressure, trappers have to set longer and longer trap-lines until they are past an economic point. Elsewhere there are animals to trap, though not as many as there used to be, but trapping must compete with more lucrative, more comfortable, more social and less arduous occupations. After so many centuries of living off the land, the sudden possibility of choice in a livelihood could not help but lead many away from the trap-line, however much some white men deplored the decision.

The fur industry, which once dominated the economy of the North, will remain in a secondary though continuing place. The North produces under 10 per cent of the total value of all fur produced in Canada. Even in a good year, the fur industry yields much less income than mining. In the Arctic, arts and crafts give the producer about as much money as fur in an average year, and the trend is for fur to slip behind. Muskrat, white fox, beaver, mink, marten, and squirrel are the main furs of the North. White fox was for a long time almost the only fur exported from the Arctic, but in recent years sealskin has become important. The biggest source of muskrat is the Mackenzie Delta at the edge of the Arctic and the remaining animals live only in the bush where they are the quarry of the Indian and Métis trapper. Ranchers have tried to raise mink in the Mackenzie Delta but the animals did not survive. Fur-ranching in the Far North cannot compete with southern ranching where operational costs are lower.

The fur industry's part in opening up the northern frontier has long been appreciated; its part in developing the seeds of local government is less known. In the Mackenzie District, and particularly in the Delta, the pressures of fur-trapping led to serious disputes about trap-lines among trappers and traders who carved their local empires. Maintaining the peace amidst these quarrels was one of the main activities of the police. In the present century, the trappers themselves were encouraged to organize councils which would, with the help of game officers and police, establish trapping areas and adjudicate rival claims. The trapping councils were useful and effective bodies in the later days of the fur trade's major activity because, in accordance with a fundamental principle of community development, they had something concrete to decide and to manage. The councils fell into disuse as the pressures on trap-lines were reduced. Later, they were replaced by informal and formal community councils for broader purposes of self-government.

Fishing. There have never been commercial fisheries in the Yukon, and there probably never will be. The waters of the Yukon abound in fish, but their importance, apart from domestic use by Indians, lies in the tourist industry. The Northwest Territories has encouraged both commercial fisheries and angling. A commercial fishery on Great Slave Lake began operation in 1945 with an annual quota established by the Department of Fisheries to ensure a sustained yield. The industry, based at Hay River, operates in both winter and summer. Operating a fishery through the ice in the sub-Arctic is not the easiest of occupations, but in one way Nature is on the side of the fisherman: fish are flash-frozen as soon as they are caught, by the simple expedient of leaving them exposed in this giant sub-arctic refrigerator. A million and a half dollars' worth of whitefish and trout from Great Slave Lake is frozen annually in this way and exported to the United States.

The catch on Great Slave Lake is always well under the quota set by the Department of Fisheries. A new approach to marketing might justify larger catches. Some commercial fishing has been tried on other lakes of the Mackenzie, but the scale is small. An attempt at commercial fishing by private interests on Nueltin Lake in the southern Keewatin District was a commercial failure, and the native people, attracted to it in high hopes, were the main losers.

As part of the administration's search for diversification in the arctic economy, small and highly successful commercial fisheries were started in many Eskimo communities. Some earlier attempts at new economic enterprises had foundered when resources did not live up to expectations. To avoid such tragedies, each of these new projects was preceded by a thorough research survey. The Department of Northern Affairs began experimentation in the Ungava region of Arctic Quebec in 1958. On the basis of success there, similar methods were used throughout the Arctic.

The first step was to divide the North into survey regions; these covered the Arctic and the lower Mackenzie, partly because of the particularly urgent need of better resource use in the Arctic, partly because the Indians of the upper Mackenzie were the concern of another government department.

The regions are listed by priorities based mostly on the economic need of the local people, partly on the known potential. The timing of surveys depends upon money and men available. If the department continues to make two or three per year, it will take until 1975 to complete the basic inventory of renewable resources of the North.

The first step in the regional survey is to assemble all known written information from files, reports, and various records from government and non-government sources. A party of up to four men then spends a summer season in the field interviewing Eskimos and other old-time residents as well as conducting practical tests. The search extends to any kind of resource that will diversify and strengthen the economy, including logging, sea mammals, and arts and crafts. The main fish sought for exploitation is Arctic char, but in some places whitefish, cod, and herring are worth developing.

Following examination on the ground, the possible resource projects are worked out with projected balance-sheets. The marketing aspects of any proposed program are taken in hand by market-research people in the department. If all aspects of production, transportation, and marketing reveal the prospect of a successful small industry, the plans are next taken to the local people for their views and advice. If the Eskimos wish to go ahead, the project usually starts the summer after the survey, with technical specialists present to help set it up. At this stage the project is generally financed by the government, which provides equipment and technical services. The Eskimos are paid for labour or for production, as appropriate; the profits, if any, go to the government.

When the project is reasonably well established, both in economic terms and in the minds of the local people, a co-operative officer takes up with the Eskimos the possibility of forming a co-operative. The administration then withdraws as quickly as possible, to use its limited resources elsewhere, though continuing technical advice is generally needed. In the establishment of the co-operative, the administration provides advice and financing through the Eskimo Loan Fund. It may, in the early stages, hire an outside expert on contract to help, but the co-operative is expected to make its own way as soon as possible. The Eskimo co-operative may employ its own staff of whites, which is a nice reversal on the Arctic of old. In the first five years of the co-operative movement of the North, after the enabling legislation was passed by the Council of the Northwest Territories, twenty co-operatives were established in the North. Most are engaged in fishing. Many are producing arts and crafts. Others have banded together to run a sawmill, build houses, or run stores.

Modern marketing of northern products, especially fish, has had a lively history. Arctic char was highly regarded by most whites in the North, though fish was generally treated with indifference by the Eskimos, except as dog food. In Newfoundland, char was salted and sold for as little at ten cents a pound. To build local fisheries in the North, the Department of Northern Affairs therefore had first to create a whole new market for char. It did so amid the discouraging prognostications of northerners who doubted the capacity of Eskimos to run the fisheries, and of southerners who were aware of Canadian resistance to fish-eating. The image of the char was established among the most reputable hotels and restaurants of Canada as a rare delicacy through a publicity campaign involving the restaurateurs and their leading chefs. When char was sold to the public it was able to command retail prices approaching two dollars a pound and the price obtained by the co-operatives selling to wholesalers steadied between seventy-five and eighty-five cents a pound.

In dollar value, the importance of arctic fisheries is modest: about $85,000 a year. In local terms, they have had great significance. Even a small amount of added cash means a great deal where the money income is so low, and the fisheries have a steadying influence on an economy hitherto subject to the big swings of the fur trade. Perhaps most important, they have provided a base for co-operatives which have then gone on to other small industries and, above all, to other realms of community development.

Some of the fish taken in the Arctic is used by the people who catch it, some is sold to local people, and some is exported from the North fresh; most is exported frozen. Experiments in smoking and canning char have been successful, and ready markets are waiting but are not yet used because there is an even easier market for fresh and frozen char. Other processes still being developed serve as a future reserve against changing market conditions.

The administration has also carried on extensive experimentation with other specialty foods to find uses for Arctic fish and sea mammals, large parts of which are put to little use. These products could be sold locally to satisfy Eskimo tastes and reduce the costs of importing food from the south, or they could be marketed as exotic foods for southern use. Muktuk, whale goulash, seal meatballs, seal heart, sweet and sour, and pickled char belly are some of the products at the stage of experimental production and market research. They are unlikely to become staples of the North American diet, but they will be bought by enthusiastic advocates who have developed the taste, and by cocktail hostesses looking for exotic conversation pieces: either way, they mean money to the Eskimos.

Tourism. In the early 1950s, tourism looked like one of the least likely resources of the North. The attempt to run river boats down the Yukon River had failed. In the Northwest Territories, there was only one road, and it went just over the border to Hay River. Many of the mainline air services still demanded fortitude, determination, and patience. Beyond, the hinterland seemed inaccessible and hopelessly expensive. Those who claimed an enormous potential for the northern tourist industry were voices crying in the wilderness. Enthusiastic missionary work was done by a few private citizens and members of the administration, but it was not until 1959 that a single person was employed full time anywhere for tourist promotion in the northern third of Canada. The few fishing-camps and outfitters did what they could on their own, but they found little support. Part of the trouble was that most people thought of northern tourism in terms of southern travel.

Even by southern standards, the Yukon had a lot going for it. It had roads and a railway, exciting angling and big-game hunting, magnificent and unfamiliar landscape, and an historically interesting focal point, Dawson City.

Big-game hunting or angling trips by chartered aircraft into remote lakes do not figure largely in the statistics of tourist entries, but they bring large returns per capita. This kind of carriage trade is the basis on which much of the industry in the North can be developed. For the right market, the small differential in cost between a northern hunting and fishing trip, and one in the longer-used areas of the continent is of little consequence. People accustomed to holidaying in remote places of the world now find the Canadian North a good bet for immediate satisfactions and a place where the man down the street has not yet been.

Tourists of another type turn to the White Pass and Yukon Railway not just because of scenery different from the continent's other watering-spots, but because it is part of the evocative Trail of '98. At its far end lies Dawson, scene in 1962 of one of the boldest tourist projects ever tried in Canada. Tourists coming so far from the forty-ninth parallel contribute far more to the Canadian economy than American visitors driving within that 150-mile belt of the U.S. border where 80 per cent of the Canadian population lives. The federal government restored as an historic site the magnificent old Palace Grand Theatre which had been one of the major cultural centres of Canada at the turn of the century. Some of the most respected names in North American show business collaborated to produce a musical comedy called *Foxy*, set in the days of the Klondike gold rush. It had an enormously successful première and first season in Dawson City prior to a New York opening. No one concerned with the venture expected this lavish stage show to make money; it was to be the publicity lure to make Dawson City once again a household name in North America for future travellers. On the other hand, no one expected the show to be as expensive as it turned out to be for the federal and territorial treasuries. Whether the experiment succeeded or failed is difficult to judge, for only the immediate costs were known. The benefits came in increasing revenues from tourists who heard of the modern Yukon and were determined to seek it out.

The tourist industry of the Yukon received two handsome gifts from the United States. One was the Alaska Highway itself, connecting Alaska with the heartland of the continent. The other was Alaskan statehood, which encouraged many Americans to visit their farthest and biggest state. The impulse to drive to Alaska was a big reason for the sixty thousand tourists entering the Yukon each year in the 1960s: quite an influx for a permanent population of twelve thousand. An active tourist department in Whitehorse is helping private interests to persuade the transients to prolong their stay in the Yukon.

There is no comparable traffic in the Northwest Territories. Nevertheless the single highway, which goes around the west end of Great Slave Lake to just beyond Yellowknife, was attracting 6,500 tourists a year by 1965 – a figure increasing rapidly each year since the road went through. Some came just to reach the end of the road. Others used Yellowknife as a jumping-off place for fishing holidays by air, boat, or canoe. However they come, tourists are putting more than half a million dollars a year into the economy of the Northwest Territories.

Many other tourists do not take time to drive into the Territories. They come by mainline aircraft to towns like Yellowknife or Inuvik and then fly into one of the growing number of fishing-camps. These camps offer their clients some of the best angling in the world in waters which until recently had never known a hook and line. So popular had this sport become that in 1964 serious overcrowding developed on the Tree River near the Arctic Ocean. Pressures were rather less elsewhere in the million and a half square miles of the North.

In the Eastern Arctic carriage-trade tourism was building a small but brisk industry. Cape Dorset in the early 1960s received many parties mainly interested in its art. The co-operative did not continue to develop tourism, though Povungnituk in Arctic Quebec, another well-known centre of sculpture and graphics, maintained determined and successful efforts to bring in airborne travellers. Dozens of other arctic communities are developing plans to lure and welcome the tourist. The airlines are working on arctic flights to carry the traveller on tourist trips parallel to the Arctic Circle during the weeks of the midnight sun, while private interests are planning a passenger service to carry travellers down the North's one major navigable river to the Arctic Ocean. Everywhere in the North there are signs that the tourist industry bids fair to become second only to mining and oil as an economic resource of the future. The tourist industry is achieving more than profits. It is drawing the North into Canada.

12 | The Modern North: The Social Legacy

Eskimos, in their short recorded history, have been all things to all men. The manner of their life, Michael Lok recorded of Frobisher's first meeting, was 'very strange and beastly'. Captain Lyon, 260 years later, romanticized their quaint and exotic ways. To a distinguished missionary, Bishop Fleming, they were 'sullen, wild, dirty pagans'. To the trader, Eskimos were part of a neat commercial organization: '. . . you will work with our post manager as one large happy family, you following his advice, as if he were your father, for he does the things which I tell him and I want you to do the things which he tells you.' And then there was Robert Louis Stevenson:

> Little Indian, Sioux or Crow,
> Little frosty Eskimo,
> Little Turk or Japanee,
> O! don't you wish that you were me?

219

The Indians of the North were less embarrassed by sentimental attention. They were never really thought of as the noble savage. Instead they are usually called the Indian problem.

Indians and Eskimos are also statistics. In 1956, 1,578 Eskimos with active tuberculosis were in sanatoria. That was one-seventh of the Eskimo population, and it did not include Eskimos fallen prey to other diseases or accidents. The largest Eskimo communities were the tuberculosis wards of hospitals in the cities of southern Canada. By 1965 tuberculosis among Eskimos had dropped to a point where it was only eight times the national average. The infant mortality rate for Eskimos and northern Indians is more than six times that of the rest of Canada.

In the early 1960s an average Canadian girl at birth had a life expectancy of seventy-three years; a boy sixty-eight years. An Eskimo of either sex had a life expectancy of about twenty-five years.

The social legacy was part of the economic legacy, the dwindling food supplies, the thin clothing, the wretched shelters. In 1954 not one Eskimo in a hundred lived in the kind of dwelling prescribed as a minimum for human beings by the laws of the Northwest Territories. The Indians were slightly better off because they had in the surrounding bushland at least the means of making a shelter. The only statistics on malnutrition are the figures for disease and death. Until the late 1950s, starvation was a regular occurrence among groups of northerners beyond immediate help.

Out of a population of nearly 9,000, only 117 Eskimo children went full time to school in the Northwest Territories in 1949; about 1,000 others of Indian, Métis, or white origin were in classrooms of the Northwest Territories. No northern Indian or Eskimo had yet reached matriculation. After being in the Northwest Territories for a hundred years, the white man had not succeeded in giving higher than a grade-four education to more than half a dozen Eskimos; most of these achieved their smattering of instruction by being hospitalized for tuberculosis. None had ever received a vocational training course. None could aspire to a job higher than trapping for the white man, or being his servant and possibly interpreter. No intellectual attainment or career was open to native people. This was in Canada – in the mid twentieth century.

All social services are significantly more expensive in the North than in the South, medical treatment most of all. Yet in 1939 the total medical expenditure of the government on Eskimos was four dollars per capita, three-quarters of which was spent on staff. In 1961-2, Canada spent one hundred times as much. The financial cost of the years of indifference was the need, by the 1960s, to spend three million dollars a year on the health of twelve thousand Eskimos. No one has measured the human cost.

Not everyone was indifferent. Missionaries, officials, and others in the North were keenly aware of the problem, but they had no resources to meet it. Earlier attempts to provide health services provide a rather seamy story. The churches established hospitals in the Mackenzie District with niggardly government support. There was tension between church and state: the government thought its financial support should give it some say in standards of medical facilities, as well as in their location, but the churches resisted what they regarded as interference in their own affairs. One church was loath to see the other have a monopoly on hospital care in a given community, and so duplication and over-building resulted in some places, while in thousands of square miles there was no medical care of any kind for a broken people. In 1926 both the Roman Catholic and the Anglican churches built large hospitals in Aklavik despite the vigorous efforts of the administration to persuade the former to put its institution in the Roman Catholic community of Fort Good Hope, where medical help was badly needed. When the Indian Affairs Branch refused to finance new equipment for the Roman Catholic hospital on the grounds it had fallen below agreed standards of care, the church appealed for funds to the Council of the Northwest Territories, and got them. The administration accused the churches of using the hospitals as charitable homes and charging the government for patient care. And so the acrimonious arguments continued while the chaotic medical situation produced too many beds for some areas and none at all for others. By the outbreak of war, the Mackenzie had 233 beds, quite a considerable number. On the average day, two-thirds of them were empty, and those who used them were often far from their homes and families. This problem was less marked in the Arctic than in the Mackenzie District. The Arctic had a Roman Catholic hospital at Chesterfield Inlet, and an Anglican one at Pangnirtung.

The administration had a few doctors of its own whom it paid partly as medical officers, partly as administrators. The medical officer cum Indian agent at Resolution got a pre-war salary of $1,461, a living allowance of $420, an administrative stipend of $1,461 from Indian Affairs Branch, and a grant from the Northwest Territories of $520.

The administrative revolution had its first effect on the medical side. In the late forties the small but growing staff had its hands full with epidemics of diphtheria, poliomyelitis, typhoid, measles, and influenza, as well as its main job of fighting tuberculosis. With survey teams travelling by ship on the Eastern Arctic Patrol, and by light aircraft all over the Arctic, a tremendous drive was mounted for both prevention and cure. Thus saturated, the North quickly moved from being neglected to becoming one of the most efficiently surveyed regions of Canada, with annual X-rays of as much as 80 per cent of the scattered population. It was a triumph in logistics and determination as well as in medical skill. In prevention, immunization could be totally effective as a defence against many diseases so dangerous to remote people. The only way to prevent the other diseases was to change the traditional way of life, especially its food and shelter.

The medical program had almost universal support from those affected, from those paying for it, and from those watching it. The only serious controversy arose from the policy of hospitalization. Strong voices were raised, notably in the churches, against treating Eskimos in southern hospitals. It was claimed that their psychological welfare, and therefore their total well-being, would be served better by keeping the Eskimos in hospitals closer to home. The medical administration argued that even if enormous sums of money were spent on northern hospitals to raise their standards – money that would reduce the funds available for other urgent programs – the northern hospital could never be as good for the treatment of tuberculosis as the major southern institution with its highly qualified specialists and sophisticated equipment. The doctors produced impressive statistics on the rate of Eskimo deaths during treatment in northern and southern institutions. Finally, they pointed out that even a well-heated hospital in a northern settlement was utterly foreign to an Eskimo accustomed to the igloo and the camp; while he might expect occasional visits from his family in the northern hospital, it was worth spending the money to make possible the same kind of visit to a southern hospital rather than sacrifice treatment standards for a people so desperately in need.

Some white men had such strong convictions that they tried to persuade Eskimos to refuse hospitalization if it meant going away to government hospitals. Any reluctance the Eskimos felt is natural enough. For anyone, the prospect of an indefinite stay in a hospital is worrying. To an Eskimo or a northern Indian it is a particularly alien world. He could understand only dimly the alternative of worsening disease and contamination of families and friends.

In these circumstances, the program of hospitalization was astonishingly successful. Though the Northwest Territories, like most parts of Canada, has legislation requiring compulsory hospitalization for certain communicable diseases, it rarely had to be invoked. In its place there was an educational campaign on the meaning of tuberculosis. Films and slides were used to make hospital life less strange and terrifying. Systems of communication were set up between patients and their families, with regular letters, monthly progress reports from the hospitals, exchanges of photographs, and tape-recorded messages. Social workers often accompanied the doctors to make immediate provision for the families of patients. One of the most persuasive instruments of all was the word of the returning patient who came back to his community, cured. When the massive campaign against tuberculosis began, only a trickle of Eskimos returned, because few had gone out, and because the long years of neglect produced a relatively low proportion of complete cures. As the program gained momentum, hospitalization was accepted with perhaps the same regret, but less hesitation.

Progress was rapid, but not always steady. While the incidence of tuberculosis was dropping reassuringly, feelings of warm satisfaction could be suddenly dashed. In 1962 one of the most accessible communities in the Arctic, an area which had gained more than average attention, had a sudden flare-up. In one spring the doctors hospitalized forty people out of a population of only about two hundred. In financial terms, the tragedy at Eskimo Point cost the taxpayers of Canada about $100,000 a year until the sick from that one village were cured. For some it would take a year; for others, longer. Medical officers concluded that the outbreak was directly related to housing conditions. To provide minimum safe housing for those involved would have cost about $75,000. Once again, no one could write the balance sheet of social costs.

The answer seemed simple. Some went to the extreme of advocating the resettlement of the entire Eskimo population in the cities of the South, or to a new southern town of ten or twelve thousand Eskimos. Others suggested that it would be cheaper to move the whole Eskimo population to the larger hotels of the country. The resettlement of northerners would have saved endless trouble for the doctors and the rest of the administration. It might have done wonders for the consciences of those who prefer not to worry about the complexities of the human voyage through a cold wilderness.

The administration gave prolonged study to the possibility, not of wholesale resettlement, but of a southern nucleus community that might attract some Eskimos willing to make the total break. In the end, the government rejected major resettlement on two grounds. First, all the grandiose schemes of resettlement overlooked the wishes of the Eskimos. A gradually deepening contact with the Eskimo mind produced no evidence at all of an Eskimo desire to become southerners. Canada had had enough history of imposed migration for administrative convenience.

The second ground for rejection was the vulnerability of northerners to competition in the South. Voluntary resettlement may hold promise in future years, but only when those resettling have learned to compete with the white man on his own ground. In short, the educational level of the migrants must approach a national average, they must learn enough of southern ways to accept the disciplines with the material rewards, and their knowledge of twentieth-century North American society must be wide enough to permit them to evaluate an alien setting. It would be tragic for Eskimos to become dependent upon the paternal advice of well-meaning white men; it would also be a mistake for them to be thrown on white charity when they were defeated in the jungle of the big city.

To persuade Eskimos to enter the maelstrom of the southern city would be a heavy responsibility. In times of unemployment, local or national, it is easy to predict who would be the first to suffer; it would be the least-educated workers, unsure of even oral English or French, unaccustomed to the monotonous routines of industrial society, susceptible to its pitfalls. If the government compensated for these short-comings by such devices as sharing the cost of wages with employers, the Eskimos would only incur the lasting enmity of the unions, and yield up their rights to be independent citizens, in fact as well as in theory. Of course, Eskimos are free to move south whenever they wish, and they get government help in doing so – but only when those moving are sure they are equipped for this particular kind of adjustment.

In the Arctic, Canada could afford the housing needed by every underprivileged Eskimo. The medical profession actually pressed strongly for an immediate and massive housing program. The need was eloquently stated in one figure: the 1964 death-rate of Eskimo children between one and four was thirteen times the national average. The northern Indians were already becoming the beneficiaries of a plan of housing aid which, in effect, gave an Indian a complete house for an investment of his own labour and as little as twenty-five dollars in cash. The program of low-cost housing in the North was slowed by physical difficulties, such as the short shipping and construction seasons and the shortage of even semi-skilled labour for erecting prefabricated homes. It was slowed by lack of money. Even when the massive onslaught on northern social problems was made, funds were by no means limitless. With soaring costs for education, health, welfare, and the development of new resources, the housing program was not set aside but was phased over several years.

Housing assistance was also limited by the administration's anxiety – perhaps over-anxiety – to avoid causing Eskimos to emerge from neglect into total dependence on the white man's largess. If we are going to treat the North as part of Canada, we should maintain something of the equations between effort and reward, between rights and responsibilities, that are part of the general Canadian scheme of things. If the government built and maintained free houses for Eskimos it could meet many problems of health and its own conscience: it could also be creating a permanent problem of dependence, of wards, of half-citizens. If at all possible, the administration hoped to meet the housing need without sacrificing the position of the Eskimo as an independent citizen in a free society.

The administration began by looking for a thousand-dollar house that could provide dry warmth at low cost both in building and in maintenance. It would have more living space than the average igloo, but it would be only a transition between the old and a permanent, larger house that would be built when the owner himself felt the need and was willing to make the sacrifice to pay at least part of the cost of more commodious living. The first answer was the so-called rigid-frame house characterized by inward-slanting walls to give strength with little material. Its basic size was sixteen feet by sixteen feet, but it could be elongated in units of four feet. With stove and insulated chimney it cost about $880 delivered in the average arctic community.

There followed a series of designs for small dwellings, each generally larger and more expensive than the last. When the cost edged towards $2,000 and beyond, the government applied a subsidy of $1,000. Federal and provincial governments had accepted responsibility for aid in slum-clearance programs across the country. The Arctic was in effect treated as one giant housing slum, different in aspect, but not in principle, from the depressed areas of large cities. The sensible method of applying slum-clearing aid to the Arctic was to offer an individual subsidy to housing of approved design, since happily there were no costs for land acquisition or clearance. Any Eskimo wanting to buy a house with up to three bedrooms could apply both for the subsidy and for a loan at 5 per cent interest through the Eskimo Loan Fund; he was expected to invest his own labour in the house as well as a cash down payment and monthly payments. The house did not have to be of government design as long as it passed the National Building Code for safety; in practice, most took advantage of the government drawings which were, with varying degrees of success, specifically created for arctic conditions and which could be bought at the savings achieved through bulk purchasing. Most of the low-cost houses were prefabricated, since this proved to be a cheaper approach, especially for areas where building skills and certain mechanical trades were lacking.

For those who could not afford to buy outright, there were welfare houses owned by the government and available for use without cost on the basis of need. For those who aspired to larger houses, but dwellings below the standards required by financing under the National Housing Act, there was yet another plan; the territorial governments of the Northwest Territories and the Yukon provided second mortgages and a scheme of assistance which in effect wrote off $1,000 after ten-year occupancy. This plan was made available to all races.

These housing schemes helped bridge the gap between the high costs of northern building and the low incomes. Even government expenditures of more than a million dollars a year on low-cost housing did not produce immediate solutions to the backlog of need in the Arctic. Some feared that the housing program would create new problems by hastening the process of attracting people off the land into the communities, as had happened in the sub-Arctic. Fortunately, the Eskimos lived almost entirely on the sea-coasts. Housing could, therefore, be taken right to the hunting-camp which, in much of the Arctic, was a more or less permanent fixture. Thus housing could be a means of persuading people to stay on the land and exploit its resources rather than to come to an unproductive village. Housing might counteract the attractions of the community with its social life and its services.

The housing program itself did not solve the problem of heating. The Arctic is probably the only place in the world where it is easier to build a house than heat it. There are no trees, grasses, or peat bogs to serve as fuel. While animal oil can be used, as it traditionally was in the igloo, its efficiency as a fuel is low, and its side effects of smell and smoke through imperfect combustion are obnoxious in the extreme. The Eskimos may have grown accustomed to it in small doses, but they have been as unenthusiastic as anyone else when faced with nausea and near-asphyxiation.

Heating-oil is expensive. When transported by forty-five gallon drum to the High Arctic it can cost more than a dollar a gallon, or nearly six times the common price in southern Canada. If the cost of heating is not to be twelve or eighteen times the cost in southern Canada, a house must be compact, extremely well insulated, its few windows triple glazed, with porches, and with snow banks in winter to break the wind. A man with a small, well-designed, and well-maintained house in the Arctic can, if he is careful, burn about the same amount of fuel as the owner of a three-bedroom ranch-style bungalow in Winnipeg or Ottawa, but each gallon of fuel will cost him more.

To reduce the price of oil, the government began building 100,000-gallon bulk storage tanks wherever it could not persuade private enterprise to do so. Fuel costs in some places dropped to less than half the level of barrelled oil, even with provision for amortizing the cost of the tanks over fifteen years. Since it would be unfair to enable a few to enjoy this benefit by the accident of their proximity to new tanks, while poor people in remote places went on paying astronomical oil prices, the government regionalized the price of fuel to spread the benefits across the North. The price of oil in the Eastern Arctic fell to less than fifty cents a gallon everywhere. In the higher-cost central Arctic, the price dropped by almost half, to about sixty-five cents, in 1965. As each new tank was built, the regional price dropped. Some advocated an even bolder program, to subsidize oil to such an extent that it could be sold everywhere for roughly the price prevailing in the higher-costs areas of the provinces. Others, like the Council of the Northwest Territories, addressed themselves to a subsidy on electricity. Still others sought a program of massive support to all costs of living and operating in the North. All such proposals presented enormous complexities in the manipulation of a whole economy and in the patterns they might set in policies of regional development elsewhere. Could the federal government finance such subsidies for the Northwest Territories and deny them to Newfoundland, for example? In 1966, though no one believed that any solutions to housing and living adopted up to that time were final, the programs of social development – whether right or wrong, too slow or too fast, niggardly or excessively paternal – still had a sense of direction they had lacked in the years of indifference.

The provision of food and clothing seemed to raise less gigantic problems than housing. At first it was simply a matter of providing relief for those in distress. Before the administration came actively on the scene the government authorized its police and the traders to issue relief. The shocking inadequacy of that program cannot be laid at the door of those involved in its distribution: indeed the traders could be commended for resisting the temptation to increase their trade simply by multiplying the store goods handed out through the charity of the Crown. Like the police, the traders acted faithfully within their terms of reference, but these terms were too narrow, both in the amount of assistance provided, and in the coverage of scattered population. The best medical advice available held that a considerable proportion of the northern native population in the mid 1950s was suffering from malnutrition. Some said half.

Even by then there had been a revolution in welfare from an unexpected source. When Canada instituted family allowances in 1944, no one involved in the decision foresaw their consequences in the Arctic. The effect of an assured monthly cheque for twelve dollars or twenty dollars is of significance in indirect proportion to the size of a family's total income. For a family earning $20,000 a year it is pin money. For a family that sees only $200 in cash a year it is an economic revolution. Overnight, the family allowance wiped out the practice of infanticide against which white men had been inveighing for generations. The Eskimos killed infants, especially girls, not through indifference to human life, but simply as a matter of necessity when it was a choice between death for some and death for all. The family allowance changed the unproductive child, girl or boy, from a burden to an asset.

Family allowance was at first paid in kind to native people in the North, or at least it could be used only for certain defined purposes. The same was true of relief. By the 1960s the last Eskimos were put on the same footing as other Canadians, receiving cheques for family allowances, as well as other payments such as old-age pensions and blind persons' allowances. For relief, the native people of the North did not receive cheques like most welfare recipients in the South, but they were given credits of money for food, fuel, and clothing; within these categories they could make their own purchases.

In the North, as in the South, controversy surrounded the administration of relief. Some urged that northerners be put on exactly the same footing as other Canadians, with all assistance being paid through cheques. Others, generally more vocal, called for more direct controls on relief. As in the South, cases were cited of some families receiving more money through welfare than others did through honest toil. Anxiety was expressed over the misuse of relief for alcohol or frivolous purposes. It was held that some northerners were beginning to look upon living on relief as an honourable vocation preferable to the uncertainties of the hunt or the job. Others answered, not by denying the abuses, but by pointing out the greater threats of mass malnutrition or worse, if children in particular were not guaranteed adequate food and shelter. Some urged the removal of the child from the care of apparently irresponsible parents: others protested such a threat to home life. The only point in common among the disputants was to blame the public servant who had to remain silent while working for the people of the North and carrying out the policies of governments. Fortunately, the native people themselves showed a gratifying degree of maturity amid the debates. While they were quite free to express their views, both orally and in letters, local councils generally displayed such good sense in their criticisms and their approvals that the administrator could depend increasingly on them for advice.

The welfare program that developed with the new administration was concerned with much more than relief. Child welfare presented unusual complexities, not only because of the accumulated need to straighten out difficulties of children in undesirable circumstances or in various informal stages of adoption, but to relate modern law to long-established native traditions. Suffering from an acute shortage of professional staff, the administration centred its efforts on assistance in designing territorial child welfare legislation and in dealing with cases of immediate need. The formalities of adoption proceedings fell far behind.

In the late 1950s, the welfare service tackled a rehabilitation program made especially urgent by the many people suffering from physical or emotional disabilities in the wake of tuberculosis. In earlier days, men and women might be left in hospital when it was clear they could not survive a return to the harsh life of the land, but continued hospitalization was unproductive and very expensive. Retraining and readjustment opened up more hopeful avenues. Rehabilitation centres were established at Frobisher Bay and Inuvik. Rehabilitants, with their families, lived in cottages where they learned new occupations and skills while gaining physical and emotional strength to face an independent life. The program was useful, especially when the hospitals were discharging many people with severe disabilities following long, undetected illnesses. The program scored successes but also developed shortcomings because the rehabilitation centres were becoming ghettos for people no longer able to cope with life outside. In 1965 the rehabilitation program underwent a fundamental change. Rehabilitation was no longer seen as a colony for special effort, but as a function – a method of helping people who lived in the community at large, rather than in buildings separate from it.

Another important aspect of welfare was the corrections program. Convicted northerners were inadequately jailed in police lock-ups because there was nowhere else for them to go except to institutions far away in the provinces. These lock-ups were usually simple steel cells lodged in an R.C.M.P. detachment. The police, unequipped to act as jailers, were anxious to be relieved of the role. The federal and territorial governments saw in this need for penal institutions a chance to implement the kind of reforms often advocated in the provinces, but difficult to achieve there because of the existence of jails of the wrong kind, and staff trained in methods no longer considered acceptable by modern penology. In 1965 both the Yukon Territory and the Northwest Territories at last initiated new corrections systems. The central part of each was a small maximum-security institution with medium-security lodging alongside to permit the rehabilitation of convicted persons as part of a community effort. These jails were scheduled to open in 1966, together with corrections camps whose whole emphasis would be on rehabilitation rather than on simple isolation from society. The success of the program cannot yet be assessed, but it has begun with the support of prison reformers across the country.

As well as this positive corrections program, other, simultaneous efforts were even more directly designed to hit the cause of crime. In the mid fifties there was almost no organized youth activity outside a few of the larger northern centres. The lack was critical, for no age group in the population was so in need of guidance as the teen-agers. By the late 1950s a campaign for northern scouting was under way across the whole North. In both the Yukon and the Mackenzie District local Boy Scout and Girl Guide groups could grow with community resources, but the movement in the High Arctic needed outside help. Through an Arctic and Northern Scouting Committee, local projects got advice, material help, and introductions to chosen southern Canadian groups with which they were 'twinned'. Thus the program for youth activity in the North brought the useful by-product of a growing understanding between young Canadians of south and north. At Povungnituk the first northern Sea Cadets were organized in 1959. With the aid of the organization in southern Canada and visits of Royal Canadian Navy ships to this outpost, the experiment was a spectacular success. As well as being a healthy outlet for youthful energies, scouting gave young Eskimos a sense of confidence and purpose and helped them to master English.

People of good will, from inside and outside government, threw their energies into this youth work as a major means of combating the dangers of the sudden adjustment to community life and to the changing role of the family and home. The evil effects of the changing life were visible in liquor violations or minor crime; these misdemeanours were dwelt upon by those who continued to deplore the alteration of the old ways, as though there were any way to stop their alteration. The positive effects of youth organization were real enough to those who worked in the communities. The youth work was not confined to Scout or Guide troops.

The North did not escape the mania of curling, and many communities overcame high odds to provide themselves with rinks. Since these projects usually needed government help, it was possible to ensure that in operation they would not exclude any race or creed. In the Northwest Territories, federal and territorial governments together agreed to match local contributions for the construction of halls, curling rinks, and such community facilities, so that local people paid only half the cost. The proportion of federal and territorial contributions depended upon the proportion of Indians and Eskimos in any community. In the Yukon, outside aid usually took the form of territorial grants related to the liquor profits. In the Arctic, it was usually impossible for the local people to raise even half the cost of a hall. National benevolent organizations made up the local share of money needed for materials, while the residents of the community contributed their labour. The finished facility was then turned over to the full ownership of a community group. The Imperial Order Daughters of the Empire sponsored three such halls and the Canadian Handicrafts Guild sponsored one.

The community projects program provides many a northern community with more than a building or a rink; it also acts as a catalyst that brings all elements of a community together with a sense of purpose, and a subject for decision-making. The finished project makes possible inter-racial community activities. For adults as well as youth, it gives the opportunity for a sense of involvement in community affairs which is one of the more positive features of changing northern life. The halls may be used for relatively passive recreation like movies or club life, or for that extraordinarily energetic participating sport that is dancing in the North. The Federated Women's Institutes have done a remarkable pioneering job of promoting club activities through the Yukon and the Mackenzie District. Their program is an effective soft-sell in adult education.

Education. Beyond a doubt, the most staggering social task facing the administration in the 1950s was education. Only the barest start had been made in providing space where children could go to school. In 1950 eight different authorities operated schools in the North. The Department of Northern Affairs provided only three classrooms. Though it paid grants to other agencies to run classes, the classroom standards were uneven. Some schools operated only four hours a day, four days a week. One teacher in three held no teaching certificate of any kind. Only 117 of all the Eskimos got full-time schooling. There was no vocational education of any kind, no adult education, and no teaching for the growing ranks of hospital patients.

Equally discouraging, there was no policy, no curriculum for northern needs, and no training for northern teachers. The teaching materials provided for Tuktoyaktuk were those used in the city of Edmonton. Progress in the classroom, as measured by achievement of grades, was glacial. The organization of education, the physical facilities, and the content of instruction all made nonsense of any pretence of equality of educational opportunity for northern residents. The first task was to reduce the proliferation of educational authorities. The Department of Northern Affairs took over from the Department of Citizenship and Immigration the responsibility for Indian education in the Northwest Territories, thus paving the way for the first completely racially-integrated school system in Canada. Mining companies were required to provide space for teaching but were not required to run the schools. Nothing was done to disturb the school district of Yellowknife; on the contrary, every encouragement was given to the formation of both public and separate school districts in communities large enough to support their own educational system. For a long time to come, however, the provision and operation of schools will be the responsibility of the territorial or federal governments in almost all settlements of the Northwest Territories.

The major task in establishing a comprehensive school system was to reach an understanding with the Roman Catholic and Anglican churches which had a considerable vested interest in schooling. The casual teaching done by remote missionaries in the absence of any other education provided no serious problem. Proper classrooms with qualified teachers could only be welcomed, not just as a service to the community, but as a means of relieving the pressures on hard-pressed missionaries. More complicated was the church investment in large residential schools.

Through its long delays, the government ran into good luck. Most of the church-run residences and schools in the Mackenzie District were old and needed replacement or expensive renovation. The churches were prepared to abdicate this costly field in return for certain government guarantees of church interests. The only churches involved were Roman Catholic and Anglican. The government agreed to build new residences and schools at public expense to replace all the church-owned buildings, and in some cases to compensate the churches for their abandoned facilities. The residences were built and operated to preserve religious separation of the pupils, at least between Roman Catholic and non-Roman Catholic. The residences were then turned over to the Roman Catholic and Anglican churches to operate at public expense. The schools, however, were run by the Department of Northern Affairs, with certain guarantees respecting religion.

The agreement on the operation of residences covered those

settlements in the Mackenzie where the churches already had educational institutions. The new residences were built at Inuvik (Roman Catholic, 250 pupils; Anglican, 250 pupils), Fort McPherson (Anglican, 150 pupils), Fort Simpson (Roman Catholic, 150 pupils; Anglican, 50 pupils), Fort Smith (Roman Catholic, 200 pupils). Shortly afterwards, the government agreed to buy and partly rebuild a 100-pupil hostel built by the Roman Catholic church at Chesterfield Inlet. The staff in each hostel, whether clerical or lay, is hired by the churches, which also take full responsibility for administration under contract with the government. The hostels are large and expensive. By far the largest, at Inuvik, cost almost four million dollars. Besides dormitories, kitchens, and other usual features of a residential institution, there are four gymnasiums (two for Roman Catholics, two for Anglicans), and two chapels appointed appropriately for the operating churches.

Inuvik and Fort Simpson are the only settlements where hostels are run by the two churches side by side. Here the schools are also divided into separate wings by religion. The teachers in the Roman Catholic wing, as in Fort Smith and Chesterfield Inlet, are both clerical and lay, while in the Anglican wing they are all laymen, not necessarily Anglican.

The agreement with the churches also provides that, in all schools of the Northwest Territories, the government chooses Roman Catholic teachers for every class with a majority of Roman Catholic pupils. The principal is of the same religion as a majority of the teachers. This policy is not without complications, for it is difficult to know six months in advance of the school year how classes and grades can most effectively be organized: a school with fifty-five Roman Catholic pupils and forty-five non-Roman Catholic might be organized to have four Roman Catholic teachers or two. Again, if all the children of one religion in grades 1, 2, and 3 are put together in one classroom to achieve complete religious homogeneity, not only will that class have a teacher of the same religion, but the room itself may be decorated with religious objects appropriate to the denomination.

The final major provision on behalf of the churches is the guarantee of half an hour at the end of each day for religious instruction throughout the Northwest Territories. In mixed classes, the children are appropriately separated for this period, and the privilege of religious instruction is not confined to Roman Catholics and Anglicans. In the Mackenzie District, where the Pentecostal Church is strong, their representatives are invited to participate in these religious exercises. The choice of religious class is left to the parents. Not all missionaries take advantage of this religious period.

The only public school district in the Northwest Territories is still the one established in Yellowknife in 1939. There are separate school districts in Yellowknife and Hay River. These receive 50 per cent of all capital costs as a grant, and the remaining capital needs as a loan from the territorial government. There are operating grants based on the number of pupils, the rest of the cost being raised by local taxation. In the Northwest Territories separate and public school supporters are thus on exactly the same financial footing. Separate school taxes are frequently lower.

Having accepted full responsibility for the school program, the government went on to make what seemed prodigious expenditures to provide the necessary buildings and equipment. Between 1955 and 1965 a capital investment of more than $25 million was made for schools and hostels in the Northwest Territories alone, quite apart from the federal program for Eskimos in Arctic Quebec and the support given to Yukon school construction. The number of classrooms in the Northwest Territories rose to 266. By 1965 there were schools to house almost all the pupils of the sub-Arctic. The lack of hostel beds and classrooms in the Arctic left a fifth of the Eskimo population still outside any educational program, with little hope of facilities for universal education in the North – and thus in Canada – until the early 1970s.

The Arctic is, of course, much the hardest region in Canada to service with schools. The money required to build in these high-cost areas, the difficulties created by the short construction season, and the long transportation routes are not the most serious problems. Schools or schooling cannot be brought to every place where children live. Although some one-room schools were built, experience proved the imprudence of leaving a teacher alone and isolated from professional consultation in remote places. The much more effective two-room school is justified only by a school population of more than thirty – far more pupils than in the average Eskimo camp. Itinerant teaching was tried by energetic and devoted teachers, but the results were close to total failure because Eskimo adults, having had little or no schooling, were usually utterly unable to help children with lessons sent by correspondence or left by the teacher.

The government was reluctant to build more of the large hostels like those in the Mackenzie District to replace the church residential schools. There was criticism of big institutions that take children so far from home in both the physical and psychological sense. The children were now returned to their homes each summer, but there was no denying the gulf between hostel and home life. As a sort of half-way house between these residences and the typical Eskimo home, the Department of Northern Affairs started building small hostels. Holding eight children, under the care of Eskimo house-parents, each hostel is a little like an Eskimo family unit, and close enough to home to permit periodic visits by parents. The hostels, whose management is under the general supervision of some experienced housekeeper in the community, teach silent lessons in cleanliness and good management. As an instrument of classroom education, they are a poor second to the larger institutions where the learning process continues long after school hours. There the children use English with supervisors and with one another, and are constantly exposed to books and games that carry on the work of the classroom. In the small hostels the house-parents, still of a generation that had no schooling, cannot give the academic help and encouragement one expects in an average Canadian home.

The building of the educational system was thus far more than a matter of applying tens of millions of dollars, wood, and glass. Building the classrooms and the dormitories was much easier than finding the right compromises to add new intellectual depth without unduly disturbing the social fabric. The small hostel for the younger child and the larger one for the older pupil of more advanced grades seemed a reasonable approach, since more of the children who reached higher grades would be on the path away from the land, and would therefore need to learn about life in the towns of the North or of the South.

In 1966 most of the teaching in the schools of the Northwest Territories was still in the first four grades. Only in Inuvik, Yellowknife, Frobisher Bay, and Hay River are high-school classes taught for local people. Yellowknife has a large high school and vocational school with a 200-bed hostel to serve the whole of the Territories. There is a 250-bed hostel with classrooms and shops at Churchill, Manitoba, for Eastern Arctic children needing vocational education, high school, or advanced primary-school classes. The Sir John Franklin School and Akaitcho Hall in Yellowknife is a particularly interesting and successful experiment in integrated education. Operated by the government, it is the only major institution in the North where children live and work together without any lines of creed or race.

The northern educational system is supplemented by the use of other resources in southern Canada. Many vocational courses are taught either as special northern classes in southern institutions, or by feeding northern pupils into regular southern instruction. The Northwest Territories was the first region in Canada to provide free university education for all. Loans and grants are made to cover travel, tuition, and board for any pupils going to a southern university; all obligations are written off after the student has returned to the North. For the territorial government, this was more sensible and much cheaper than rushing into the building of higher education facilities. For the young people of the North it was an act of generosity removing almost all financial barriers to higher education.

The third and most important part of the education program is the policy itself. The problems of organization and construction are small, in comparison with the questions of what to teach and how to teach it. The government was not lacking in advice. Some held that education should be introduced slowly in order not to damage the family by separating educated children from their untutored parents. Pressure was sometimes put on parents to refuse permission for their children to go off to the residential schools. At the other extreme, some believed that teaching could be carried out effectively only with the complete integration of northern pupils into classrooms of southern Canada. Some held that the northern curriculum should be based on the skills of the land, in order not to draw the children from their homes and make them unfit to return. Others thought in terms of a northern educational system almost identical to those in the South, so that the pupil could move easily into a competitive position anywhere in Canada. Many others questioned the purpose of education if there were no jobs on graduation.

At first, the government had little choice in what to teach or how to teach it. Using teachers qualified in southern Canada, it had nothing to give them but the curricula of Alberta, Ontario, or Quebec, and leave to the teacher any adaptation she thought possible or desirable. Then gradually a northern curriculum was developed.

The thinking behind the program was that in future years the children of the North might want to return to the land of their fathers; they might want to live and work in northern towns in occupations requiring a good formal education; or they might want to make their way in Canada as a whole, with no limit at all to the ceilings of their intellectual ambitions. The school had to provide for all. The prospects for employment of the school graduate were bright. Even with no increase at all in the economic activity, even with a total failure of every plan and hope for development of the resources of the North, employment was likely for all qualified to take it, simply by replacing the southern Canadians now brought such distances to do jobs normally performed by local residents. In southern Canada, one does not usually advertise for a store clerk, a nurse, a tractor driver, or a radio technician a thousand miles from home. One does so in the North only because of the temporary vacuum in schooling. In other words, the major problem in the North is not unemployment: it is the serious imbalance that produces a critical lack of skilled and semi-skilled workers alongside a surplus of unskilled. Given an average Canadian standard of education, the northerner has little to fear in his economic future. He is in a highly advantageous position when competing for northern jobs where he is at home. He is cheaper to hire because he is less likely to give up the job. He is less likely to need expensive transportation for himself and his family, on recruitment, resignation, or annual vacation. If the educational system works, he should be able to compete for southern jobs on the same terms as other Canadians.

Having established this position, the government maintains that the aim of its educational system is not job training: it is preparation for citizenship in a broader sense, the pupil returning to the trap-line being just as important as the potential nuclear physicist. The purpose is to open doors, particularly to a culture with a written literature. The teaching of English or French is of paramount importance, not simply as an economic tool, but as the avenue to world literature and world thought. In practice, English became the language of universal instruction because it has been the language of the community, even in Arctic Quebec.

One of the liveliest debates in education centred on the question of language. Critics called for instruction in the Eskimo language and used such provocative phrases as 'cultural genocide' to describe the use of English in classes. The administration by an argument that is discussed in Chapter 15 regards itself as the most effective protector of the Eskimo cultural tradition. It is prepared to use the local language in the lower grades, but as a matter both of principle and of practicality it is heavily committed to English. It is a matter of principle because a liberal education can be achieved only by the use of a major language. The Danes used Eskimo in Greenland but found themselves under criticism from the Greenlandic people themselves, who considered that total proficiency in only the Eskimo language put them at a cultural and economic disadvantage: Danish now predominates in Greenland schools. English is used as a matter of practicality in Canada because there are virtually no qualified teachers who can teach in either an Eskimo or an Indian dialect. As the educational system matures and produces its own teachers, the local vernacular will be used in the schools as a second language.

The new curricula are designed to adapt teaching to local environment. Supplementary readers have been produced, many with the help of northern pupils themselves, so that northern youngsters can learn vocabulary or arithmetic in terms of seals and bears instead of cows and pigs. The use of these materials is limited by the teachers themselves, who are accustomed to southern teaching methods and who have usually had only short experience with northern life and culture. The turn-over in the teaching profession across Canada is remarkably high. Though it is somewhat lower in the North, education is bound to suffer when the average stay of a teacher is about three years, with only a week or two of instruction to prepare for this very different teaching role. Administrators, on the other hand, are allowed in the field only after nearly a year of training, including instruction in the Eskimo language.

Despite the barriers of language and culture, despite the problems of curricula to fit two worlds and of staff teaching across a gulf, progress has been made. In terms of achievement of grades, it has been less rapid than in southern Canada, but gradually successes have been chalked up.

By 1966 a few northern Indians were in Canadian universities. No Eskimos have reached matriculation, but the time is not far off when they too will reach the higher levels of education. Meanwhile, many are equipped with enough background and basic skills to provide some variety of career choice, and some intellectual interests beyond what was conceivable a dozen years ago. The brightest hopes still lie far in the future. No one associated with the North has illusions about the setbacks ahead before all doors are opened to the newest generation. Still, after the forgotten centuries, the start has been made. The people of the North have a chance to conquer something bigger than their shrinking world.

13 | The Modern North: Political Development

The modern political history of northern Canada began on July 15, 1870. On that day, through the authority of an imperial Order in Council, Great Britain transferred to Canada that immense region known as Rupert's Land and the North Western Territory, stipulating that the combined area should be known as 'The Northwest Territories'. A second imperial Order in Council of July 31, 1880, confirmed the transfer of Britain's arctic islands to Canada.

The Canadian government had previously passed an 'Act for the Temporary Government of Rupert's Land and the North Western Territory when united with Canada', an indication of prescience far from characteristic of all parliamentary handling of its frontier affairs. The area included all of the Yukon Territory and the Northwest Territories, all three prairie provinces, and parts of Ontario and Quebec. In 1870 a small part of the new territory, including

243

the Red River Settlement, was organized as the province of Manitoba and admitted to Confederation. The lieutenant-governor of Manitoba became lieutenant-governor of the Northwest Territories for five years.

Parliament then passed the Northwest Territories Act to give a more permanent form of government, appointing a resident lieutenant-governor and making provision for a council that would in time become a legislative assembly with a maximum of twenty-one members. The seat of government, originally at Battleford, was moved to Regina in 1883. The boundaries shifted like the sands, for the Northwest Territories came to be regarded as a vague frontier area off which units would be split as their development warranted some further degree of local self-government. The District of Keewatin was created in 1876 in present-day Manitoba, and withdrawn from the government of the Territories. Manitoba was considerably enlarged in 1881. The Yukon became a separate territory in 1898. Alberta and Saskatchewan were created as provinces in 1905. In 1912 northern Quebec, Ontario, and Manitoba reached their present dimensions, and the Northwest Territories emerged as it was to remain for at least the next fifty years.

The absence of mind that Prime Minister St. Laurent spoke of, referring to the administration of the Territories, was particularly marked in the early days. The Northwest Territories Amendment Act of 1905 provided for the appointment of a Commissioner of the Northwest Territories to administer the Territories under instructions of the Governor-in-Council and the Minister of the Interior. There was to be a council of up to four appointed members, with Ottawa as the seat of government. Lieutenant-Colonel F. White, comptroller and deputy head of the Royal North West Mounted Police, was appointed the first commissioner. No council was appointed and not a single ordinance was passed for sixteen years. Colonel White was superannuated from the force in 1912, but continued as commissioner for another six years. During all this time, such administration as there was remained largely in the hands of the police.

In 1918 Colonel White died; two years later W. W. Cory, Deputy Minister of the Department of the Interior, was made the commissioner. The next year the government appointed a council of four men, soon raising their number to six. This was the real beginning of government of the Northwest Territories as it exists today. This interest in the North was awakened, like many other projects of the time, by the oil rush at Norman Wells. Still, it was an interest of narrow limits. The councils appointed during the next thirty years included much intellectual and administrative talent, but the meetings at first were infrequent in number and thin in content. Until 1929 they averaged fewer than one a year. In the 1930s they were stepped up. The old ordinances enacted with prairie conditions in mind were gradually revised. Legislation relating to employment, schools, and liquor was more often discussed. Gradually the council evolved a body of law that was related to a modern frontier community rather than exclusively to western farmers, or northern hunters and trappers. Still there was no ground-swell of aspiration, political, economic, or social. The Indian, Eskimo, and Métis population had no knowledge whatever of territorial government, and even among the few relatively educated whites interest was restrained. There were no elected representatives to whom the residents of the Territories could turn, either in the federal Parliament or in the wholly appointed territorial council. Most of the whites were employees of large institutions that did not encourage political activity among their servants. They were also, in large part, transients, rather than family men who had cast a permanent lot with the North. As a consequence, the main concern of government, as of administration, was the welfare of the native peoples, in a passive way, of course. No revolutions were likely, if only because of a lack of resources during the depression. Voices that might have touched a conscience were voteless voices, crying in a northern wilderness.

In the late 1930s the seeds of a real northern government were planted as more independently-minded individuals entered the Territories after the mining rush around Yellowknife. Their efforts were focused first on local government. Had the war not intervened, the pressure for some kind of elected territorial representation might well have grown quickly.

The growth of a new class, just before and after the war, was a healthy sign in the political growth of the Territories. The North was no longer the almost exclusive property of the government, the churches, and the Hudson's Bay Company. The unhealthy identity between government and administration was on its way out, and in its place there began to grow the kind of relationship that is known in Ottawa and in the provincial capitals. The first sign of change was the appointment to the council in 1946 of a resident of the Territories. The next step, in 1951, was the enlargement of the council to eight members, three of them to be elected. At least one meeting each year would take place in the Territories. The Northwest Territories Act was amended again in 1954 to make an additional constituency.

At this stage – a stage that lasted until 1966 – the government of the Northwest Territories consisted of a Commissioner of the Northwest Territories, and a council of nine members. The commissioner was a civil servant appointed by Order in Council. From Mr. Cory's appointment in 1920 until the resignation of R. G. Robertson in 1963, the commissioner continued to be the Deputy Minister of Northern Affairs and National Resources. The appointment was then given to B. G. Sivertz, who for a few months combined this role with his position as director of the Northern Administration Branch of the Department of Northern Affairs. Early in 1964 Mr. Sivertz relinquished the post of director to become the first full-time Commissioner of the Northwest Territories. In 1966 the council was further enlarged to include three new elected members from the Arctic. Shortly afterwards, the first elected Eskimo member, Simonie, was elected to the council, joining Abraham Okpik, who had been appointed the year before.

The commissioner is the appointed head of both the government and the administration of the Territories. As head of the government, he sits with the council and presides over its meetings. His role is similar to the speaker of the House of Commons, but it is far more. It combines features of the offices of prime minister and lieutenant-governor. The commissioner requests the chief electoral officer of Canada to issue writs for elections. He convenes sessions of the council. With a ceremony of dignity borrowing features from federal and provincial parliaments, he opens sessions of the councils, preceded by a mace-bearer, and reads a Speech from the Throne. He prorogues sessions. In all these duties are the beginnings of parliamentary forms which, as time goes by, are expected to develop in the hands of separate officers into the customary Canadian parliamentary patterns. Some day there will no doubt be a lieutenant-governor, a speaker, and party divisions, with a government, a premier, cabinet ministers heading departments, and an official opposition.

The council includes among its appointed members a deputy commissioner who sometimes deputizes for the commissioner in council debates, and takes the chair, as do other council members, when the council is sitting in committee of the whole. In day-to-day administration his responsibilities are much more precise and important. He has the commissioner's authority to act under countless territorial ordinances and regulations – a system that was all the more necessary when the commissioner himself carried other burdensome offices that often kept him far away from affairs of the Northwest Territories.

From its earliest days until 1963, the council's appointed membership included civil servants other than the deputy commissioner. In fact, until the appointment of the first territorial resident to the council, all the members were public servants, generally officers of departments with extensive northern experience and interests. The pattern was broken when two public servants retired to private life but retained their legislative appointments. One was C. M. Drury, who resigned as Deputy Minister of National Defence in 1955 but was not replaced in the council by his successor in the public service. When the Commissioner of the R.C.M.P. resigned his office in 1960, following a difference of opinion with the federal government, he stayed on the territorial council. When eventually he retired from the council, he was not replaced by a representative of the force.

Gradually, therefore, the role of civil servants in the council diminished. When the appointments to the new council of 1964 were announced, the only civil servants left were the commissioner and the deputy commissioner. The appointed members included two businessmen, a labour leader, and an academic. The elected members in that council were all northern businessmen, active or retired.

If one thinks in terms of a power struggle between local residents and an overpowering Ottawa government, one might expect that the council would find itself constantly dividing between appointed and elected members. In practice, there is no such line between members. In the history of council debates and divisions, there are few instances of divisions along the lines of appointed versus elected members, let alone a continuing cleavage. The explanation is to be found partly in the calibre of all the council members, partly in the consciousness of the appointed members of their peculiar responsibilities for representing the will of northerners. Appointed members have also tended to take a special interest in those vast areas of the Northwest Territories that were not directly represented by elected members until 1966, the four older constituencies all being in the relatively populous Mackenzie District.

The system of appointed members is not accepted as a permanently desirable northern institution. To many northerners, the existence of appointed members in a legislative body has a tinge of colonialism which should be ended as a necessary early step in constitutional development. They have been reassured by the gradual disappearance of civil servants from the legislative body.

This was not the view of the elected members of the council itself. Between the late 1950s and 1962 the council engaged in long deliberations about the future of the Territories, culminating in a major resolution to the federal government. The council then voted unanimously in favour of keeping appointed members, at least until the electorate was broad enough to produce legislators of many different callings and backgrounds who could manage the increasingly big business of territorial government.

The council is served by a secretary and a legal adviser. Like most of the territorial administrators, these officers have been supplied and paid by the federal government. The council has frequently called upon the resources of the federal administration to prepare papers and draft legislation.

The scope of the council of the Northwest Territories is as wide as that of any provincial government: the division of functions between federal and provincial authorities as defined by the Canadian constitution applies to northern as much as to southern Canada.

The powers of the territorial government are, however, different from those of any province. The federal government did not turn over to Alberta and Saskatchewan ownership of their natural resources when they became provinces in 1905; in fact, the transfer was delayed twenty-five years. That transfer has not taken place in the Northwest Territories or the Yukon. Except for specific grants in communities, Crown land is in the title of Ottawa, which also retains responsibility for surface and sub-surface minerals, including oil. The expenditures relating to these resources still far exceed their revenues to the government. Unlike the provinces, the territories can borrow money only with the permission of the federal government. These are the only legal distinctions in powers between the provinces and the territories.

In practice, there are other differences. The minister certainly exercises a greater control and influence over the commissioner than the federal government lets any provincial lieutenant-governor have over a premier. The constitutional responsibility of the federal government for Indian and Eskimo affairs gives it a large stake in operations in such provincial fields as education and welfare. Finally, the fact that the Northwest Territories is overwhelmingly financed by the federal government with funds raised from federal taxpayers gives the federal government an active voice and responsibility.

Those who look at constitutional development in the North in terms of Canadian colonial history or of American struggles for statehood are in danger of being gravely misled. There are northern voices in favour of immediate provincial status, but they are few. While it is universally accepted that provincial status is desirable as soon as either territory has the resources to sustain it, there is an almost equal realization that the granting of provincial status too quickly would slow northern development. The northern territories would then lose their special position, involving heavy investment of national public funds, and be on the same bargaining basis as any other province. That would not be an enviable position, when the revenues are so small and the development needs, through sheer geography, so staggering. Public statements by leaders of succeeding governments have indicated federal desire to create Canada's eleventh and twelfth provinces just as soon as possible. The timetable remains as uncertain as the success of the search for rocks and oil beneath the ground, and the availability of men to develop and to buy them.

Certainly, federal government in the first half of the century could be faulted for the paucity of its northern investment. In more recent years the picture of a forgotten colony and an Ottawa colonial office reluctant to cast off the bonds of servitude has not stood up to scrutiny. When the old battle-cries of Canadian history have been voiced anew to make a case for more rapid political development, one target for complaint has been the partially appointed council. It is worth remembering that the proposal for a fully elective body was made by the Ottawa-resident commissioner and appointed members in 1960, and rejected by the elected territorial representatives. If there has ever been a struggle between grass-roots democracy and appointed legislators, the debates of the territorial council have concealed it. Perhaps it would be better to have a fully elected council with non-voting advisers, as some have suggested: it is not vested interests that have stood in its way, but federal caution in moving without the clearly expressed will of northerners.

How difficult the federal government has found it to foster political development to accompany the huge expansion of social and economic services was illustrated in the debate on the proposed division of the Northwest Territories. Most students of Canadian history had assumed that the sprawling Territories, which had been split so often as sections of them became ready for greater self-government, would be split again to permit the faster growth of its more populous part. The idea of a separate Mackenzie Territory had long been discussed. The assumption was that, like the Yukon Territory in 1898, it would be split off with a government and administration of its own to operate independently of the much less developed Eastern Arctic. By 1958 the idea was being actively discussed in the council of the Northwest Territories; the debate continued over several sessions in the Mackenzie and the Eastern Arctic, as well as in its Ottawa meetings. In fact, it was the first time in Canadian history that the political division of the frontier had been subjected to prolonged debate by legislators, instead of being a matter of federal administrative decree. By an informal form of plebiscite, the people of the Eastern Arctic were asked to choose a new name for the residual part of the Northwest Territories; a name that would obviate geographical contradiction when applied to the Eastern Arctic. The Eskimos chose 'Nunassiaq', the beautiful land.

The council recommended the creation of a Mackenzie Territory and a Nunassiaq Territory. The proposals of the administration on some vital points were not accepted, notably the boundaries of the units and the elective principle in the Mackenzie council. Whether the decision of the council would be proved right or wrong, the legislators showed a healthy independence of the administration and neatly disproved allegations that the mid-twentieth-century adjustment in the Northwest Territories was a sinister design of an Ottawa administration foisted on the legislative representatives of the North. The two territories recommended by the council would have differing forms of government and administration reflecting their differing stages of development.

The federal government prepared the necessary legislation, but before it could be introduced into the House of Commons there was a change of federal government. The new administration proceeded with the bills inherited from its predecessors. Both in the House of Commons and in committee, the legislation was vigorously criticized by the new opposition – which had prepared it while in power a few months before. Then there was a territorial election resulting in a substantially new council which asked that the legislation be held in abeyance until it could re-examine the proposals. The next chapter was a further council recommendation in late 1964 for a federal commission of inquiry to consider many aspects of the future of the Northwest Territories – a request to which, in modified form, the federal government acceded the following spring.

The Carrothers Commission Report was published in the fall of 1966. Its recommendation establishing Yellowknife as the capital and residence of the commissioner was endorsed by the territorial government and accepted by the federal government a few weeks later. The Commission opposed any further division of the Northwest Territories. It made a number of recommendations for economic growth and administrative autonomy which were generally accepted by the federal government.

Meanwhile, the government of the Northwest Territories tackled its responsibilities with unprecedented activity. The creation of the office of commissioner separate from other competing responsibilities gave more opportunity for the development of new legislative programs, and it usefully emphasized the role of the Northwest Territories as one of Canada's political entities. Gradually and quietly it had acquired some of the symbols of provinciality in its parliamentary forms, in its coat of arms, and in its relations with federal and provincial agencies. In 1967 the territorial government managed a budget of nearly $14 million, most of which was provided by the federal taxpayers. The territorial government got its money not only from its own sources, such as liquor revenue, licences, and fuel taxes, but from the federal government with which it negotiates five-year financial agreements. Although ultimately the federal government thus pays a high proportion of the bills of the Northwest Territories, it does so by providing a five-year pot of money which gives the Territories a good deal of authority and flexibility in spending the funds it is given. The territorial government's authority or influence extends beyond the management of this budget. In areas where it lacks constitutional authority, notably Eskimo and Indian affairs, it does not legislate, but it may pass resolutions to the federal government which have carried a good deal of weight. It has also served as a strong pressure group urging major federal expenditures on roads and other investments relating to resource development.

The British North America Act itself raises some interesting questions about the relations of territorial and federal governments. Education, for example, is a clearly provincial prerogative, and therefore a territorial one. Should a territorial government have complete freedom in this field, it could enter into substantial commitments which would ultimately not be financed by the Territories at all, but by the federal government. An instance was the decision of the territorial government, without prior federal consultation, to provide virtually free university education through a scheme more advanced than any known elsewhere in Canada. The initial cost was modest enough, but as the educational level rises each year, the future commitment may be great. Legally, the federal government could have vetoed, or simply ham-strung, the plan before it started. It did not do so. The case provided an interesting example of the power of the territorial government over money, most of which it did not have to raise. Other provinces might envy its position. Commoner examples of the capacity of the territorial government to commit the federal government to spending are in a host of minor laws and regulations applying to all residents of the territories. With roughly 60 per cent of the population of the Territories classified as Indian or Eskimo, and therefore a responsibility of the federal government under the constitution, territorial laws can involve commitments by the federal authorities. The same situation is true to some extent in any province. In the North, where the proportion of native population is highest, the degree of federal involvement is far greater.

As long as funds for northern administration and development are voted by the Parliament of Canada to the appropriate minister, he must be responsible to Parliament for the prudent use of that money. There is a limit in the extent to which he can turn over those funds to another government and surrender control over their use. The proper degree of delegation to the territorial government is part of complex Canadian political science. Meanwhile, the answers to questions of growing territorial autonomy are not to be found in the misapplied slogans of Canada's colonial days.

Without awaiting a new balance of fiscal power born of northern prosperity, the Northwest Territories will advance towards independence through the creation of its own administration. Although by the 1960s most of the federally provided civil service for the North was living in the field, it was a system with complications. The civil servant, when concerned with welfare, operated under the laws of the Northwest Territories and under the policy directions of the commissioner; but when work concerned Eskimos, the civil servant's line of direction was less clear. Eskimos must be governed by the laws of the territory where they live, but development programs for Eskimos are a federal matter. While the Northern Administration Branch, which provided much of the northern civil service, is part of a federal department and responsible to its deputy minister, it also receives directions from the territorial government. At each session of the territorial council, members of the branch appear as witnesses to report on their stewardship.

Change is needed. Though there was logic in the federal operation of the northern administration in the earlier days of passive development, and though there are still real advantages in using all the resources of the federal administration, the Northwest Territories cannot be self-sufficient without its own workers directly under its own control to carry out its own wishes. Succeeding territorial governments have usually been generous in their praise of the work of federal employees, but this is no substitute for staff on a direct territorial payroll. The Northwest Territories has, in fact, long had a small civil service of its own, operating the territorial liquor stores. Other employees were later added for hospital insurance, physical fitness, and archives. The major shift from a predominantly federal administration to a territorial administration remains to be accomplished.

Political development in the North has advanced not only at the territorial level. To promote local government, the Northwest Territories has devised five different stages through which settlements can pass so that the power of local decision-making can match the willingness and ability of local people to take responsibility for their own affairs. Most northern communities are at the stage of unorganized settlements. The beginnings of local government are commonly found in the community council or residents' association. Where there is a resident administrator these groups have been more active. Their vitality varies from place to place and from year to year, but one pattern can be found: where the local people have some decision-making power and are not merely vague advisers the council tends to work relatively well. Where there are community halls or curling rinks to be built or managed, the job brings people together in an important exercise in community development. This process was accelerated in 1964 when the federal government made available a $100,000 Community Development Fund to be spent at the instance of arctic community councils, with only the loosest kind of control from the administration. As well as paying for a host of small community projects, the fund added scope to local decision-making on which local government could grow.

In the development area, as in the unorganized settlement, no local taxes are raised. The powers of the advisory council are limited, but with the authority of the commissioner it is possible to enforce local regulations. For example, in an unorganized settlement, the people might be interested in a project to develop certain land for local recreation, but there is nothing to prevent anti-social citizens from using it as a dump. Regulations in a development area could help the local will prevail by ensuring the intended recreational use of the land. A bold regulation in the development area of Inuvik provided penalties for cutting down trees; as a consequence this is the only community on the edge of the tree-line which has not been swept clear of the attractive but painfully slow-growing bush which usually ends up in local stoves.

In the local improvement district, modest land taxes are collected. The local council does not have legal control over the tax revenue, but in practice its advice is generally taken, not only in the spending of locally-raised funds, but in projects of senior governments in the district.

The village is a more formal kind of local government. The council has six members, three appointed by the commissioner and three elected. It has control of its own budget, and can borrow money, subject to the approval of the commissioner. A village is generally expected to raise more of its own funds than the earlier stages of local government, though the mill rate is not necessarily higher than in a local improvement district. Village status began only in 1963; in 1966 Fort Smith was the only village in the Northwest Territories.

The final phase of local government is the town, which has a mayor and a fully elected council of eight members. The town government takes full responsibility for town planning, municipal development, and all local services, though it is financially assisted by senior governments. Yellowknife and Hay River have town governments.

In the realm of federal government, all adult residents of the Northwest Territories have won the federal vote. The Northwest Territories lagged far behind the Yukon in getting a representative in the House of Commons. The first device used to meet the electoral aspirations of the Mackenzie residents was to enlarge the Yukon constituency to embrace most of the Mackenzie District, in 1947. Five years later, when a new constituency of the Mackenzie was created, the first member was M. A. Hardie. One of the most engaging political tales of the time concerns a visiting governor-general who was approached by a northerner interested in the political vistas opened by enfranchisement. 'I want your advice,' the latter said. 'I think I'll run for Parliament, but I don't know which party to run for.' 'Sir,' His Excellency is said to have replied, 'you have just asked the one man in Canada who cannot advise you in that respect.'

The new constituency still left nearly a million square miles of Canada unenfranchised because of the administrative difficulties of conducting balloting in remote arctic areas. The omission irritated articulate northerners, who occasionally wrote vigorous letters declining to pay their income tax until represented in Parliament. The lack of a federal vote for any qualified citizen was a blot on the political map of Canada which was finally removed in 1962.

The imperfections in electoral representation applied to territorial elections until 1966. It is worth noting that when anyone has lacked a vote, territorial or federal, it has been for regional rather than racial reasons. Eskimos and northern Indians have always had the same federal voting privileges as their neighbours. Eskimos in Arctic Quebec were voting before residents of any race were casting their ballots in the Mackenzie valley or Baffin Island.

The Yukon. The story of political development in the Yukon is simpler, for it leap-frogged over many stages through which the Northwest Territories passed. The Yukon, which had been made a provisional district of the Northwest Territories in 1895, was made a separate territory by Act of Parliament on June 13, 1898, a prompt reaction to the sudden pressures of the gold rush.

Under the original Yukon Territory Act, the government consisted of a commissioner and an appointed council of not more than six members. The next year, an amendment provided seven members of whom two would be elected, and in 1905 three more elected members were added to bring the total to ten. In 1908, long after the gold rush was over, there was enough confidence in the Yukon's future to alter its form of government again. The council was now made wholly elective. To parallel the constitutional growth of the Northwest Territories and the provinces that had been carved from it, a speaker was provided from the council, a provision absent in the present-day Northwest Territories.

The creation of the office of speaker set the Yukon on a course of constitutional development differing from the latter-day Northwest Territories, where the commissioner performs the role of speaker, as well as of premier and lieutenant-governor. In the Yukon, the council began to sit separately from the commissioner. The Yukon's system of government has more in common with the American idea of the separation of powers than with any other legislature in this country.

The Yukon's political forms soon proved out of step with its economic development. As the long doldrums set in, the territory seemed in danger of losing its elected legislature. In 1918 the Governor-in-Council was given the power to abolish the council and substitute two appointed advisers. Instead, the ten-member council was replaced the following year by an elected council of three members which survived thin times until the Yukon started again on its upward path during the Second World War. In 1951 the elected council was increased to five members, and in 1960 to seven members.

The character of government has been noticeably different in the Yukon Territory and in the Northwest Territories. In Whitehorse, Ottawa influence has been weaker. This is not particularly a factor of distance: psychologically, central Canada seems farther from the Yukon, whose contacts with the outside are more often with the Pacific coast than with the prairie provinces or eastern Canada. Ottawa has been the seat of government for the Northwest Territories, and the commissioner, by the personal prestige of his position in the federal hierarchy, as well as by his place in council, has had a strong role in all legislative debates. In the Yukon, the commissioner operates the administration. His relations with the council have ranged from hostile to correct and even cordial, depending in part upon personalities of the time. Never did he have quite the commanding role in the council chamber that his Northwest Territories contemporary generally assumed.

Suspicion of Ottawa has been a venerable rallying-cry for Yukoners, though Ottawa has had relatively little to do with the administration of most Yukon affairs. From its earliest history, the Yukon has run its own show with a completely separate territorial civil service carrying out territorial functions. The commissioner is a federal employee, but the only federal members of his staff are those managing resources such as land, mining, and forestry. Ottawa uses the territorial administration as its agent for engineering projects, an interesting switch on the Northwest Territories, which has employed the central administration for a host of territorial functions. Ottawa's hand is mainly felt in the federal-territorial financial agreements which provide the major basis of the Yukon's financing, and in expenditures for roads and other forms of resource development. Ottawa has spent much more money for roads in the Yukon than in the Northwest Territories.

One thing the Yukon council wants is greater control over the administration. A system of cabinet government is some time off. There are no party distinctions in the Yukon council, and even if there were parties controlling the territorial government and serving as the opposition, the council itself is too small to permit the usual kind of cabinet government. It is generally assumed that any significant growth in that council will have to await growth in the Yukon's population and economy.

In 1960 two major changes were made in the Yukon Act. The section prohibiting the commissioner from sitting with the council was repealed. He does not preside over the council, as in the Northwest Territories, but he may sit with it. This arrangement makes it easier for him to advise and inform legislators, and brings legislature and executive closer together. The second change created an advisory committee on finance of three council members nominated by the council. The commissioner was to consult the committee on the preparation of his estimates, but the method and extent of consultation were left undefined.

There were vain hopes that detailed examination of estimates by a delegated committee would relieve the council itself of a painfully slow process. The advisory committee, whose membership rotates each year, does give council members a chance for more detailed understanding of the administration both in the Yukon and in Ottawa, which it visits each year in company with the commissioner.

The Yukon has long since achieved the independence and local authority toward which the Northwest Territories is now driving. There is talk in Whitehorse of provincial status and of the need for major mining developments to bring in new wealth and people.

The Yukon has had no struggles over the right to federal parliamentary representation. The Yukon has had its own member since it was first created as a constituency in 1902 and, except for the short period from 1947 to 1952, that member has represented the Yukon alone. In the ratio of constituents to members, the Yukon has done well.

Some Canadians refuse to think of the political growth of the Yukon and the Northwest Territories only in terms of evolving local governments. The alternative is union with the provinces, the elimination of the two territories entirely through the extension of provincial boundaries north to the arctic seas.

This proposal has appeared in occasional public speeches and newspaper editorials since the 1920s. In 1937 Premier T. D. Pattullo of British Columbia suggested the extension of the eastern boundary of his province northwards to the Arctic Ocean, which would give him all of the Yukon and most of the Mackenzie valley. Alberta would have none of this. 'The Mackenzie Valley is already annexed to the province of Alberta geographically and commercially,' proclaimed the Edmonton *Bulletin* of April 14, 1938. The following March, a resolution of the Alberta legislature called for the extension of the province's boundaries northwards to the Arctic Ocean. After the war such provincial dreams were revived from time to time, with no noticeable support from the North. Northerners, with their own wry sense of humour, answered these claims by proposing the incorporation of northern parts of adjacent provinces into the territories.

In 1964 the proposal for provincial expansion northwards was made more seriously than ever before. The occasion was the Whitehorse meeting of the government heads of the Yukon, Alaska, and British Columbia. Premier W. A. C. Bennett of British Columbia made this an opportunity for a warm invitation to the Yukon to join his province. Yukoners showed keen interest, but newspaper polls a week or two later indicated that they were still reluctant to give up their identity.

The proposals may well continue to be made, but they are unlikely to be accepted. Alternatives to Ottawa rule do not seem so desperately needed, as Ottawa delegates its responsibilities increasingly to the North. As the reins of one absentee landlord are loosening, it is unlikely that northerners would wish to seek another senior partner. There is also a question of the attitude of other provinces. Saskatchewan and Manitoba have occasionally talked wistfully of expansion to the north, though perhaps with less zeal than their western neighbours. The provinces that have nowhere north to expand, except to the sea, might resent this upset in the balance of Candian federation. In any event, the interest of the provinces in northern imperial dreams is flattering to the North, and an indicator of confidence that northern wealth cannot now be far away.

14 | Science, Literature, and the Arts

Science. The history of scientific endeavour in the North reaches back as far as the records of northern travellers. With the possible exception of the whalers whose purposes were frankly commercial, and whose knowledge was jealously guarded, virtually all expeditions to the North until the last century were at least partly scientific. Their first concern was knowledge that would facilitate travel — mapping, sounding, meteorology, and the study of ice. Research into the land and the people who lived there generally came later.

By the late nineteenth century, scientific interest in the Far North had broadened to include fields of investigation more remote from the immediate purposes of transportation. Though many had already written of the native peoples and their customs, Franz Boas was the first scientist to journey north specifically for anthropological investigation. Vilhjalmur Stefansson and Diamond Jenness established a tradition that was to enrich northern anthropology and sociology. Knud Rasmussen left in the records of the Fifth Thule Expedition a towering monument to early scholarship in northern social science. The work was carried on by Tom Manning and Graham Rowley who, like the pioneers, were totally absorbed in the life of the country.

The voyages of the Eastern Arctic Patrol following the First World War provided a floating base for itinerant scientists of many disciplines. But these journeys brought a diminishing return by mid century; everything within range of the ship's brief ports of call had been seen and noted. Serious scientific work required longer sojourns and expensive transportation. One of the contributions of the Royal Canadian Air Force in the earlier days of arctic development was to provide transportation to many a shoe-string research project. Though the development of civil aviation spurred the opening of the North, the scientist could only regret the loss of government planes for free transportation, to stretch his limited budget.

Everyone concerned with northern development agrees that Canada's investment in northern research today is sadly inadequate. Though the tempo has obviously quickened in terms of northern expeditions and of southern agencies involved, the work is pitifully short of the need. Northern research is both applied, in the sense that it seeks practical ways of opening up and living in the North, and pure, in the sense that the North is a laboratory for research of broader application. In terms of need, it is more relevant to the average scientist that a third of Canada is in the North, than that only one-fifth of one per cent of the population lives there. In terms of resources, the northern scientist, like the industrialist, finds that the effort and the cost are great, but that the returns seem at least commensurate.

Government, industry, universities, and private foundations are engaged in northern research. The efforts of the wide range of government departments concerned with scientific work in the North are co-ordinated by the Northern Research and Co-ordination Centre of the Department of Northern Affairs, which also provides liaison with universities and private research institutes. It also has funds for direct sponsorship of research projects, notably in the social sciences, and for general assistance to academic work in the North. Since 1962 the centre has paid out about $500,000 in grants to universities and scientific expeditions. It also supports scientists through contracts to the extent of about $25,000 a year. The money is far short of what the universities would like, but the program has the twin advantages of immediate results from specific projects, and a longer-range interest on the part of many universities which a few years ago had no departments showing any interest in research above the sixtieth parallel.

Most of the projects undertaken by the centre are linked with the needs of the administration, and the administration itself commissions considerable applied research. Its most ambitious continuing investigation has been in resource surveys, and there are many minor contracts for operational research into such subjects as hostel management or curriculum development. The centre operates one permanent scientific station in the North. The laboratory, opened at Inuvik in 1963, serves as a base for scientists in the Western Arctic. Laboratories and a library have been established to provide support for the widest possible range of disciplines.

The Department of Agriculture has two northern experimental farms, at Haines Junction a hundred miles north of Whitehorse, and at Fort Simpson, though its research projects range far beyond these permanent stations. The Department of Transport's meteorological stations provide a base for scientific work in other fields besides meteorology; the Dominion Observatory has staff working on continuing magnetic observations, for example; and the National Research Council has put magnetic equipment where Department of Transport employees can read and maintain it. When intermediate sites of the DEW Line were declared obsolete in 1963, some of them were made available for the use of scientists. All these permanent posts, while extremely useful for occasional specific tasks, have a limited value for northern science in general, since they do not happen to be where scientists want to go.

The northern scientific work of all government departments ranges from the National Research Council's work in the upper atmosphere to the Fisheries Research Board's continuing investigations under the surface of the seas. It involves the mapping of the land and the bottom of the ocean, the collecting of insects, the analysis of glaciers, pure physics, the design of underwear, town planning, and linguistics. The scientific work has included an impressive series of co-ordinated projects involving many disciplines, such as the programs of the International Geophysical Year in 1957-8. One of the I.G.Y. projects, on Lake Hazen in the centre of northern Ellesmere Island's mountain ranges, continued until 1961 as a base for major studies in glaciology, meteorology, geology, and archaeology. The Polar Continental Shelf Project, which began in 1959, is an ambitious scientific program; ranging far and wide by surface and air, its purpose is to discover every detail of the continental shelf stretching a hundred miles outwards from the arctic islands and of the islands themselves and the channels between them. The McGill-Jacobsen Expedition began about the same time, as an intensive study of the physical sciences on Axel Heiberg Island.

In addition, the University of Alberta focuses its northern work in the Boreal Institute which brings together many disciplines in a co-ordinated program of northern research. The University of Saskatchewan has an Institute of Northern Studies whose interest in the physical sciences in the northern part of the province also extends into the Northwest Territories. Le Centre d'Etudes Nordiques at Laval University has emphasized research in northern Quebec. The University of British Columbia and the University of Toronto, while not formalizing the direction of their northern work in any institute, have contributed many scholars to scientific research in the Northwest Territories, the Yukon Territory, and Arctic Quebec.

Literature. The literature of the Canadian North has an impressive catalogue, but little of it was written by its permanent citizens. It is almost entirely the product of white men who went north as visitors to a strange land. When they returned, the most reticent of men sometimes found themselves caught by an overpowering compulsion to write. From the pens of the least gifted came some moving tales of majestic simplicity. Once away from the influence of the North they never wrote again.

Almost every expedition to explore the North produced its journals. These began with the odysseys of the Vikings, who gripped the imagination as much by what they left unsaid as by what they recorded. This was in fact the earliest Canadian literature of all, and later generations owe a seldom-voiced tribute to these literate travellers who paused to write in the midst of their strange adventurings. Fortunately, Sir Martin Frobisher had his chroniclers who set down more than the path of his voyage and the strange phenomena of man and nature that he met: through four centuries is preserved the spirit of anxiety of men confronted with forces desperately beyond their control – a feeling familiar to those who know the unchanging seas of the modern Arctic:

> Being thus encompassed with danger on every side, sundry men with sundry devices sought the best way to save themselves. Some of the ships, where they could find a place more clear of ice, and get a little berth of sea room, did take in their sails and there lay adrift. Others fastened and moored anchor upon a great island of ice, and rode under the lee thereof. And again some were so fast shut up and encompassed that they were fain to submit themselves and their ships to the mercy of the unmerciful ice. These crews strengthened the sides of their ships with chunks of cables, beds, masts, planks, and such like, which being hanged overboard on the sides of their ships, might the better defend them from the outrageous sway and strokes of the said ice. Some other men, having spikes, pieces of timber, and oars in their hands, stood by almost all day and all night, without any rest, bearing off the force and breaking the sway of the ice, with such incredible pain and peril it was wonderful to behold; which ice otherwise had no doubt quite stricken quite through and through the sides of their ships. And yet many of the ships, even those of greatest burdens, were heaved up between islands of ice a foot out of the sea above their watermarks, having their knees and timbers within board both bowed and broken therewith.
>
> Amidst these extremities, whilst some laboured for defence of the ships and sought to save their bodies, others of more milder spirits sought to save the soul by devout prayer and mediation to the Almighty.

So wrote George Beste, Frobisher's second-in-command. He might have been speaking for a host of unchronicled voyages into the mysteries of the Arctic.

In the tortured journal of Jens Munk there is an awful pathos, born not merely of the catalogue of death and destruction, but of the simple acceptance of the incomprehensible forces confronting man in his early arctic probings.

On June 4th which was Whitsunday [1620], there remained only three alive, besides myself [Munk wrote, at what seemed the climax of the terrible ordeal of that dread winter at the mouth of the Churchill River]. All lying down unable to help one another. The stomach was ready enough, and had appetite for food, but the teeth would not allow it. The cook's boy lay dead beside my berth, and three men on the steerage. Two of the living were on shore, and would gladly have been back on ship but it was impossible for them to get there as they had not sufficient strength. We had now, for four days, had nothing for the sustenance of the body. Accordingly I did not now hope for anything but that God would put an end to thise my misery; and thinking that it would have been the last I wrote in this world, I penned as follows: 'Inasmuch as I have now no more hope of life in this world, I request for the sake of God, if any Christian men should happen to come here, that they will bury in the earth my poor body, together with the others which are found here, expecting their reward from God in Heaven. And, furthermore, that this, my journal, may be forwarded to my most gracious Lord and King (for every word that is found herein is altogether truthful) in order that my poor wife and children may obtain some benefit from my great distress and miserable death. Herewith, goodnight to all the world; and my soul into the hand of God.'

Jens Munk lived to serve his king in glory, but never again to record the ebbing of life on the dark side of the moon. Others who followed sometimes wrote not in despair but in triumph, or in simple chronicling of days that passed. Each precious journal was read and re-read by those who followed in their wake, for the crumbs of arctic knowledge were then so few. Today, their fragments of fact are long since outrun by the accumulated data of science. Their stories have more than the excitement of early adventure: they have a quality of disciplined emotion that makes them among the most rewarding of literature to emerge from any Canadian frontier from the sixteenth to the late twentieth century.

The journals of the early explorers did not suffer from contemporary indifference. Arctic literature of centuries ago apparently had its ready market. Not surprisingly, the journals had an enormous influence in shaping men's minds about the nature of northern Canada. Captain Lyon was one of the most influential of all. His highly literate descriptions of Eskimo life a century and a quarter ago, illustrated with drawings of great competence and sensitivity, make one wonder how many sailors or merchants of today are schooled to achieve such elegance on the printed page. Captain Lyon's journals formed the basis of the popular, sympathetic notions of the Eskimo that crept into English, and later North American, school books. The romanticizing of Eskimo ways that has persisted through the changing realities of their modern life can be traced in large part back to Lyon's journal. The Indians had no such image-makers, and this is reflected in the ethnic patterns of modern Canadian life.

In nearly all the arctic books in the three centuries following Frobisher there runs the thread of superhuman determination, of terrible struggle, of frozen fear. The Canadian North was unbelievably harsh to those early mariners in their ill-equipped venturings. It was no wonder that in their every waking hour they thought of the ice and the cold and the forsaken loneliness. If, on the other hand, Eskimos had been writing books at the same time, it is a reasonable guess that they would have said far less about the climate and the odds of nature. They had mastered this environment, but the white man had not.

When the white man began to come to terms with the Far North, the legend of the virtual invincibility of Nature still persisted. Those who survived the experience were heroes. This attitude can still occasionally be found among those who have served a year or two amid the hot and cold running water of modern arctic suburbia.

It was not always the fault of the writer that the travails of the Arctic were overplayed. Publishers wanted to sell their books. Many wrote to help raise funds for their particular northern calling, and any false modesty about northern experience would hardly help the cause. For these and other reasons, the North got the name of being a rather nasty place – much more so than it has deserved in modern times. Vilhjalmur Stefansson was the iconoclast who felt his mission was to smash this outworn image, and replace it by the concept of the friendly Arctic. He earned the far from friendly comment of many of his arctic contemporaries for doing so. Quite apart from his scientific contribution, Stefansson thus started a new literary trend which helped balance the picture of northern life.

Not everyone was his disciple. The era of the northern newspaperman began in 1921 with the Mackenzie oil rush. Some of these writers were astonished to find long, hot summer days instead of igloos, lush vegetation instead of ice-floes, mosquitoes instead of polar bears. But the past died hard; in the finest traditions of the circulation office, their stories included hair-raising tales of the hardships of the wintry North they never saw. Martin Frobisher would have smiled.

The Yukon was far from the literate sea captains of old, and its early literature is relatively thin and prosaic. It made up for this deficiency in one vivid explosion of verse from a poet laureate who penetrated men's emotions the world over with his extrovert love of the growing legend of the Klondike.

> There are strange things done in the midnight sun
> By the men who moil for gold. . . .

Not the least of the strange things was the poetry of Robert Service himself. He was in California when the rush began. While people all around him were caught by the frenzy, he remained indifferent to the spell of the Yukon, and drifted south towards Mexico from job to job, guitar in hand. The rush was really over when he made his way to Whitehorse, where he served as a bank teller. He wrote his first poems there, long before he had ever set eyes on the Klondike. He did not even bother going to Dawson City until the bank posted him there in 1908. Before he arrived, all his best-known verse had been written. He left the Klondike in 1912, and never returned.

Sam McGee was a real person, and his cabin still stands in Whitehorse. He never forgave Service for immortalizing him through his celebrated cremation. Other characters, such as the lady that's known as Lou, became as real as the Malemute Saloon, and many is the old-timer who will recall with conviction being present at the famous shooting. But if people like Lou and Dan McGrew never existed, they should have. Robert Service was right to remedy the Creator's oversight.

Gold was not the only bonanza from the Klondike. More than a hundred books have been written about Canada's most traumatic frontier experience. A few of them are very good indeed; but some writers made the error of exaggerating a phenomenon whose strangeness needed no imaginative embellishment. In every old-timer who survived the long quiet years to live half by the creeks, half in the Sunset Home, there is an unwritten book. No sourdough is really satisfied with any book that anyone else has done.

The gold rush produced more than prose and poetry. It was one of the first events of international importance after the portable camera became popular. Pictures by the thousands were taken, and most were lost. The emulsion was wiped from countless precious plates to provide window-glass for log-cabins in those thin days when the rush was over. Other plates were simply abandoned and destroyed by weather and time. Still, many hundreds of pictures remain to provide a further proof, where words might fail, that it all really happened.

The twentieth century has produced no such stimulus to literature anywhere in the North. Nevertheless, the shelves have quickly filled. Besides the growing volume of scientific record, a considerable literature of personal reminiscence of the 'I Lived in an Igloo' school of varying literary merit has accumulated. The work of Farley Mowat has, to say the least, been controversial. Although his evalutions have been vigorously questioned, his infinite capacity for moral indignation and his sensitivity to the mood of the Arctic undoubtedly enabled him to produce some of the modern North's finest writing. Most reporters from Outside have gone too rarely or stayed too briefly to develop perspective, let alone any sense of what the North is all about. Bob Hill of the *Edmonton Journal*, the first southern reporter to have the North as a full-time beat, was a pioneering exception.

The North has produced an impressive group of publications. Whitehorse has two newspapers, and gave to Canadian journalism Harry Boyle, who had the flair to be the North's Bob Edwards but disappointed readers by leaving newspaper work for radio. Yellowknife, Fort Smith, and Hay River also published newspapers of refreshing vitality. Outside the North, the Hudson's Bay Company's quarterly, *Beaver*, and the Department of Northern Affairs' *North* chronicle the past and present of the North.

The literature of the North is almost all in English. Though there has been little conscious fiction in English, the relatively limited French literature section includes one novel of consequence, *Agaguk* by Yves Thériault. Almost the only writing by Indians has been in English, notably reminiscences by John Tetso of Fort Simpson. The first major work by an Eskimo was an autobiography entitled *I, Nuligak*, published in English translation in 1966.

Until about the beginning of the present century, the Eskimos had no means of writing anything. The syllabic system of writing devised by the Reverend James Evans for the Cree Indians and adapted for the Eskimos by the Reverend E. J. Peck was a tremendous boon at the time for those it reached. It was easy to learn and provided a rapid means of communication for an illiterate population. Over a longer period, it has many limitations. Being based on a representation of sounds, it has the disadvantage of imprecision. A group of symbols may stand for up to half a dozen different words, with only the context to give the correct meaning. The use of added symbols or superscripts would clarify the writer's intention but would create more complications in the writing itself and reduce the advantages of speed. Though easy to master, syllabics are difficult to reproduce, not only because the symbols are often mistaken one for another when written without care, but because there are so few machines to reproduce them. Typewriters with syllabic keys are scarce and expensive; linotype in syllabics is non-existent. Syllabic writing in book form is therefore expensive to produce for a small market.

A more fundamental objection to the syllabic system of writing is that it created an orthographic island among the Eskimo people who are already too small in numbers to afford such divisions in their culture. While the syllabic system of writing spread around Hudson Bay and the Eastern Arctic, Eskimos of the Western Arctic and of Labrador picked up a system of writing in Roman characters. Eskimos in Greenland and Alaska also use Roman letters. As a consequence, an Eskimo of the west coast of Hudson Bay, for example, cannot write a letter to a friend near the Mackenzie Delta. He cannot read what a Labrador Eskimo has written, and he has no access to the quite considerable Eskimo literature produced in Greenland.

The Department of Northern Affairs, not long after it was formed, began an ambitious program to strengthen Eskimo culture. The department was convinced that Eskimo culture might die unless the Eskimo language could be written in a standard form in which all Eskimos could communicate, and in which a truly Eskimo literature could survive and flourish. This would have to be a simple but exact system of Roman characters, partly because of the problems of printing, and partly because Roman characters are already used in the world's major Eskimo literature, in Greenland.

The new standard orthography for Eskimos was the product of many minds and prolonged research. Chiefly responsible for devising it was Dr. Gilles Lefèbvre. The work of elaborating it and adapting it to the needs of various dialects was done by Alex Spalding and an able corps of Eskimo assistants under the direction of Raymond C. Gagné.

Northern Affairs decided to introduce the new orthography gradually so that the older generation would not feel the familiar syllabics slipping away in favour of a system of writing they might not wish to learn. Gradually documents were rendered in both systems of writing to give encouragement to the newer and to provide, incidentally, a means of absorbing it. The younger people, by learning and using the new system, are expected to find it easier to hold on to their language. The Eskimo response has generally been enthusiastic.

In Canada, almost the only written Eskimo literature by the mid twentieth century was religious, laboriously translated by scholars of the Anglican and Roman Catholic churches. Except for private letters, and some interesting verse, little was produced by the Eskimos themselves. In 1959 Northern Affairs began the first Eskimo periodical, a quarterly called *Inuktitut*, The Eskimo Way. It was edited and illustrated by Mary Panegoosho. All the contributions were from Eskimos. It was produced in a syllabic version as well as in Roman characters. Although it was not produced as regularly as its publishers hoped, it was a break-through which had a stimulating effect on the latent literary talent of the Eskimo people. It gave promise that Canadian Eskimos would produce as creatively as Greenlanders and contribute to a culture that could survive the onslaughts of modern civilization as well as the Welsh or Scottish have done.

Though perhaps outside the classification of Eskimo literature, a major work for Eskimos deserves mention. It is called *Qaujivaallirutissat*, or the 'Q-Book' for short. It traces its ancestry to a *Book of Wisdom* published by the Hudson's Bay Company in English and Eskimo in 1930 to give Eskimos some general idea of the wide world about them. The government followed it up after the Second World War with a series of pamphlets by the well-known Eskimo linguist Leo Manning, under the title *Eskimo Book of Wisdom*. It was of a more practical nature, and touched upon such subjects as public health and hygiene. The 'Q-Book' is much more ambitious than its predecessor. It is a sort of Eskimo encyclopaedia, or at least the first volume of one. Its three hundred large pages in English, Eskimo syllabics, and new Eskimo orthography, cover such broad subjects as civics, education, health, safety, care of equipment, and business. It is distributed free to all Eskimo families. Any major work in Eskimo has an immediately appreciative audience because of the paucity of materials in the language; this appears to be especially valued because of the wealth of material put together by the team of Eskimos and whites who worked two years to produce the book.

The Arts. If the literature of the North is overwhelmingly the creation of the new-comers, the significant arts are mainly the possession of the native people: such has been the critical and popular acclaim of the Eskimo arts that they have almost completely overshadowed the contributions of whites.

The chronology of northern art should not omit those same journals that form the core of northern literature. Not many of the journals were illustrated by more than meticulous cartography, but the engravings of Lieutenant Back, who accompanied the Franklin land expedition, and of Captain Lyon remain as faithful reproductions of a way of life long gone. In more modern times artists of repute in southern Canada were attracted by the possibilities of the

North. Oddly enough, in those days of apparent indifference and thin resources, the government of the Northwest Territories commissioned A. Y. Jackson to paint in the Mackenzie valley, just after the Second World War. He recorded the sombre Barrens and the brooding head-frames of the new mining industry. Even earlier, the restricted passenger list of the Eastern Arctic Patrol of 1927 included an artist who for a season took the place of a cinematographer. In later years the photographer was back and the painter disappeared, but Frederick Varley went to the Eastern Arctic in 1938, following Lawren Harris, whose canvas of Bylot Island is particularly well known.

Native arts in the North have a much longer and more exciting history than the works of the new-comers. Assessment of their accomplishments is troubled only by definitions. Ambitious men have tried to divide their work today into arts and crafts, starting with the simple proposition that the drawing or engraving hanging in the gallery is art, and the duffle slippers are crafts; the magnificent statuary of Inukpuk is art, and the trivial carving of some unknown and uninspired whittler is craft. As the line becomes finer, arts tend to be defined as what one is enthusiastic about, and crafts as what one likes less well. Long before this point, the wise man has abandoned both the classification and the definition.

And yet, by common consent, not only do the crafts – the tool-making, the weaponry – of northern people stretch back at least twenty-five hundred years: their arts do also. The Eskimos added elegant ornamentation to their objects of utility, and carved figures whose significance was spiritual or artistic. The nature of the art has not remained static, because of both individual experimentation and external stimulation. The sailors who came in growing numbers in the nineteenth century, especially the whalers, were glad to trade their wares for these exotic souvenirs of arctic voyages. Captain Lyon referred to the fineness of their carvings in ivory, which were by then (1824) being offered in exchange for the white man's luxuries. The economic motive was firmly entrenched among carvers long before the white men took up permanent residence in the Arctic. It is a motive, oddly enough, that is decried among the Eskimos but considered acceptable and untainting by successful white artists and their agents. Nevertheless, increasing commercial acceptance enormously increased the amount produced. The immense surge of creativity in the mid twentieth century stimulated some bad art (or was it art?) and much that was startlingly good.

Since the commercial history of Eskimo art was so long established, it may seem odd that the Hudson's Bay Company did little to encourage what was to become, through government promotion, a lucrative business for the company. In 1928 the company began a development department, but it was abandoned during the depression. In 1950 the average per-capita income to Canadian Eskimos from all arts and crafts was seventeen cents.

The person most responsible for the recent flowering of Eskimo art is James Houston. In 1948, while on a private painting trip in eastern Hudson Bay, he was so struck by the quality of Eskimo stone carving that he re-awakened the interest of the Canadian Handicrafts Guild which had organized an exhibition as early as 1930. The guild gave Houston $1,500 with which he bought about a thousand pieces, which were offered for sale in November 1949, with instant commercial success. The government then provided $31,000 in grants to finance Houston's continued work in the Eastern Arctic. Carvings were bought through Hudson's Bay Company stores, and sales were carried out through the company and the guild in southern Canada.

The reputation of Eskimo stone- and ivory-carving rapidly established itself in Canada and abroad. Public demand far outran the supply. The Department of External Affairs, understandably sensitive about the popular foreign image of all Canadians as igloo-dwellers, nevertheless accepted the importance of this newly recognized Canadian art and organized exhibitions at leading galleries throughout Europe. It was soon safe to say that, among foreign gallery-goers, Canadian art was generally thought of in terms of remote Eskimos whose names were rarely known and almost never pronounced.

Success brought its problems. The government, concerned about continuing standards in the face of undoubted economic pressures, studied the course of native arts abroad in order to find, and if possible to avoid, the pitfalls. The government found itself in one of its familiar dilemmas of wishing to help maintain standards and yet to avoid pressure, direction, or interference; it was particularly apprehensive about administrators making judgements on art. Yet a completely *laissez-faire* attitude would court the disaster that has befallen comparable artists abroad, who have been subjected to the immediate commercial pressure for mass production that quickly excludes creativity.

Fortunately, the North was far enough away to reduce the temptation for unprincipled entrepreneurs to exert direct pressure for a massive increase in production. The purchase of carvings through the Hudson's Bay Company was some guarantee of the preservation of principles, but not every store manager or administrator is an authority on art. Inevitably he had a deep influence, however much he might regret or be awed by his responsibility, because he had to price some carvings high and some low. At least patent copying and mass production could be fought, and so could the grosser forms of prostitution. Gifted artists were discouraged from accepting orders for polar bears with ash trays in their backs or whales with pencils in their mouths. When any community seemed to be more concerned with the fast dollar than the feeling they had once expressed, the government sometimes employed an artist to talk with the local artists in the hope of encouraging them to regain their potential. Similarly, in areas where there had been little carving, usually because of the disappearance of suitable local stone, material and encouragement were provided. The result has generally been both an artistic and a financial success.

Houston helped to open up new media to Eskimo artists after the stone sculpture had achieved acceptance in the outside world. The genesis of print-making was the traditional incising on ivory. Houston, then serving as area administrator at Cape Dorset, got leave, but no financial help, to study print-making in Japan. The techniques he learned were then passed to the artists of Cape Dorset, who took to the new medium with immediate enthusiasm. The West Baffin Eskimo Co-operative at Cape Dorset bought from its members large numbers of pencil drawings. The print-makers either made stencils or carved stone blocks from which fifty impressions were made on fine-grade paper. They were first offered for sale in 1959, and met with an extraordinary response. Within a few days, almost all the year's work was sold. The return to the co-operative in the first year was $3,500, in the next year it was $60,000, then $100,000. In 1962, looking for new media, Houston went to study engraving under William Hayter in Paris – this time at government expense. A new dimension was now added to the Cape Dorset work, a dimension that still retained a close relationship to the traditional incising on ivory.

Unlike carvings, which are too heavy and bulky to be collected and evaluated at a central point, prints can be readily transported. Taking advantage of this, the Department of Northern Affairs established a group of voluntary advisers representing gallery directors and private collectors. The West Baffin Eskimo Co-operative gave authority to the Canadian Eskimo Art Committee to pass judgement on which prints would be marketed, and to assign prices – wisely deciding that this was a job far beyond the competence of artists utterly unfamiliar with distant markets. The *cachet* of the Canadian Eskimo Art Committee would also influence prospective purchasers.

The growing income from art enabled the West Baffin Eskimo Co-operative to branch out in its commercial operations, to open a retail store at Cape Dorset, and to hire its own non-Eskimo staff, notably Terrence Ryan, who for many years was to be its artistic adviser. This was a satisfying development; a decade before, no one would have imagined Eskimos hiring whites.

Other communities experimented in print-making but failed to reach acceptable standards without careful instruction in techniques of production. Povungnituk was the next community to succeed, under the guidance of Viktor Tinkle, an artist employed by the Department of Northern Affairs to help the co-operative. Later, Eskimos at Holman Island and Baker Lake gradually learned to produce work of high quality different in approach from that of the Eastern Arctic.

With the rapid economic and social change in Eskimo lives, with a tendency towards urbanization, certainly with increased exposure to white influences, Eskimo art might be expected to decline in interest, validity, and creativity. Remarkably, the 1950s and 1960s brought a cultural renaissance, as Eskimo artists found new outlets for their work and new media for their ideas. Cape Dorset was to be the crucible in which many of the ideas were tried, although experiments in pottery made there did not develop as far or as quickly as at Rankin Inlet. Cape Dorset artists long had an interest in fabric design, and by the mid 1960s seemed on the verge of commercial production. They even submitted a design for a mural for a public building in a national competition; they did not win, but once again they impressed the Outside with their vitality and imagination. They did get the commission for an important artistic project at Toronto International Airport for which they provided three massive *inukshuks* – agglomerations of rough-hewn, unmortared rocks in the vague likeness of human figures, used as landmarks, or to mark overland routes, or to form defiles in which caribou could be herded for slaughter.

Cape Dorset artists justly gained an extraordinary reputation, strengthened by two remarkable films made by the National Film Board on their work: 'Legend of the Raven', about carving, and 'Kenojuak, Eskimo Artist', about print-making. But Cape Dorset is only one of the many Eskimo communities making striking contributions to Canadian art. Povungnituk has been the most active and productive of artistic colonies, branching from carving into prints and other graphics. The National Gallery of Canada bought, for $500, a head carved by an artist of Frobisher Bay. Other galleries collected the work of such small and distant communities as Repulse Bay. Increasingly, collectors sought out individual artists, and were prepared to pay for work as sculptors, rather than as northern souvenirs.

At the same time, the production of crafts increased rapidly. Eskimo women, traditionally skilful seamstresses, had only to be encouraged, to produce marketable items. No doubt the most famous craft of all was Ookpik, the sealskin arctic owl designed by Jeannie Snowball of Fort Chimo. The Fort Chimo Co-operative, which hired its own business manager and lawyers to handle its affairs, licensed the name and design of Ookpik to manufacturers, while continuing to make the original sealskin owls on a small scale. Tuktoyaktuk followed suit with the first of the 'friends of Ookpik', a representation of the mythical arctic ice-worm called Sekoosie. The program of arts and crafts, which had meant so little in the early 1950s, was bringing the Eskimo population nearly a million dollars a year by 1965. This new cottage industry made as much money as the arctic fur trade without being subject to fluctuations as is the white fox. It was an industry that could be carried on by women as well as by men, an industry that could bring the arctic economy some of the diversification it so badly needed. Perhaps most of all, success brought a moral victory to the Eskimos: the conviction that they need not be merely the white man's hewer of wood and drawer of ice. The Eskimo as a citizen had something of his own to contribute, without apology and without condescension.

The Indians of the Yukon and of the Mackenzie District had no such success. In art, they produced nothing so dramatic as did the Eskimo or the Indian artists of the west coast. They were capable of highly competent crafts, but their slippers and beadwork had to compete with machine copies (sold even in the North) and with other Indian work from the South. Crafts provided some local income, but the northern Indian was not able to achieve the artistic reputation of his more northerly contemporary. The reasons may be left to the conjecturing of the art historian or the sociologist.

15 | The Still Point

The polar seas may be the Mediterranean of the late twentieth century, but most Canadians are scarcely aware of them. While Canadians are decidedly more conscious of the northern third of their country than they were fifteen years ago, they still know very little about it. The rest of the polar basin, in which Canada has such a large interest, is almost as remote as the 'canals' of Mars.

When Canadians first reproached themselves with their indifference to the North and its people, the needle to their conscience was often a comparison with other northern lands. There were the industries of the Soviet Union, the cities of Alaska, the advanced social programs of tiny, impoverished Greenland, to mock proudly rich Canada with its absence of mind. The comparisons are worth making, for Canada can learn from every proprietor of a northland, but it would be a mistake to assume direct parallels between the Canadian North and any other.

Alaska. Geographically, Alaska is Canada's closest northern neighbour. It was from Alaska that Canada's original Eskimo population came. Even in recent times some Alaskan Eskimos have moved to Canada, drawn perhaps by our family allowances. Alaska has little in common with Canada's Yukon or Northwest Territories, and even its arctic people and regions are different. Its total area is well over half a million square miles, but only a small part of the inhabited land is arctic. The population is about 226,000, of which about 16,000 are Eskimos and 18,000 are Aleuts, Interior Indians, and Maritime Indians.

Alaska, both before and after its purchase by the United States in 1867, had an economy based on fur and fish. Land animals are less important than seals. Whaling was carried on longer there than in the Western Canadian Arctic, but it died out just after the turn of the century. Gold was prospected in Alaska before the mid nineteenth century. Though there was always enough produced to keep alive men's hopes and recently to yield about $25 million a year, there was no Alaskan phenomenon quite like the Klondike. There is a modest mineral industry yielding copper, silver, coal, gypsum, and oil.

Commercial fisheries, which have long been much more important in Alaska than in northern Canada, have tended to advance the movement of population into settlements. More than a third of Alaska's population live in towns. Alaska has a major reindeer industry with 600,000 animals brought originally from Siberia, but it is not notably profitable. There is a good deal of arable land, but agriculture is limited. Communications are much more highly developed than in northern Canada. A 451-mile railway from Seward to the interior was finished soon after the First World War. Roads lead to the sea and into the Yukon.

The major industry of modern Alaska is defence. Military requirements have poured money in prodigious quantities into the building and maintenance of fixed installations. While defence has been an enormous boon to the economy, it has also done some damage to the economy by drawing the labour force away from marginal resource industries which cannot compete with the high wages offered on military projects. Defence has sharply increased the population, especially in the major cities such as Fairbanks

(35,000), and Anchorage (65,000). About two-thirds of Alaska's working population is employed by the government in its civil or military operations. Harvesting of natural resources uses about a tenth of the labour force.

Greenland. Canada is the ancestral home of the Greenlanders. The émigrés moved across the narrow gap of water from Ellesmere Island to northern Greenland as long as four thousand years ago, with a major migration perhaps shortly after the Vikings established themselves near the southern edge of the island. In between was a stretch of vacant arctic coast – a narrow passage of rock between the ice-cap and the sea, barren, harsh, and possessing few resources beyond those that could be harvested from the water. Only in the south was the land gentle. When the Norse had gone, and where the Eskimos were to follow, there were grass-covered valleys where sheep might graze, low willows, and ice-free ports. The Eskimos from the north eventually made contact with the settlers in the south, and the thirteen Viking colonies disappeared, presumably by inter-marriage, or bloodshed, or both. Not until the Danish missionary Hans Egede came to Greenland in 1721 was contact with Europe re-established.

Modern social development in Greenland dated from that visit. Egede had a burning ambition to bring education to the Greenlanders. Though progress was slow in the next hundred years, the process was well started – in striking contrast to the situation on the Canadian side of the water. The social program of contemporary Greenland, which is often justly praised, was not begun until the end of the Second World War, but it was built on an established tradition of education. During the long period of slow awakening, the Danes were paternal and solicitous governors who allowed no competition, either in religion or in trade. The price structure in the stores was related to social purpose rather than to profit, an arrangement possible only in a state monopoly resigned to losing money. Goods of high nutritional value were sold below cost, while teeth-decaying luxuries were made very expensive indeed. Alcohol was banned entirely to Greenlanders, though it was accessible to the European Danes in Greenland.

In its sudden intensity, the social and economic program launched by the Danes after the Second World War had analogies in Canada in the mid 1950s, though Canada was starting almost from scratch. Greenland's schooling was expanded, medical services improved, housing programs pushed, political institutions developed, and new industries started. It was a courageous program for Denmark in this far-off territory with so little in common with the mother country and so little to contribute to it. After more than two hundred years, Greenland has never come close to paying its own way, and it is doubtful that it ever will. Apart from a little coal, and cryolite which Canada bought in quantity for its aluminum industry in the Second World War, Greenland's mineral prospects are few. The fisheries, which have been modernized, are productive, though hardly profitable enough to carry the whole cost of the social program for Greenland. They are relatively new, for until the present century the waters of the east Greenland coast were too cold for fisheries. A sudden and unexplained rise in water temperature sent the arctic sea mammals north and brought in cod, halibut, herring, and shrimp. Greenlanders sometimes ask what would happen to the large factories and fishing fleets if the water temperature ever dropped again.

In contrast, the Canadian North was a net producer of wealth when the fur trade was thriving and development programs cost nothing because they did not exist. There is a firmly held conviction among even cautious observers that the Canadian North will be a net producer again: a producer of far more than enough wealth to pay for the present level of human development. Unlike Denmark, Canada has a pressing moral obligation to do something about its northern regions, simply because they are contiguous.

It was, then, a noble effort that Greenland made and, as a social program, a successful one. Canada was able to learn more from this next-door example than she learned from Alaska. Even Greenland's disappointments were useful to study. Alcohol was one. The attempt to impose a racial line on drinking did not work there any more than it has worked anywhere else in the world. It quickened the desire of the Eskimo to drink, and no police force on earth could stop it. Drinking in a wild, irresponsible way was more than a form of relaxation from the cares of the day: it was a statement of social protest, an assertion of racial equality. When the barriers were let down, the adjustment was exceedingly difficult. It was a little less difficult in Canada because Canada had not tried for so long to maintain racial restrictions on alcohol.

Greenland's educational system produced many graduates who went on to higher education in Europe. It developed an educated class who read the literature of the world in Eskimo and produced its own literature, music, and art. From the beginning, Greenlandic writing was in Roman characters. In one vital respect, the Greenlandic administration encountered a serious difficulty. Nearly all teaching was in Greenlandic, and Danes wishing to teach in Greenland had to gain proficiency in it. The old language was certainly preserved, but the younger generation of Greenlanders claim that their economic horizons are limited because they cannot speak Danish fluently. The curriculum, modified to give much greater emphasis to Danish, has been brought closer into line with the principles underlying the Canadian school system in the North.

Canada has been catching up on Greenland's medical and welfare program, but it will take time to reach the educational level of the Greenlanders. In some ways the Canadian North has gone ahead, notably in the co-operative movement. In political growth and other respects, Canada can only patiently await the passage of time. Greenlanders who have taken an articulate and leading part in local government for a hundred years, now have a national council and their own representatives in the Danish parliament. In business and in the professions there will doubtless continue to be a large number of Danes for many years to come. In Greenland, as in Canada, it takes a long time to develop a wholly local administration.

U.S.S.R. While one might briefly refer to all the European cohabitors of the higher northern latitudes, the only other country important for comparison is the U.S.S.R. Its North, if we use the sixtieth parallel as a convenient line of definition, is two or three times as large as Canada's; in other words, its North is about the same size as all Canada. The proportion of Arctic in the two countries is sharply different, for the temperatures at comparable latitudes bear no resemblance at all. The Soviet North, generally much colder than comparable Canadian latitudes, produces low temperatures far beyond any Canadian record. Yet this is within the tree-line; the Soviet North has summer temperatures high enough to promote the growth of trees.

All in all, the Soviet Union is far more fortunate in the physical characteristics of its North than is Canada. Forest growth, which lowers costs of construction and heating, provides an economic base for vast areas that are virtually uninhabited in a comparable Canadian latitude. At least as important, the U.S.S.R. is blessed with a series of navigable rivers running northwards to the sea. Those Soviet rivers are now linked by the transcontinental rail system and by a transcontinental northern sea route open for about seventy days in the year. The northern rivers of the U.S.S.R. are open to shipping for about the same period as is the Mackenzie, that is, roughly one hundred days. The Soviet North has soil cover. The last ice age, which scraped northern Canada almost clean, dealt much less harshly with Russia. With warm summer temperatures and good soil, northern agriculture has been readily developed to provide local food, to lower northern living costs. In mineral wealth, the Soviet Union is well endowed, though perhaps not so richly as Canada.

The Soviet North is immensely more developed than the Canadian. Murmansk has been known as a gateway for traders for nine hundred years. By the mid seventeenth century, Siberia had been crossed by land, though its major settlement and development was a twentieth-century phenomenon. As in Canada, an early reason for the move to the frontier was showing the flag and establishing sovereignty. With the industrial revolution of Soviet times, the timber and mineral resources of the North became important for their own sake. Normal economic standards could be overlooked because of the Kremlin's urge to be independent of the West for its raw materials. Northern products such as fur and timber could be sold in foreign markets to get badly needed exchange. The northern sea route could ease the heavy burdens on the Soviet rail system. Forced labour could be put to productive use in the North to build industries and communities which would later be taken over by free labour. Forced labour in the Soviet North had an interesting political result. Many of the later Soviet leaders were obliged in tsarist times to spend an early apprenticeship in Siberia, where they gained an impression of the potential of the North and shed some of the wilder misconceptions. Canadian statesmen have not undergone a similar period of training.

In the Soviet Union today, five million people live above the sixtieth parallel, as contrasted with 32,000 in Canada's comparable latitude. There are ten Soviet northern cities with a population of more than 50,000: Archangel is about the size of Ottawa; Murmansk not much smaller; and Norilsk has over 100,000 inhabitants. About twenty-five citizens in every thousand of the U.S.S.R.'s population live in the North.

These people are cultivating about a million acres of land. They are harvesting a sixth of their country's timber. Their fish and fur production exceed by many times the Canadian levels. Nickel, copper, cobalt, gold, diamonds, tin, tungsten, platinum, iron, and oil are among the minerals in significant production.

The northern people represent many ethnic groups including a few Eskimos. Little is known in the West about their living conditions or their state of social development, since the Soviet North has long been closed to foreign travel. The U.S.S.R. claims an extensive educational and health system. Certainly a far higher proportion of Soviet than of Canadian northerners live in major settlements where such services can be provided with relative ease. Lacking objective information, it may be reasonable to infer that the standard of social services in the Soviet North falls not far short of those available outside heavily populated European Russia. Since the operation of the Soviet North no longer depends upon forced labour, the Kremlin has been obliged to provide reasonable services, as well as incentives, for work in high latitudes.

Even though the direct basis for comparison between the Soviet North and the Canadian North may be sketchy, the Soviet example is of particular interest in Canada. Whatever their difficulties, the Soviet Union has proved that it is possible to develop a highly sophisticated economy in extreme climates. This should encourage Canadians as they contemplate their own northern resource potential.

Labrador. The Canadian North has been treated thus far in terms of those parts of the Arctic and sub-Arctic that lie above the sixtieth parallel of latitude: the Northwest Territories and the Yukon. The definition is not so neat in eastern Canada where the true Arctic stretches far below the sixtieth parallel and where there are sub-arctic conditions still farther south. Though most of Arctic Quebec and Labrador lie below the sixtieth parallel, they have much in common with the larger northern territories.

By the second half of the eighteenth century, Labrador was beset by feuds between the resident Eskimos and the visiting Newfoundland fishermen. At the instance of Governor Palliser, the Moravian Brethren were invited to establish themselves along the coastline. Their first mission was opened at Nain in 1771, the second at Okak, about a hundred miles to the north, in 1775, and a third at Hopedale, about a hundred miles to the south, in 1781. A fourth settlement, begun much later, was completed in 1835. All four settlements had churches and schools, and Okak had, in addition, a hospital.

The pattern of arctic settlement in Labrador was thus different from the history of the Northwest Territories. The church and the administration did not follow the fur trade, though the Labrador fishing industry had prompted the arrival of the church. As in Greenland, there was almost no religious competition. The missionaries had time and resources to develop education of a higher standard than that of more westerly regions, and they used the Roman alphabet for the written Eskimo language. Later, many more settlements were started, and some soon abandoned. In 1919 the worldwide influenza epidemic reached even the distant outpost of Okak and almost wiped it out. The Hudson's Bay Company operated six posts in Labrador which were taken over by the government of Newfoundland when the company withdrew in 1942.

At the time of the union of Newfoundland with Canada, the concern in St. John's for the social welfare of the Eskimo population was reflected in a provision for $200,000 worth of federal aid in the building of welfare, health, and educational facilities, and the instigation of an anti-tuberculosis campaign. Under the terms of Confederation, Eskimo affairs remained the responsibility of the provincial government, partly because of its long familiarity with the Labrador situation, partly because the high degree of integration between Eskimos and others in Labrador made impractical the segregation of Eskimo people for specific administrative programs.

In all Labrador, there are about 450 Indians and 1,000 Eskimos out of a population of 25,000.

Despite the efforts of the Newfoundland government and the long work of the Moravian missionaries, the social and economic situation of the Labrador people remains a cause for concern. The land is sterile, and the yield from the sea is thin and hardly won. Handicrafts have brought only limited income. The population, despite net immigration, has not even held its own in the past two hundred years. Living standards remain low. The Eskimos have made the transition from the old life, but find opportunities limited in the new because they have not reached an educational level that would allow them to compete outside.

Arctic Quebec. Like Newfoundland, Quebec has discussed Eskimos with the federal government in the 1960s, but the circumstances have been quite different. The Eskimos of Arctic Quebec have tended, far more than the people of Labrador, to be treated as part of the community of Eskimos in the Northwest Territories. The trader and the missionary moved into Arctic Quebec when they took up residence in the Territories. The whaler, long before, had never been aware of any administrative boundaries around Hudson Bay. The inhabitants of Arctic Quebec were as far from the mind of the federal government as all other Eskimos were.

Just before the Second World War, the federal government tried to get reimbursement from the provincial authorities for the relief it had paid to Quebec Eskimos. Quebec refused to pay, on the grounds that the British North America Act made the federal government responsible for Eskimos and Indians. The case was heard in the Supreme Court of Canada in 1939 where the Quebec interpretation prevailed. The decision was to have been appealed to the judicial committee of the Privy Council in London, but the war intervened. Here was a curious irony. In the view of the legal advisers to the federal government at the time, there was a good chance that London would have affirmed Quebec's rights and responsibilities to Eskimos within its borders. Twenty years later, the wheel had turned, and this provincial responsibility was vigorously advocated by the Quebec government.

When the federal administrative revolution in northern affairs began in the 1950s, the Quebec Eskimos were fully included. Education, welfare, and health measures were brought to Eskimos living along the coast of Hudson Bay from Great Whale River in the south, to Hudson Strait, and east to the Ungava Bay area bordering almost on Labrador. The northern co-operative movement had its birth around Ungava Bay. The Quebec communities shared in the surge of arts and crafts, and the char fisheries prospered.

Even though the federal government was active in Eskimo affairs in Quebec, its role was not the same as in the Territories. Even the titles of field officers reflected the difference: the local administrator was known not as an area administrator but as a northern administrator, to avoid the implication that he was responsible for a specific area of land. The federal government took no direct part in major resource development as in the Territories; except as it affected Eskimo employment, housing, and other such native affairs, mining was a provincial responsibility. The R.C.M.P. had long maintained Arctic Quebec posts largely for administrative purposes, since they were not responsible for provincial law. When the Department of Northern Affairs had established its services, the federal police withdrew. In Fort Chimo, they were replaced by a provincial detachment. The federally built schools, nursing-stations, and administrative buildings, as well as Eskimo housing, were mainly on provincial land. In the operation of welfare and of inland fisheries, federal officers worked closely and harmoniously with provincial officials.

Early in the 1960s Quebec began to express growing interest in taking over all administration in *Nouveau Québec*. In 1962 intense discussion went on between the federal Minister of Northern Affairs, the Honourable Arthur Laing, and the provincial Minister of Natural Resources, the Honourable René Lévesque. They did not reach a harmonious conclusion.

The federal government argued that, constitutionally, Eskimo affairs were a federal responsibility. It was quite prepared to consider delegating to Quebec responsibility for administration of the affairs of Eskimos in its province, and to withdraw completely if the change-over was acceptable to the Eskimos. Both governments agreed that it would not be practical to take a plebiscite of Eskimo opinion. Before making any agreement with Quebec, Ottawa wanted to sound out and reassure the Eskimos, who had already expressed doubts about their welfare at the hands of the province. Well satisfied with recent federal measures, they recalled earlier days – before the coming of the federal administration – when they felt indifferently treated. Quebec, on the other hand, wanted to complete the principles of an administrative transfer before consulting the Eskimos. The difference of viewpoint became a matter of national interest in the context of federal-provincial relations.

Lacking agreement for transfer, the federal administration carried on, while provincial officials became increasingly active. Quebec established a directorate for the affairs of this part of the province, and sent resident representatives to many arctic communities to learn the language and the local situation in preparation for an eventual change-over of administration. In Povungnituk they immediately threw provincial funds and energies into the building of the local co-operative, with notable success. At Great Whale River, the departure of the military establishment in 1965 gave the provincial authorities the opportunity to take over all the municipal functions that the Mid-Canada Line base had formerly provided. Relations between the provincial and federal representatives on the ground were generally good. The responsible conduct of the provincial representatives could go far to alleviate Eskimo concern over any change in administration. A smooth change was something that all men of goodwill warmly desired if the Eskimos indicated their consent. Certainly the administration of Eskimo affairs as part of normal provincial services, rather than as a separate ethnic problem, was in accord with long-term federal plans for Eskimo administration in Canada.

The Canadian Arctic of the Future. In fifty years, will the Canadian North look at all like the Soviet side of the globe? Not a chance. In a few hundred thousand years, the natural differences might begin to even out as a blanket of soil is gradually created over all Canada – based on the unlikely assumption of no change in climate in either place. By then all manner of things could happen, such as another ice age, or the damming of Bering Strait and the pumping of the Japanese current into the Arctic to produce a climate as temperate (and as foggy?) as southern England. Or as a winter works project, someone might decide to dam Fury and Hecla Strait to alter the ice in Hudson Bay. Or they could dam Davis Strait, if they have a mind to arrest the cycle that may create America's next ice age. This last project might displease arctic Boards of Trade who had examined the implications of an ice age. If New York had not already been completely submerged as a consequence of the Bering Strait dam and pumping project, its buildings might well be hung with icicles while the jet set retreated to the salubrious forests of Baffin Island. It has happened to the climate before.

More immediate predictions are not much easier to make. It is reasonably certain that settlement will follow the pattern of northern Ontario. There will be settlements, generally of a few thousand people, very much like mining towns farther south, separated not by farmland but by thousands of miles of inexpensive real estate. The ranch-style bungalow, inappropriate as it is, will move north to illustrate the continuing ascendancy of human tastes over scientific logic; or in fifty years it may be Mexican haciendas. The bold dreams of cities under plastic bubbles will remain dreams, not because they are entirely unreasonable, but because they could be built only with a degree of community planning and social discipline, against which Canadians rebel. North American freedom, after all, rejects attempts of the state to impose conformity when individuals can conform so much more eagerly themselves.

On the other hand, igloos will be as rare as the kayak, now known only from museum models, is today. The life of those on the land will have changed as much in the Far North as in southern agricultural belts. The increased productivity of labour, largely through improved transportation, will siphon off many of the people who now live on the land and give the rest the opportunity for a better kind of living. There will be hunting and trapping, with supplementary wage employment; but those so occupied will tend to work out from permanent settlements, where they and their families can enjoy social services which by then will be the birthright of all Canadians.

The native people of the North will have eased their way into many callings. They will no longer be a geographical entity to anything like the present extent. Some will have moved to southern Canada and abroad, where a few will have earned great distinction in public affairs, the professions, and industry, while others drift in aimless misfortune: their chances will be very much like those of their fellow citizens. Most of the native people of the North will stay there, taking over the occupations for which, today, outsiders are brought great distances to fill. Their culture will not be lost, nor their language. Those in the towns may develop their own equivalent of Burns Night and even – may they be forgiven – their own version of the haggis over which each year they will weep, homesick for a life to which they would never dream of returning. They will treasure their own heritage, which will by then be preserved in a growing literature. The National Film Board will produce colour films of their appealing ethnic rites, before they return next morning to the respectability of their white collars, nurses' caps, or miners' hard hats.

The population of the North will continue to grow in something greater than the proportion of new mines and oil-wells, simply because there is no getting around the high northern birth-rate; this applies to Russia as well. In fifty years it will still be about the most sparsely settled land on earth, though the distance between those oases of human settlement will shrink. In fifty years, northern airlines will run on time; only a cynic would suggest that the planes they will then be using are today lined up on southern airfields.

The dog-team will have gone the way of the kayak and the igloo. Tracked vehicles will be the standard means of land travel in winter, though the faster and more comfortable ground-effect vehicle will commonly be used for longer journeys. Vertical-take-off and short-take-off aircraft will provide access to remote places, while relatively conventional planes operating from relatively conventional landing-fields will fly northern townspeople to the Outside.

The pattern of water traffic on rivers will probably not change greatly, except that there will be more passenger vessels for the tourist trade. There *will* be changes at sea, where nuclear-powered ice-breakers will permit standard vessels to operate farther, faster, more safely, and therefore more cheaply than today. The first of the nuclear-powered freighter submarines may well prove themselves in places where the underseas pipelines for oil and for solids do not reach.

The network of conventional roads and railways will spread into the north-east Yukon, and far north of Great Slave Lake. It will be possible to drive from the forty-ninth parallel to the Arctic Ocean, or westwards from Hudson Bay into the barrens. Development roads will have been built from the seashore into the interior of those arctic islands whose mineral wealth is being mined. The tourist traffic by all modes of transportation will be heavy. People will complain about Canadian meals and lack of native cuisine.

The annual production of minerals in the Yukon and the North-west Territories will be valued in the billions of dollars and will employ a labour force almost as big as the whole northern population today. Oil may have passed its heyday, though the most accessible wells will still be producing. The population of the North, including the employees of supplementary industries and their dependants, will exceed a hundred thousand. In some terms, it will not be a dramatic growth, but it will be backed by balance-sheets of northern development, all in black ink.

In fifty years, the North will have contributed two new provinces to Canadian federation. Their small legislatures, cabinets, and judicial systems will include representation from all ethnic groups. Their relations with the federal government will be the same as those of other provinces. Ottawa will no longer be their whipping-boy (except to the extent that it is for any province), and this will cause deep emotional disturbances until a substitute can be found. Psychiatrists will practise in the North, and undertakers will at last be able to make a living because northerners will less often retire to Victoria to die. Politicians will make speeches about the vast untapped resources of the North. Some people will insist that southern Canada should be developed first. Others will suggest that the income tax in the North should be lightened.

Like weather forecasts, long-range predictions about the North are easier than assessments of its immediate future. The North as it stands in the mind and emotions of Canada today is hardest of all to see. Undoubtedly, Canadians are far more conscious of the northern third of their country now than they were fifteen years ago. The mystic appeal of the North has been demonstrated in many ways, not least in one notable national election when most observers felt the North was a potent force working on the emotions of Canadians.

Other Canadians regard Eskimos as a national institution, even though they know very little about them, and still less about northern Indians. A poll among people expressing an interest in the North put the Eskimo population close to ten times its actual figure. Perhaps that is not surprising in view of their habit of creeping constantly into the newspapers, magazines, or films, or the acceptance of their art in galleries and on mantelpieces everywhere. No Canadians are consciously unkind to these new-found countrymen: in fact, many seek a cheap path to glory through self-appointment as spokesman and champion for the Eskimos; rarely have so many people claimed to have spoken for so few with so little authority. Neither need medals be struck for those who gain an easy notoriety by demanding simply that more be given by government, by churches, by commerce, or by industry – without stopping to weigh whether, as has been true of other aboriginals, the short-term 'more' is the long-term 'less'. Having a real live Eskimo at your national conference has become *de rigueur* in certain quarters. No Indians need apply. Students of race relations may wonder whether this is the smoothest path to national acceptance. The real heroes of modern Canada are those who can forget the race of the man or woman opposite, be he Indian, Anglo-Saxon, Jew, French, Irish, or Eskimo. Of course, if there is a language barrier, no one can forget, but he can treat that other Canadian as an equal, not as superman or serf.

Northerners sometimes complain bitterly about the press, and with some reason. In all Canada, there is hardly a southern journalist who has fully informed himself on the North. Northern reporting by southern writers usually takes the form of a brief flight from ignorance, the most superficial of briefings, fast talks with a few of the articulate whites who tend to meet the planes, and a rapid retreat to the South. Next time, the same paper will send a different reporter. It is a system that provides neither breadth nor depth. It does provide monumental inaccuracies and strange dimensions. In defence of the press, the North is an expensive place to visit, and one does not spare highly paid reporters for long excursions.

If the glitter of the North is sometimes tarnished by the press, the northerners often have themselves to blame: they are the ones who inform the wandering reporter, who retail the latest horror story about mismanagement, disaster, or mayhem to this new audience. And they are the ones who are most surprised by the cynicism of the resulting story, a cynicism that communicates itself to the public. These growing pains are inevitable when the chance for perspective is small. When the great northern awakening began, Canadians devoured the stories of igloos past and oil-wells yet to come. Perhaps they were over-sold. They may have expected sudden solutions to problems centuries old. They may have anticipated instant riches from rocks that have lain fallow since time began.

No one close to the North expected such immediate and gratifying results. In fact, the level of resource development is not far from the reasoned hopes of the experts a decade ago. The layman, unfamiliar with the long chain of exploration, development, testing, marketing, and building, before any mine comes into production, realizes even less how long each phase is stretched when that mine is north of sixty degrees. It is all a matter of perspective. When the new North is a little older, its frustrations and triumphs will be accepted with more objectivity and more understanding. It will be an interesting story of nation-building for later generations to recall.

The record will start with an absence of mind. If it tells its story well, it will not tell it in terms of dollars and manpower. It will look at the empty places where now the children are taught to find a broader horizon. It might quote the figures, however incomplete, of those who not so long ago starved to death, of those who died unnecessarily because no medical help was near, of those who slowly slipped from life when the hunt had failed again. The record would chronicle the revolution in human minds as northerners improved their own living conditions through co-operatives and community development. There would be milestones to record in terms of human accomplishment, of lives now saved, of artistic creation.

The record would show the failures too: the projects that ended dismally through inexperience, haste, or sheer bad luck; the sudden epidemic, the drop-outs from school, the cases of liquor offences before the magistrate.

The credit side could list many assets. There would be the physical development – the northward push of resources production, the ferment of a people who, however demanding their present lives and however sorry their poverty in relation to other Canadians, have come from the chronic social and economic despair of a few years ago. Strongly on the credit side would be that corps of devoted Canadians who have given so much of themselves to service of the North in a hundred callings. Rarely thanked, sometimes reviled, they are in large part the authors of the past success and the source of future hope. From sorry beginnings, the record would surely show human and physical accomplishment perhaps unsurpassed in speed and depth among administrations serving underdeveloped areas anywhere in the world. It has been a good start.

> . . . and do not call it fixity,
> Where past and future are gathered.

Index

Advisory Committee on Northern Development, 169
Akaitcho, 65
Aklavik, agriculture, 181, 207; climate, 180; communications, 147, 194; hospital, 156, 221; Hudson's Bay Co., 74; Lindbergh's visit, 139; logging, 206; permafrost, 21
Alaska, 284-5; air route, 150; church, 122; climate, 6, 23; commerce, 68, 284; Eskimos, 29, 31, 32, 272, 284; geography, 5, 22, 284; gold rush, 86, 87, 88, 90, 284; military, 151, 192, 284-5; pipeline, 109, 151; purchase, 68; road, 184, 215, 284
Alaska Highway, airstrips, 188; construction, 150, 151; land-line, 193; length, 150; maintenance, 191; permission to build, 108, 150; route of Eskimos, 36; take-over by Canada, 184; tourists, 184, 185, 215; in Yukon, 155
Albanel, Father, 61
Alert, 8, 13, 14
Aleuts, 284
Alexandra Falls, 22
Amadjuak, 76
Amundsen, Roald, 55, 107
Anchorage, 285
Anglican Church, 77; at Aklavik, 147, 221; in the Arctic, 120-9 *passim*, 147; and education, 126-7, 234-6; and Eskimo literature, 273
Animals, *see* Fauna
Archangel, 289
Arctic, 108, 149
Arctic Archipelago, 6, 7, 20, 110, 113, 190, 204
Arctic Bay, 80, 149
Arctic Circle, 10, 185
Artillery Lake, 62
Athapaskan Indians, 36
Atlin, 145
Aurora Borealis, 14, 15, 196
Axel Heiberg Island, 7, 103, 105, 106, 107, 266
Aylmer Lake, 66

Back, Lieutenant, 274
Back, George, 65, 66
Back River, 66
Baffin, William, 48, 49
Baffin Bay, 116, 117
Baffin Island, agriculture, 207; church, 124, 125; climate, 294; communications, 191, 195; Eskimos, 80, 118; exploration, 44, 45, 49, 51, 54, 55, 103, 108; falcons, 43; geography, 7, 8, 9; Hudson's Bay Co., 76; mapping, 46; mining, 149, 187, 202; transportation, 183
Baillie Island, 118
Baker, Faye, 139

Baker Lake, 14, 62, 124, 130, 131, 134, 174, 278
Balikci, Asen, 35
Ballistic Missile Early Warning System (BMEWS), 192
Banks Island, 102
Barrens, 11, 36, 136, 137
Bathurst Inlet, 65
Bear, 17, 18, 25, 44, 115, 209
Beaufort Sea, 118
Beaver, 272
Belcher, Sir Edward, 53
Belcher Islands, 125, 148, 202
Bell, James Mackintosh, 135, 148
Bell, Robert, 135
Bell Telephone Company, 194
Bellot Strait, 53, 80
Bennett, W. A. C., 259
Bering Sea, 22, 29, 87, 183, 293, 294
Bernard, Captain Joseph, 74, 123, 130
Bernier, Captain Joseph, 99, 102, 103, 105, 106, 108, 149
Beste, George, 46, 267
Big Island, 69
Birds, *see* Fauna
Black, George, 155
Blacklead Island, 76
Bloody Fall, 62, 65
Boas, Franz, 55, 263
Boats, 68, 70, 182
Bompas, Bishop W. C., 122, 123
Bonanza Creek, 89, 97
Booth, Felix, 51
Boothia, Gulf of, 52
Boothia Isthmus, 52
Boothia Peninsula, 67, 80
Boyle, Harry, 271
Breynat, Bishop, 122
Buffalo, 24, 25
Button, Sir Thomas, 48
Bylot, Robert, 48
Byrd, Richard, 107, 108, 137

Cabot, John, 44, 57
Cambridge Bay, 138, 183, 189, 193
Campbell, Robert, 67
Camsell, Charles, 135
Canada Tungsten Company, 202
Canadian Arctic Expedition, 103
Canadian Broadcasting Corporation, 194, 195, 196
Canadian Eskimo Art Committee, 278
Canadian Handicrafts Guild, 233, 276
Canadian National Telegraphs, 193, 194
Canadian Shield, 11
Canadian Wildlife Service, 18
Canoe, 37, 182
Canol Pipeline, 109, 110, 151, 185, 188, 191
Cape Columbia, 6

Cape Dorset, Eskimo art, 277, 278, 279; Eskimo culture, 30, 32; Eskimos, 157; geography, 8; Hudson's Bay Co., 76; tourism, 215
Cape Dyer, 48
Cape Hope's Advance, 152
Cape Morris Jesup, 6
Carcross, 155
Caribou, 24, 69; population, 18, 24, 31, 79, 154, 170, 206; skin, 17, 34, 38
Carmack, George Washington, 88, 89, 145
Carmacks, 185, 201
Carrothers Commission, 251
C. D. Howe, 111
Chantrey Inlet, 66
Char, 18, 211, 212, 213, 292
Chesterfield Inlet, church, 124; Dickins's trip, 137; doctor, 156; Hearne's trip, 62; hospital, 221; Low's voyage, 102; radio station, 152; school, 235; Tyrrell's trip, 134
Chilkoot Pass, 87, 90, 91, 99
Chipewyan, 63, 120, 121
Christian I, King of Denmark, 44
Church of England, *see* Anglican Church
Churchill, airfield, 109, 152, 189; Button's voyage, 48; church, 124; climate, 180; Fort Prince of Wales, 61; Foxe's voyage, 50; harbour, 148, 183; MacAlpine's trip, 138; radio station, 152, 196; R.C.M.P., 131; school, 238; tree-line, 10; Tyrrell's trip, 134
Circle, 88, 90, 97
Clothing, 38
Clyde River, 76
Coats Island, 76
Columbus, 41
Commercial Airways, 138
Commissioner of the Northwest Territories, 131, 244, 247, 249, 251-2
Commissioner of the Yukon, 169, 175, 256, 257-8
Committee Bay, 54
Con Mine, 148, 153, 201
Constantine, Inspector, 88, 130
Cook, Dr. Frederick, 54
Cooper, Sir Patrick Ashley, 78
Co-operatives, 212, 277, 278, 279, 287, 292, 293
Coppermine, air service, 189; church, 123; copper, 34; exploration, 51; Franklin's trip, 65, 66; Hearne's trip, 62, 65; logs, 206; MacAlpine's trip, 138; R.C.M.P., 130
Coral Harbour, 109, 152, 157
Cornwallis Island, 8, 16, 80, 189, 191
Coronation Gulf, 65, 123
Corrections, 231
Cory, W. W., 244, 246
Coudert, Bishop, 123
Council of the Northwest Territories, 212, 221, 228, 244, 246, 247, 248, 250

Craig Harbour, 106
Crocker Bay, 80
Cruikshank, Andy, 139
Cumberland Sound, 117, 124
Cyril Knight Prospecting Company, 148

Davis, John, 48
Davis Inlet, 120
Davis Strait, 53, 116, 294
Dawson City, 20, 23, 134, 144, 270; agriculture, 181; air service, 138, 188; church, 122, 123; Dempster Highway, 185; gold rush, 86, 88-97; LaBine's trip, 138; mining, 153; R.C.M.P., 130, 133
Dease, Peter Warren, 65, 67
Dease Lake, 67
Defence, 191
Des Groseilliers, Médard Chouart, 59, 60
Devon Island, 7
Dickins, 'Punch', 137, 138
Discovery, 48
Discovery Mine, 201
Distant Early Warning Line, 111, 171, 190, 192, 209, 265
Dogs, 33, 37, 182
Dolphin and Union Strait, 66, 124
Dominion Explorers, 138
Dominion Government Telegraphs, 193
Dorset, *see* Cape Dorset
Drum dance, 35, 36, 127-8
Drumlins, 12
Drury, C. M., 247
Dubawnt River, 134
Duchaussois, Father, 121
Dundas Harbour, 80, 81
Dyea, 91

Eagle Plain, 203
Eastern Arctic Patrol, 111, 222, 264, 275
Echo Bay, 135
Egede, Hans, 285
Eldorado, 89
Eldorado Mine, 135, 148, 153, 201
Ellesmere Island, 5, 6, 7, 8, 9, 266; Bernier's voyage, 105; climate, 13; Eskimo migration, 80; Greely's trip, 55; Lowe's voyage, 102; MacMillan expedition, 106, 137-8
Ellsworth, Lincoln, 55
Ennadai Lake, 174
Erebus, 52
Eric the Red, 42
Eskers, 9, 11, 12
Eskimo Point, 124, 157, 223
Eskimos, administration, 170; arts and crafts, 274-80; church, 125, 127, 128, 129; early life, 28, 29, 30, 31, 34; Eastern Arctic Patrol, 77; employment, 173, 192; government, 35, 245, 246, 249, 253; influence of Europeans, 79-80, 81, 116, 118, 119; interracial contact, 173; Labrador, 290; law, 35, 166; in literature, 269, 273-4; migration, 174; orthography, 272, 273-4; Que-

bec, 291; radio, 196; reindeer, 154; reputation, 35, 36, 297; resource development, 211, 212, 213; social problems, 35, 157, 219-41 *passim*; transportation, 181, 182; use of copper, 62; use of rifle, 75, 79; use of wood, 206; whaling, 117; writing, 35, 120
Eureka, 8, 14
Evans, the Rev. James, 120, 121, 272
Excelsior, 90

Fairbanks, 284
Falcons, 43, 115
Faraud, Father Henry Joseph, 121
Fauna, 17, 18, 19, 24, 25
Federated Women's Institutes, 233
Field, Ted, 139
Finnegan, James, 139
Fish, 25, 34, 37, 38, 57, 58, 210, 211, 212, 213
Flat Creek, 185
Fleming, the Rev. (later Bishop) A. L., 124, 219
Flora, 15, 16, 24
Fort Chimo, 109, 152, 157, 189, 279, 292
Fort Enterprise, 65
Fort Fitzgerald, 184
Fort Franklin, 65, 66
Fort Good Hope, 69, 71, 121, 207, 221
Fort Liard, 70, 135, 203
Fort McPherson, 86, 121, 130, 185, 235
Fort Norman, 69, 70, 71, 121, 123, 130, 136
Fort Prince of Wales, 61
Fort Providence, 121, 122, 207
Fort Rae, 69, 70
Fort Reliance, 66, 87, 88
Fort Resolution, 65, 69, 121, 122, 130, 148, 222
Fort Ross, 80, 81
Fort Selkirk, 68
Fort Simpson, 70, 136, 137, 156; agriculture, 69, 207, 265; church, 121, 122; climate, 24; communications, 147; fur route, 69, 71; Hudson's Bay Company, 65; radio, 196; R.C.M.P., 130; road, 185; school, 235
Fort Smith, 255; air service, 188; church, 122; climate, 23; Dickins's trip, 137; newspaper, 271; schools, 157, 235; transportation, 136, 184, 185
Fort Yukon, 68, 71, 86, 122, 123
Fortymile River, 87, 88, 89, 90, 122
Fox, 17, 18, 75, 79, 118, 153, 208, 209, 280
Fox, 53
Foxe, Luke, 50
Foxe Basin, 30, 50
Foxy, 214
Fram, 5
Frances Lake, 67
Franklin, Sir John, 52, 53, 54, 65, 66, 67, 101, 138
Frederick II, 43

Frobisher, Martin, 45, 46, 49, 54, 119, 267, 270
Frobisher Bay, airfield, 109, 152, 189, 191, 192; defence, 191; Frobisher's voyage, 45, 46; Hall's voyage, 54; Hudson's Bay Company, 76; rehabilitation centre, 230; school, 238
Frobisher Exploration Company, 153
Fullerton, E. G., 136
Fullerton Harbour, 102, 130
Fury and Hecla Strait, 51, 294
Fury Beach, 52

Gabriel, 45, 46
Gagné, Raymond C., 273
Geological Survey of Canada, 89; administration, 163, 164; Robert and J. M. Bell, 135; support Stefansson, 103; Yellowknife ore, 144, 148
Giant Mine, 153, 201
Girling, the Rev. H., 124
Gjoa, 55
Gjoahavn, 55
Glaciers, 8, 165
Goat, 25
Godsell, Philip, 75
Gold Bottom, 89
Goose Bay, 109, 152
Gorman, G. W., 136
Grandin, Father (later Bishop), 121
Grant, Cuthbert, 64
Great Bear Lake, 22, 65, 66, 135, 137, 138, 147, 153
Great Slave Lake, church, 121; communications, 194; fisheries, 69, 210; geography, 22; mapping, 66; mining, 135, 136, 144, 148, 202; trading-posts, 65; transportation, 184, 185, 202, 215, 296
Great Slave Lake Railway, 187
Great Whale River, 11, 292, 293
Greely, Adolphus W., 55
Greenland, administration, 166, 240; church, 128, 129; DEW Line, 192; history, 285-7; ice-cap, 6, 7; literature, 272-3; permafrost, 20; polar ice, 5; settlement, 29, 30, 32, 42, 43, 44, 116
Grey Nuns, 122, 207
Grise Fiord, 8
Grolier, Father Peter Henry, 121, 122
Gulls, 19

Haines, 68, 184, 188, 265
Hall, Captain Charles, 46, 54
Hall Beach, 189
Hardie, M. A., 255
Hares, *see* Rabbits
Harper, Arthur, 86, 87
Harris, Lawren, 275
Hay River, communications, 194, 195; doctors, 156; fisheries, 210; geography, 22; government, 255; newspaper, 271; schools, 236, 238; transportation, 183, 184, 185, 187, 189, 213

Hayter, William, 278
Hearne, Samuel, 62, 63
Henderson, Robert, 88, 89
Henry, Alexander, 63
Herjolfsson, Bjarni, 42
Herschel Island, 74, 118, 119, 124, 130
Hill, Bob, 271
H.M.C.S. *Labrador*, 112
Holman Island, 278
Holt, George, 87
Home Bay, 125, 132
Hopedale, 290
Hospitals, 156, 221, 223
Housing, 225, 226, 227, 228
Houston, James, 276, 277-8
Hudson, Henry, 48, 49, 116
Hudson Bay, Eskimos, 31, 117, 292; Foxe's
  voyage, 50; geography, 11, 294; Hudson's
  Bay Company, 76; Hudson's voyage, 48;
  mining, 134, 149; ownership, 112; Radis-
  son and Des Groseilliers's voyage, 59;
  transportation, 183, 189, 201
Hudson Strait, 13, 45, 48, 76, 112, 183, 292
Hudson's Bay Company, *Book of Wisdom*,
  274; church, 121, 124; communications,
  193; competition, 130, 144, 147; early
  flying, 137; Eskimo carvings, 276-7; exploration, 61; history, 60-82, 87, 154, 246;
  industry, 156; Labrador, 290; land, 101;
  mining, 149
Hunter, Archdeacon, 121, 122
Hyslop and Nagle, 130

Ice Age, 27, 137
Ice-islands, 6, 113
Iceland, 42, 44
Igloo, 32-3, 294
Imperial Oil Company, 136, 147
Imperial Order Daughters of the Empire,
  233
Implements, 38
Independence, 29
Indian Affairs and Northern Development,
  Department of, 164
Indians, administration, 73, 163, 170, 210,
  211, 232; Alaska, 284; arts and crafts,
  280; early life, 28, 31, 36, 38; fishing, 37,
  210; fur trade, 58, 59, 68, 72, 87, 144, 209;
  government, 245, 249, 253; hospitalization, 223; housing, 225; Labrador, 291;
  literature, 269; living standard, 72, 220;
  reputation, 297; schools, 234, 240, 241;
  social contact, 72, 173; transportation,
  182; writing, 120
Ingstad, Helge and Anne, 43
Inukpuk, 275
Inuktitut, 273
Inuvik, communications, 192, 196; construction, 205; cutting trees, 255; rehabilitation centre, 230; research, 265; schools,
  235, 237; transportation, 183, 188, 189,
  215

Investigator, 53

Jackson, A. Y., 275
Jacobshavn, 7
James, Thomas, 50
James Bay, 43, 50, 61
Jenness, Diamond, 263
Jesuits, 61, 122
Johnson, Albert, 139
Joy, Staff Sgt., 106
Judge, Father, 122, 123

Kayak, 33, 117, 182, 294
Keewatin, caribou, 28; church, 124; climate,
  14; communications, 196; Eskimos, 30,
  79, 173, 174; fisheries, 210; government,
  244; Knight's voyage, 51; prospecting,
  148, 201; transportation, 189
Kelsey, Henry, 61
Kendall, Mate, R. N., 66
Keno, 153, 184, 201
'Kenojuak, Eskimo Artist', 279
Kent Peninsula, 65
King, Dr. William, 102, 105, 119
King, William Lyon Mackenzie, 104, 106,
  107
King Point, 55
King William Island, 53, 55, 67
Kirby, the Rev. W. W., 121, 122
Klengenberg, Captain Charles, 74, 75, 130
Klondike, geography, 22; gold rush, 85-97,
  108, 144, 145, 146, 200; literature, 270;
  sovereignty, 109
Knight, John, 51
Komatik, *see* Sled
Kudlik, 34

LaBine, Gilbert, 135, 136, 138, 147
Labrador, church, 120; Danish voyages, 44;
  Eskimos, 30, 31, 272, 289-91, 292; Vikings,
  43; whalers, 116
Ladue, Joseph, 89
Lady Franklin Point, 194-5
LaGuardia, Fiorello, 109
Laing, Arthur, 292
Lake Bennett, 92, 93, 145
Lake Harbour, 14, 76, 124, 149, 157
Lake Hazen, 266
Lake Lindemann, 91, 92, 93
Lakhtine, W. L., 112
Lamprey, 50
Lancaster Sound, 7, 8, 49, 51, 52, 53, 102,
  112
L'Anse-aux-Meadows, 43
La Pérouse, Comte de, 62
La Pierre's House, 71
Lefèbvre, Dr. Gilles, 273
'Legend of the Raven', 279
Leif the Lucky, 43
Lemming, 17, 18
LeRoux, Father, 123
Lesage, Jean, 105, 170

Lévesque, René, 292
Liard River, 22, 65, 69, 87
Lindbergh, Charles, 139
Little Cornwallis Island, 203
Little Whale River, 124
Lofthouse, the Rev. J., 123
Lok, Michael, 46, 219
Lomen Brothers, 154
Lomonosov Ridge, 4, 6, 113
Louise Falls, 22
Low, A. P., 102
Luddites, 72
Lyon, Captain George Francis, 31, 219, 269, 274, 275

MacAlpine, Colonel C. D. H., 138
M'Clintock, Leopold, 53-4
M'Clure, Robert, 53
McConachie, Grant, 139, 140, 149
McDonald, Robert, 122
McDonogh, John, 137
McGee, Sam, 270
McGill-Jacobsen Expedition, 266
Mackenzie, Alexander, 63, 136
Mackenzie River, agriculture, 146, 208; church, 125; climate, 24; communications, 193; exploration, 51; fur trade, 68, 69, 209; geography, 10, 11, 12, 22; Indians, 36; oil, 203; route to Klondike, 86; settlement, 65, 66, 67; Stefansson's trip, 102; transportation, 135, 136, 138, 183-4, 185, 187, 288; wartime projects, 109; wood, 206
MacMillan, Donald, 106, 107, 137
McQuesten, Jack, 87
Manning, Leo, 274
Manning, Tom, 264
Marble Island, 51
Markham, Commander Albert, 54
Markland, 43
Matonabbee, 62
May, 'Wop', 139
Mayo, Al, 87
Mayo, 146, 155, 184, 185, 200
Meadows, Arizona Charlie, 94, 97
Melville Bay, 53, 117
Melville Island, 20, 51, 53, 204
Métis, 134, 144, 170, 209, 245
Michael, 45, 46
Mid-Canada Line, 293
Miles Canyon, 93
Milne Inlet, 202
Moose, 25, 69, 70
Moose Factory, 139
Moravians, 120, 290
Mosquitoes, 19, 150
Mount Logan, 21
Mowat, Farley, 271
Munk, Jens, 50, 60, 61, 268
Munn, Captain Henry Toke, 149
Murmansk, 288, 289
Murray, Alexander, 68

Murre, 19
Muskeg, 12
Musk-ox, 17, 18, 154, 209
Muskrat, 23, 73, 208, 209
Nahanni River, 22, 65, 87, 137
Nain, 120, 290
Nansen, Fridtjof, 5
Nares, Captain George, 54
Narwhal, 18, 19, 117
Nascopie, 77, 80
Neakoteah, 125
Negus Mine, 148, 153
Neptune, 102
Nobile, Umberto, 55
Norilsk, 289
Norman Wells, capacity, 203; Canol, 109, 151; oil rush, 147, 245; road, 185
Norsemen, *see* Vikings
North, 272
North American Trading Company, 90
North Magnetic Pole, 52
North Pole, 3, 4, 5, 8, 10, 11, 54, 104, 112, 113
North Rankin Inlet Nickel Mines Ltd., 201
North West Company, 63, 64, 71
North West Mounted Police, *see* Royal Canadian Mounted Police
Northern Aerial Minerals Exploration Company, 137
Northern Affairs and National Resources, Department of, air services, 190; DEW Line, 111, 171; Eskimo culture, 273, 278; history, 161, 163, 164, 169; Quebec, 292; research, 264; resource development, 211, 212; schools, 233-4, 237
Northern Messenger, 194
Northern service officers, 170, 173, 175
Northern Trading Company, 147
Northwest Highway System, *see* Alaska Highway
Northwest Passage, 45-55 *passim*, 63, 65
Northwest Staging Route, 140, 149
Norway House, 68
Nouveau Québec, *see* Quebec, Arctic
Nueltin Lake, 210
Nunassiaq, 251

Oaks, 'Doc', 137
Oblates, 122, 123
Ogilvie, William, 90
Okak, 290
Okpik, Abraham, 246
Old Crow, 71
Ookpik, *see* Owl
Ouyerack, Charlie, 125
Owl, 17, 279

Padlei, 76, 174
Palace Grand Theatre, 94, 97, 214
Palliser, Governor, 290
Panegoosho, Mary, 273
Pangnirtung, 80, 124, 156, 193, 221

Parry, Sir Edward, 31, 51, 53, 67
Parry Channel, 7
Pattullo, T. D., 259
Peary, Captain Robert, 4, 6, 54, 101
Peck, Dr. E. J., 124, 272
Pedersen, Captain T. C., 74
Peel Plateau, 22, 185, 203
Peel River, 22, 69, 71
Pelly River, 22, 67, 68
Penguin, 19
Penny, Captain William, 117
Pentecostal Church, 236
Permafrost, 10, 19
Permanent Joint Board on Defence, 109-10
Petitot, Abbé Emile, 122
Pine Point, 144, 148, 181, 185, 187, 202
Pingos, 12, 20
Plants, *see* Flora
Point Barrow, 20
Poirier, Senator Pascal, 103
Polar bear, *see* Bear
Polar pack, 5
Polo, Marco, 43
Pond, Peter, 63
Pond Inlet, 76, 80, 117, 149
Porcupine River, 68, 69, 71, 86
Porsild, Dr. A. E., 154
Port Harrison, 76, 157
Port Radium, 138, 148, 180
Portage La Loche, 68, 69
Portland, 90
Povungnituk, 76, 215, 232, 278, 279, 293
Precipitation, 14, 23
Prelude Lake, 22
Prince Patrick Island, 103
Ptarmigan, 17, 19

Qaujivaallirutissat, 274
Quebec, Arctic, 291-3
Queen Elizabeth Islands, 7, 8, 25, 30, 183, 203
Queen Maud Gulf, 67

Rabbits, 18, 25, 69
Radio, 193, 194, 195-6
Radisson, Pierre Esprit, 59, 60
Rae, John, 53, 67, 73
Rain, *see* Precipitation
Ramparts, 22
Rankin Inlet, 51, 148, 201, 202, 279
Rasmussen, Knud, 264
Rat River, 71, 139
Raven, 17, 19
Rehabilitation, 230
Reid, 'Pat', 137
Reindeer, 154, 156, 164, 284
Repulse Bay, 54, 67, 118, 279
Resolute, 53
Resolute Bay, 189, 190, 191
Resolution, 69, 121
Resolution Island, 13, 14, 45, 152
Revillon Frères, 81

Richardson, John, 65, 66
Rifle, 18, 24, 31, 75, 79
Ringnes Island, 105
Robertson, R. G., 246
Roman Catholic Church, in Aklavik, 147; in Arctic, 77; Eskimo translation, 273; history, 120, 121, 122, 123, 124, 126; hospitals, 221; recruitment of missionaries, 126; role of missionary, 129; schools, 127, 234, 235, 236
Ross, John, 51, 52, 66, 116
Ross River, 185
Rouvier, Father, 123
Rowley, Graham, 264
Royal Canadian Air Force, 190, 191, 264
Royal Canadian Corps of Signals, 147, 193
Royal Canadian Mounted Police, communications, 193; corrections, 231; Herschel Island, 119; history, 130-4; N.W.T. Council, 244, 247; settlements, 147; use of aircraft, 190; voyages of *St. Roch*, 55; Yukon, 88, 92, 95, 106, 108, 109, 155, 164
Rupert Bay, 59
Rupert's Land, 74, 101, 130, 243
Rupertsland, 77
Russia, *see* U.S.S.R.
Ryan, Terrence, 278

St. Laurent, Louis S., 105, 161, 244
St. Michael, 91
St. Roch, 55
Schieffelin, Ed, 87
Scouting, 231-2
Seal, 17, 18, 117
Sector theory, 104, 105
Seguin, Father, 121, 122
Service, Robert, 270, 271
Seward, 284
Shaman, 38
Sheep, 25
Siberia, 5, 6, 8, 29, 288
Simonie, 246
Simpson, Sir George, 64, 66, 67, 68, 71, 73, 74
Simpson, Thomas, 66, 67
Sivertz, B. G., 246
Skagway, 91, 92, 95, 145, 151, 186, 188
Skelton, O. D., 106
Skookum Jim, 88, 89
Skraelings, 42
Slave River, 136
Sled, 33, 37, 181
Smith, 'Soapy', 92
Smith Sound, 8, 107
Snag, 13
Snake River, 187, 202
Snare River, 65
Snow, *see* Precipitation
South Baffin Trading Company, 81
Southampton Island, 30, 76, 80, 109, 117, 118

Spalding, Alex, 273
Spence Bay, 80, 183
Steele, Superintendent Sam, 92, 93, 99, 130
Stefansson, Vilhjalmur, 103, 104, 123, 263, 269-70
Stevenson, Robert Louis, 219
Stewart, Charles, 105, 107
Stewart River, 22, 87, 146
Stikine River, 67
Strathcona Sound, 203
Stringer, the Rev. (later Bishop) Isaac O., 124
Sugluk, 76
Sverdrup, Captain Otto, 105, 106, 107
Sverdrup Islands, 105, 106
Syllabics, 120, 272, 273

Tagish Charlie, 88-9
Tanana River, 87
Tantalus, 146, 200
Telegraph, 145, 193
Temperature, 4, 8, 13, 150, 179, 287
Terror, 52
Tetso, John, 272
Thelon River, 134, 137
Thériault, Yves, 272
Thule, 30, 32, 33, 111
Tibbett, J. F., 149
Tinkle, Viktor, 278
Tornit, *see* Tunit
Tree line, 10
Tree River, 130, 215
Trout River, 65
Tuberculosis, 76, 156, 220, 223
Tuktoyaktuk, 157, 183, 184, 207, 233, 279
Tunit, 30
Turquetil, Father Arsène, 124
Tyrrell, Joseph Burr, 134

Umiak, 33, 117, 118, 182
Ungava, 9, 11, 123, 211, 292
Unicorn, 50
United Keno Hill Mine, 187, 200
U.S.S.R., 103, 104, 113, 283, 287-9, 295

Varley, Frederick, 275
Victoria Island, 7, 66, 67, 74, 130
Victory, 52

Vikings, 30, 42, 43, 44, 85, 115, 266, 285
Vinland, 43
Viscount Melville Sound, 7, 112

Walrus, 18, 116
Wann, Clyde, 139
Waterways, 136, 147, 184
Watson Lake, 23, 108, 139, 150, 151, 184, 188
Weather stations, joint arctic, 110
Wellington Channel, 53
Western Canada Airways, 138
Weymouth, George, 48
Whale, 18, 116, 118, 119, 284
White, Lieut.-Col. F., 244
White Pass, 91
White Pass and Yukon Railway, 123, 145, 146, 214
White River, 86
Whitehorse, agriculture, 207; airfield, 108, 109, 150; church, 123; climate, 23; communications, 194, 195, 196; forest fire, 206; gold rush, 93; government, 257, 259; hospital, 155; newspaper, 271; population, 146, 147, 151; refinery, 151; Robert Service, 270; schools, 155; tourism, 215; transportation, 139, 140, 145, 184, 187, 188, 189
Wolfall, Master, 120
Wolstenholme, 76
Wolves, 18, 25
Wood Buffalo National Park, 169, 185, 205
Wrangel Island, 104

Yellowknife, climate, 23; communications, 195, 196; Franklin's trip, 65; government, 245, 255; hospital, 156; mining, 144, 148, 153, 201; newspaper, 271; permafrost, 20; schools, 157, 234, 236, 238; tourism, 215; transportation, 181, 185, 188, 189
York Factory, 61, 67, 68
Yukon Council, 155
Yukon Field Force, 92
Yukon Order of Pioneers, 97
Yukon River, 21, 36, 68, 69, 87, 91, 93, 183
Yukon Southern Line, 139